London War Notes

1939-1945

"Very well then—alone"

London
War Notes
1939 - 1945

Mollie Panter-Downes

Edited by WILLIAM SHAWN

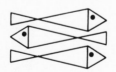

FARRAR, STRAUS AND GIROUX
NEW YORK

to William Shawn,
with my affectionate gratitude
for editing these London War Notes,
and for everything

1939

September 3

[*September 1, 1939, Germany invades Poland. September 3, Great Britain declares war on Germany.*]

For a week, everybody in London had been saying every day that if there wasn't a war tomorrow there wouldn't be a war. Yesterday, people were saying that if there wasn't a war today it would be a bloody shame. Now that there is a war, the English, slow to start, have already in spirit started and are comfortably two laps ahead of the official war machine, which had to await the drop of somebody's handkerchief. In the general opinion, Hitler has got it coming to him.

The London crowds are cool—cooler than they were in 1914—in spite of thundery weather which does its best to scare everybody by staging unofficial rehearsals for air raids at the end of breathlessly humid days. On the stretch of green turf by Knightsbridge Barracks, which used to be the scampering ground for the smartest terriers in London, has appeared a row of steam shovels that bite out mouthfuls of earth, hoist it aloft, and dump it into lorries; it is then carted away to fill sandbags. The eye has now become accustomed to sandbags everywhere and to the balloon barrage, the trap for enemy planes, which one morning spread over the sky like some form of silvery dermatitis. Posting a letter has acquired a new interest, too, since His Majesty's tubby, scarlet pillar boxes have been done up in squares of yellow

[3

detector paint, which changes color if there is poison gas in the air and is said to be as sensitive as a chameleon.

Gas masks have suddenly become part of everyday civilian equipment, and everybody is carrying the square cardboard cartons that look as though they might contain a pound of grapes for a sick friend. Bowlegged admirals stump jauntily up Whitehall with their gas masks slung neatly in knapsacks over their shoulders. Last night, London was completely blacked out. A few cars crawled through the streets with one headlight out and the other hooded while Londoners, suddenly become homebodies, sat under their shaded lights listening to a Beethoven Promenade concert interspersed with the calm and cultured tones of the B.B.C. telling motorists what to do during air raids and giving instructions to what the B.B.C. referred to coyly as expectant mothers with pink cards, meaning mothers who are a good deal more than expectant.

The evacuation of London, which is to be spaced over three days, began yesterday and was apparently a triumph for all concerned. At seven o'clock in the morning, all inward traffic was stopped and A.A. scouts raced through the suburbs whisking shrouds of sacking off imposing bulletin boards which informed motorists that all the principal routes out of town were one-way streets for three days. Cars poured out pretty steadily all day yesterday and today, packed with people, luggage, children's perambulators, and domestic pets, but the congestion at busy points was no worse than it is at any other time in the holiday season. The railways, whose workers had been on the verge of going out on strike when the crisis came, played their part nobly, and the London stations, accustomed to receiving trainloads of child refugees from the Third Reich, got down to the job of dispatching trainload after trainload of children the other way—this time, cheerful little cockneys who ordinarily get to the country perhaps once a year on the local church outing and could hardly believe the luck that was sending them now. Left behind, the mothers stood around rather listlessly at street corners waiting for the telegrams that were to be posted up at the various schools to tell them where their children were.

All over the country, the declaration of war has brought a new lease of life to retired army officers, who suddenly find themselves the commanders of battalions of willing ladies who have emerged from the herbaceous borders to answer the call of duty. Morris 10s, their windshields plastered with notices that they are engaged on business of the A.R.P. or W.V.S. (both volunteer services), rock down quiet country lanes propelled by firm-lipped spinsters who yesterday could hardly have said "Boo!" to an aster.

Although the summer holiday is still on, village schools have reopened as centres where the evacuated hordes from London can be rested, sorted out, medically examined, refreshed with tea and biscuits, and distributed to their new homes. The war has brought the great unwashed right into the bosoms of the great washed; while determined ladies in white V.A.D. overalls search the mothers' heads with a knitting needle for unwelcome signs of life, the babies are dandled and patted on their often grimy diapers by other ladies, who have been told off to act as hostesses and keep the guests from pining for Shoreditch. Guest rooms have been cleared of Crown Derby knickknacks and the best guest towels, and the big houses and cottages alike are trying to overcome the traditional British dislike of strangers, who may, for all they know, be parked with them for a matter of years, not weeks.

Everybody is so busy that no one has time to look up at the airplanes that pass overhead all day. Today was a day of unprecedented activity in the air. Squadrons of bombers bustled in all directions, and at midday an enormous number of vast planes, to which the knowing pointed as troop-carriers, droned overhead toward an unknown destination that was said by two sections of opinion to be (a) France and (b) Poland. On the ground, motor buses full of troops in bursting good humor tore through the villages, the men waving at the girls and howling "Tipperary" and other ominously dated ditties, which everybody has suddenly remembered and found to be as good for a war in 1939 as they were in 1914.

London and the country are buzzing with rumors, a favorite one being that Hitler carries a gun in his pocket and means to shoot himself if things don't go too well; another school of thought favors the version that he is now insane and Göring has taken over. It is felt that Mussolini was up to no good with his scheme for holding a peace conference and spoiling what has become everybody's war. The English were a peace-loving nation up to two days ago, but now it is pretty widely felt that the sooner we really get down to the job, the better.

September 10

The public at the moment is feeling like a little boy who stuffs his fingers in his ears on the Fourth of July only to discover that the cannon cracker has not gone off after all. When war was declared last Sunday, it was imagined that the German bombers would be over the same night, but Londoners woke up the next morning to find themselves as they were. Britons are slightly bewildered by a first week of war which has included the sinking by the Nazis of a ship full of neutrals, the accidental dropping of some bombs on Denmark, and the educational flights of the R.A.F., which seems to have constituted itself Leaflet-of-the-Month Club to the Third Reich. Laconic official bulletins have made reading between the lines the most popular sport of the hour.

In blacked-out London, millions of people are learning that it is a physical impossibility to keep the ears permanently skinned for warbling sirens, that life must go on even under the blue lights, and that boredom is nearly as potent a menace as bombs. Mr. Charles Cochran announced in a letter to the *Times* that his plans for an autumn revue are proceeding and that his young ladies are standing by; it does

seem probable that schemes for reopening theatres and cinemas will be drawn up shortly. Meanwhile, Britons find
themselves dependent for entertainment on the B.B.C.,
which desperately filled the gaps in its first wartime programs with gramophone recordings and jolly bouts of community singing stiff with nautical heave-hos and folksy non-
ny-noes. There has already been considerable public
criticism of these programs and of the tendency of announc-
ers to read out important news in tones that suggest they
are understudying for Cassandra on the walls of Troy. No
doubt in time entertainment will get back on a normal footing again. It is possible that the long winter evenings will
see a revival of those cozy Victorian family gatherings at the
piano or of the parlor game, and that popping round the
corner to see the new Shirley Temple will seem dashing indeed in a world where black is so uncompromisingly black.

One of the questions that have been bothering people
who live out in the country is the fate of the thousands of
German and Austrian refugees who are employed as servants
in remote districts where British domestics are unobtainable.
A soothing statement issued this week counselled these
aliens to act in a becomingly British manner and not to talk
German on the streets. They were also asked to report at
once to their local police stations. Countless anxious cooks
attired in their best dirndls turned up as requested and were
handed emergency orders which made it a serious offence for
them to possess without permission any explosives, motorcy-
cles, or sea-going craft, or to hoard any undeclared cameras,
maps, or nautical charts. Unbosoming themselves of any explosives which they happened to have around, they sped
happily back to their kitchens and got on with downing Hitler by bottling England's plum harvest, which is immense.

Another worry for the tender-hearted is the possible effect
of air raids on the nerves of domestic pets, and the *Times'*
kennel column carries dozens of advertisements offering
sanctuary to evacuating dogs for from 7s 6d a week. There
have also been pathetic appeals from many people to the
public to give a fair deal to the dachshund, that merry little

quadruped who had the misfortune in the last war to be linked in the popular imagination with the country of its origin. Today, so many Fritzes and Minnas rule over British hearts that he who casts the first stone is likely to find (war or no war) that he has started something.

Since every citizen has been forbidden to stir a yard from home without his or her gas mask, public ingenuity has occupied itself in this curious waiting period with the problem of how to carry the by now familiar cardboard container. A neat canvas case worn slung from the shoulder makes the whole thing as innocuous as a Kodak and is popular with the men. It has been observed that Queen Elizabeth, on her numerous smiling visits to the various women's organizations in London, carries her gas mask this way. "A woman carrying her mask in a satchel of violet velvet adorned with artificial roses caused," said yesterday's *Telegraph* restrainedly, "some curiosity." The rush to buy these cases must have been the only brisk business, aside from activity in the provisions departments, that the stores have experienced lately. Bond Street shopkeepers, struggling along gamely with skeleton staffs, have issued a list of firms which are open for business as usual; among them are Elizabeth Arden and Max Factor. The women of Barcelona, it is remembered, were always *soignée* between air raids.

How to accustom children to a war which at any moment may come right into the nursery is something that exercises everybody. The juvenile genius for accepting new conditions has already, however, reconciled many a family to a father unaccountably vanished and a mother who in a tone of determined gaiety proposes a game of Mickey Mouse in one of these amusing new mask things. The most comforting "reaction" so far reported was the remark of the little girl who countered parental whimsy with a stern "It's all right, Mummie. I know what it is. It's a gas mask, and we put it on when they bomb us."

Rationing of petrol—to the tune of enough for only two
hundred miles per month per car—was to have come into
force today, so all yesterday cars queued up at the filling stations to get a full tank with which to start the lean days
ahead. By night, most filling stations in London and the suburbs hadn't a drop, and it was a surprise when an announcement was suddenly made over the radio that the rationing
scheme had been postponed until next Saturday. To most
people, this is going to be the hardest of all the disciplinary
methods to which Britons have had to adapt themselves in
the last fortnight. With, on the whole, astounding good
humor and an obedience remarkable in an effete democracy,
they have accepted a new troglodyte existence in which there
are few places of entertainment, no good radio programs, little war news, and nothing to do after dark except stay in the
cave, because crossing a Kensington square has become
about as healthy as it was in the days of lurking footpads.
This time, it is no thug who is likely to knock one out, but
one's own familiar lamppost, which has lighted one's latch-
key into the door on countless happier nights. Coroners have
had a few stern remarks to make in the past few days about
the blackout deaths, which are likely to become more and
more frequent, and to combat which Harrod's has arranged
a window showing a plaster *élégante* neatly equipped for
metropolitan night rambles with white hat, luminous disc,
white armlet, and buttonhole of flowers. "So we'll go no
more a-roving so late into the night" has taken on a significance that Byron never intended.

The cinema ban was partially lifted today, and audiences
gladly packed into the Empire, on Leicester Square, to get
back to unreality until six in the evening with Robert Tay-
lor and Hedy Lamarr in "Lady of the Tropics," or into Studio One to take their pleasures more grimly with "I Was a

Captive of Nazi Germany." Grillrooms have been packed since the war started; so have the pubs. In spite of the difficulties of getting together after dark, Londoners want company at the moment. British reserve has cracked under stress to the extent that neighbors now chat with positively village chumminess and the total strangers in the next apartment are liable to knock on the door and ask if they can bring a bottle of whiskey and their gas masks in. It's friendlier drinking together these days.

The Duke and Duchess of Windsor came home in a blaze of public apathy. No one seemed particularly glad or sorry, but everyone felt it was natural that yet another anxious family should want to be reunited in such times. The *Express,* always a fierce Windsor partisan, devoted space to the Duke's reading on the journey "The Nazis Can't Win," and to the Duchess's travelling coat—mustard-and-black tweed. Press comment otherwise was restrained and the public was too busy thinking about the men who were going to France to be able to whip up any especial emotion over one man who had come back. Since his homecoming, the Duke has slipped quietly around London, has been photographed shaking hands with Hore-Belisha at the War Office, and has taken tea with his brother at Buckingham Palace, where the sentries have put away their red coats for the duration and now mount guard, minus tourists with Kodaks, in khaki battle dress.

London is full of soldiers marching or sitting around waiting to be marched somewhere. Hundreds of special police have suddenly appeared on traffic duty, smart in newly issued uniforms and not yet quite nonchalant enough to resist a glance over the shoulder when a snorting bus pulls up a foot or so behind their outstretched arms. Of the women's uniforms, the smartest seems to be the dark blue and scarlet of the fire service, faintly recalling a musical-comedy Zouave. The West End women's shops report better business, especially in sensible things like tweed suits tough enough to last the three years for which everyone has been told to prepare, and smart slacks or house coats in which to brighten up the air-raid shelters.

Lord Gort and Winston Churchill are undoubtedly the most popular men of the moment here. Many who thought that Churchill was too dangerously akin to a shot of high explosives in a peacetime Cabinet are breathing a good deal easier at the thought of that cherubic-faced warrior back in his old place at the Admiralty. All grades of opinion seem to feel that Gort's all right. Britain's Commander-in-Chief is young for the job, and that again is felt to be all on the right side. The fact that the name of France's little gray general also begins with a "G" makes the team of Gort and Gamelin trip off the tongue with a racy swing in the endless game of fireside strategy that everyone plays while waiting for real news from the front to be spoon-fed by the Ministry of Information. The Ministry has announced that relatives of men with the British Expeditionary Force in France will not be allowed to write to them at present; neither will the soldiers be able to write home except on official "I-am-well" cards. It seems to be the present policy in this curious hush-hush war to keep the whole thing as impersonal as official communiqués that deal in terms of "considerable advances" and "heavy artillery attacks"—not in men.

September 19

The outbreak of war found the little village which we will call Mugbourne not entirely unprepared. All through the early spring months, we had turned out on foggy nights to attend Air Raid Precautions soirées and first-aid lectures given at the Dog and Pheasant. Colonel Basing, with his staunch lady helpers, had long ago gone round the countryside cramming astonished yokels' heads into gas masks. Although surprised, no one had resisted except an old man who said it was just as he feared: he could not get his durned beard in the mask nohow and if the Colonel had no objection, he thought he would take his chance in the woods. During the summer, plans had been made for billeting London *évacués* around the village should the evacuation order ever come. On Friday, September 1st, it came. For three days, the village school was reopened to receive the relays of mothers and children from London. On Sunday, September 3rd, we gathered around the radio in one of the classrooms to listen to the King's broadcast. It was a glorious evening. The sunlight streamed through the top windows onto the samples of juvenile flower-pressing and the photographs of Their Majesties' Canadian tour, clipped from the newspapers, that decorated the distempered walls. The Quality sat around on the school forms or perched on desks, nervously fiddling with blue pencils or the buttons of V.A.D. overalls as they listened. The Village, in charge of sizzling tea urns for the refreshment of evacuated mothers, modestly clustered in the doorway. Mrs. Molyneux-Thring had brought along her embroidery, a Chippendale-design stool cover, to while away the long hours of waiting for the bus loads of evacuees to arrive. In a dignified and at the same time respectful manner, she continued to fill in a squiggly corner of leaf while receiving the words of her sovereign. Miss Potts wept quietly. Colonel Basing, standing erect by the side of Mr. Crampton, the schoolmaster, blew his nose. Suddenly they all struggled to their feet for the National Anthem. Mugbourne, officially bidden Godspeed, was at war.

For the first week of the war the weather was superb. Everybody's garden was a riot of asters and dahlias at which nobody looked, except possibly the two evacuated infants who had found sanctuary with Mrs. Wade at the Dog and Pheasant and spent their first sylvan morning toddling on rickety legs round the flower beds methodically pulling every blossom up by the roots.

The visitors from London made a great difference to Mugbourne from the start. Cockney voices shrilled over the village green, where mothers sat listlessly in the sunshine, pining for the fleshpots of Battersea, or occasionally gathered their dirty-nosed infants around them and trailed along to the village hall, where Miss Potts and Miss Bull held a tribunal to receive complaints. None of the mothers had slept a wink the first night, it appeared. "It's the 'orrible quiet,

Miss," they said plaintively to Miss Potts. Some of them were knocked all of a heap at discovering that Mugbourne boasted no Woolworth's or Co-op Stores and that the most go-ahead draper's establishment was Luff's, where Mrs. Luff still made the classic inquiry, "Will you take the farthing change, ma'am, or a packet of needles?"

On the first Wednesday of the war, Mugbourne experienced its first air-raid warning. The village itself does not possess a siren, but the neighboring town of Shepherd Parva does, and a printed official notice advised us to take cover when we heard what was rather prettily described as a warbling blast. At about 8:15 A.M., everyone was electrified to hear, coming across beautifully on the calm morning air, Shepherd Parva warbling away to beat the band. Every man, woman, and child in Mugbourne promptly stuck a head out of the window and looked up at the sky, which remained placidly blue and undarkened by hostile aircraft. The only sound to be heard, apart from warbling Shepherd Parva, was the tooting of the huntsman's horn in Stogberry Woods, for it was the first cubbing morning of the year and in the absence of young Squire (who was manning a gun somewhere in England), the old Squire had hoisted himself painfully on a horse and come out as temporary Master. Quite unmoved by the warning, old Squire and his merry men continued to tootle and crash about happily in the copses. It was felt to be an excellent gesture which would certainly infuriate Hitler if he knew.

Reactions to our first alarm were on the whole prompt and praiseworthy. Miss Chubb, one of our sub-wardens, found that she had not yet been provided with the tin hat promised by a benevolent government for such a contingency. Nothing daunted, she donned an aluminum pudding basin, which fitted to a nicety, mounted her bicycle, and shot round her section blowing blasts on a whistle with a violence which shook the pince-nez on her mild nose. Mrs. Lovell's Nannie instantly shut the twins in the night-nursery cupboard as a precaution against flying shrapnel. Mrs. Molyneux-Thring's butler gave the order for the Moor Place staff to file out into the air-raid trenches dug beyond the water garden, the evacuation to be carried out in strict order of precedence, from housekeeper to tweeny. Most spectacular of all was the departure of Miss Sybil Molyneux-Thring to take up the position allotted to her as driver of an ambulance. When Shepherd Parva started to warble, Miss Molyneux-Thring was still abed. We heard later that she had struggled out of her night attire and into most of her uniform as she ran downstairs, completing her toilet on the last lap across the stable yard, where Parker, the chauffeur, had her car waiting with the engine already running. Handing him her nightdress, Miss Molyneux-Thring hopped in blithely and drove off in a scatter of gravel, leaving Parker clasping a few yards of peach-colored chiffon to his bosom and feeling that this was war all right.

At somewhere round nine, Shepherd Parva spoke again, this time in the steady, reassuring tones of the All Clear. Mugbourne, we felt, had not behaved too badly. We had been calm but ready for anything. The only person who suffered from the experience was an elderly lady, living a good way out from the village, who had heard the air-raid sirens but not the All Clear. She and her old cook were fished out of the cellar by Miss Chubb two days later. They had sat there quite philosophically, cooking emergency rations on a Primus stove and thinking that this was a nice, restful sort of air raid. If it had not been for the milk boy, who found an accumulation of untouched bottles sitting on the doorstep and raised the alarm, they might be there still.

October 1

Criticism is in the air these days, after pretty nearly a month of this curious twenty-five-per-cent warfare. Everyone is slightly fed up with something or other: with the Ministry of Information, which doesn't inform; with the British Broadcasting Corporation, which is accused of being depressing and—worse—boring; with the deficiencies of the fish supply, which have made fishmongers hoard herrings for their regular customers as though they were nuggets; and even with the bombs which don't drop. The war of nerves has degenerated into a war of yawns for thousands of Air Raid Protection workers, who spend their nights playing cards, taking cat naps, and practically yearning for a short, sharp air raid. The fact that many of them are drawing an average of £2 10s a week for doing nothing much except waiting around has also caused a good deal of murmuring.

The Ministry of Information comes off worst with everybody. The man in the street feels, rather naturally, that he is paying plenty for this war, that he is entitled to know what is happening, and that he wants more to happen. He feels that something is rotten in a system which recently went through the most complicated acrobatics of releasing, suppressing, and releasing again even such a harmless piece of news as Her Majesty's return to London from a visit to the Princesses at Balmoral. The Englishman grumbles, but to be long on patience is one of the traditional strengths of the British.

Sir Seymour Hicks, the veteran actor, radiating his particular brand of intimate charm over the microphone in a talk on humor and the war, said that laughter was an important asset in the job of winning a war and one which the Nazis conspicuously haven't got. The English have it, and they may need it before they win this one, which everyone here sees more and more as a lineup of the forces of decency against those of thugdom. With red sky at morning giving a more than usually sinister warning of foul weather ahead, the conflict shows signs of coming into the open as an out-and-out Holy War.

October 8

Hitler's speech made no particular news here, since it was no more and no less than was expected. The orator who stole all this week's thunder was Mr. Winston Churchill, whose broadcast speech last Sunday evening turned out to be a model for such things and put new heart into countless homes where the theme song was beginning to be "Kremlin, Keep Away from My Door." The First Lord's guess as to the motives actuating that "riddle wrapped in mystery inside an enigma" may be proved wrong by subsequent events, but the fact that he made such a friendly reference to the Soviet Union has created much interest here, where the public, always carefully brought up on the idea of the U.S.S.R. as the bogeyman of Europe, is more than usually fogged as to what it's all about. Everyone wants peace, but at the moment no one can see much hope of it. Meanwhile, everyone is watching with strained interest the game of diplomatic musical chairs going on in Eastern Europe, feeling dimly that somewhere there is the answer that will settle the fate of Western Europe for years to come.*

London made several efforts last week to supply a few crumbs of nourishment to the intellectually starved public. The National Gallery came out with the announcement that it is sponsoring a series of lunchtime concerts at popular prices. All the Gainsboroughs and Van Dycks having been evacuated to the country, one will now mount the familiar steps, pay a shilling, and listen to a program of chamber music while strolling through the empty anterooms, where only discolored squares on the walls show the position of one's old favorites. "It's a good thing that someone is doing something about music," the *Times* wistfully observed. "We need the rectifying influence of music which can stand for an immutable order of being, unshaken by the shocks of politics." Unfortunately, this is not the type of music dished out at present by the B.B.C., which persists in talking under the public's head. To get anything worth listening to, people have been forced to do a little bootleg tuning-in on enemy stations, whose Bach and Beethoven make better propaganda than anything else the Nazis are likely to put on the air.

The other blow struck for the arts was the partial reopen-

* On September 17, Russia invaded Poland.

ing of the theatres under a staggered-hours plan. The first play to open since the war started will be J. B. Priestley's "Music at Night," which comes to the Westminster on Tuesday and had a tryout at the Malvern Festival a year ago. It is an experimental attempt to dramatize the reactions of a group of easily recognizable types—elderly statesman, titled harlot, young Communist poet, etc.—to the performance of a violin concerto. Played in lighting as murky as a blackout and progressing entirely through the spoken thoughts of the listeners, with occasional "Outward Bound" interruptions from the dead, who enter from the next world behind curtains, the dialogue hops briskly in and out of time, harping on the terrors of approaching dissolution in a way which may not seem exactly hilarious to an audience with a gas mask under every seat and an ear cocked at night for the sirens.

However Mr. Priestley's adventure is received, there is not much doubt of the warmth of welcome waiting for the Crazy Gang, which has announced that it will be back at the old stand at the Palladium in the near future. Nervo and Knox, Flannagan and Allan, and the rest may be relied on to concoct just the right mixture of low slapstick, honest sentiment, and legs, in that order, guaranteed to warm the cockles of the British heart through the long and trying winter evenings to come.

Getting back to the radio, as everyone does these days, one of the few simple pleasures left to us at the moment is the English broadcaster on one of the German stations, who is popularly supposed to be the British officer who was imprisoned for a while in the Tower as a traitor. He reads out the Nazi news bulletin in a voice which has ludicrous moments of seeming to parody Noel Coward at his most strangled. His frequent allusions to the *Ark Royal,* which he still insists is at the bottom of the sea, caused the irreverent to hum Mr. Coward's little ditty, "Has Anybody Seen Our Ship, the H.M.S. *Disgusting?*"

Mr. Coward himself has joined the Navy; so has one of the best British actors, Ralph Richardson. Beatrice Lillie is going around singing to the troops, and recently created quite a contretemps. One regiment planned to present the lady with a bouquet of gladiolas after her performance, but unfortunately she sang "I Hate Spring," which contains the line "I hate gladiolas." There was a hurried conference of officers, and Miss Lillie got no bouquet.

In London one never hears an airplane. The sky is quiet, patrolled only by blimps, which glitter in the sunlight like swollen fairy elephants lolling against the blue. In the country, the sound of aircraft is never absent; the planes roar overhead by day and night. The glorious weather still holds, the pheasants whirr, and the guns pop away in the woods. The evacuated children have settled down now more or less peacefully. On Sunday, parents come to see them and every village has its reunited family parties walking about in their best clothes, the children pointing out landmarks to Mum and Dad like old inhabitants. Play centres and health clinics have been organized for them, and in some cases communal feeding, when cottagers have found it difficult to provide midday dinner or transport to and from school was a problem.

The horse has made a comeback in the country. Stout ponies honorably pensioned off to the paddocks have been put between the shafts again and ancient governess carts creep along the lanes bearing the guests to the station, the children to school, and the housewife to do her shopping. Since the butcher and the grocer have announced apologetically that "owing to the petrol rationing we can only come out your way Mondays," people have had to get rid of a flock of lordly ideas. Today, when the lady of the manor goes to tea with a neighbor and the butler starts out on his half-day, they both use bicycles. It may be a healthy trend.

October 15

Mr. Hore-Belisha arose in Parliament on Wednesday and told the members about the stupendous task of moving the

British Army safely to France. Sending soldiers off to war, 1939 version, is a dark and secret business shorn of all "Cavalcade" trimmings of flags, running children, and military bands playing "The Girl I Left Behind Me." The girls these soldiers are leaving behind them very likely don't know even the dates of their men's departure, or, if they do know, are allowed to tell no one. Everything about this war is shrouded in a thick hush-hush fog confusing and irritating to a people who are accustomed to take their wars straight and imperialistic, with plenty of flag-wagging and patriotic fervor. So far, there is little of either, and people talk as though the war were some tiresome chore, inconvenient and dangerous but something that every sensible person realizes he must tackle if the house is ever going to be set in any sort of order.

Hopes of there being a short cut to peace were not very buoyant in London last week, although Chamberlain's speech was generally approved and the Stock Exchange maintained a more cheerful level than it has at any other time since the war started. Londoners brewed themselves cups of the first pool tea, whose price is controlled at 2s 4d a pound; made new jokes about the pamphlet raids, in which someone inevitably brought off a crack about "Mein Pamph"; and started to dig in philosophically for the long English winter that will be broken, so many people think, by the primroses and bombers arriving simultaneously.

Directly war broke out, American periodicals mailed to English subscribers were stopped at the docks for reasons which have not been very clearly stated. Last week, copies began to dribble in again, and Britons were able to read a more comprehensive reporting of events than any their news-starved eyes had seen since war started. At home, the fashionable periodicals, such as *Tatler* and *Sketch,* are carrying on gamely, though in somewhat leaner form, since the death of the social season did them out of most of their glossy prey. Unable to photograph peers on shooting sticks, they get along as best they can with peeresses driving ambulances, débutantes trundling fire hose, and young Guardees trundling débutantes around the Café de Paris; also with the wedding groups of couples who have suddenly heard Time's winged chariot rumbling all too uncomfortably near the war.

Map dealers are doing a brisk trade, although it is a disturbing fact that no sooner is a new map nailed in position than some fresh turn of events is likely to cancel everything and lay up more old boundary lines in lavender. Canny spenders are waiting a while before investing any more money in the changing face of Europe. Headlight regulations change just about as rapidly, and motorists have got themselves headaches trying to obey capricious official behests to paste paper on their solitary headlight, to hood it, to paint over the reflectors, or to mask the whole thing in a sort of peekaboo yashmak. Most people, having lost track after the last regulation but one, have now got mad and leave things the way they are, which is usually pretty murky.

Londoners tell country people that they don't know how bad blackout driving can be. The yokels reply sourly that Londoners have curbs to guide them and that rural drivers only have white lines which end when they get off the highroads, leaving them to grope down lanes where the road surface, the grass, and the ever-yawning ditches all look the same uniform, unhelpful gray. Since no one enjoys driving after dark, the plight of the country dweller in remote districts is truly dismal. Friends living only a few miles apart, and despairing of ever getting together at home, have been forced to fix up a rendezvous in London, where, at any rate, they are sure to have to go for a day's shopping, or to meet husbands, sons, or lovers up for a few hours' leave from their war stations.

The closing of certain tube stations in London has made a terrible congestion at bus stops in the rush hours. The wily board their bus when it gets blocked at a traffic light; otherwise, chances of getting a seat are remote. Cycles are appearing on the streets in increasing quantities, ridden by young girls in slacks, by civil servants pedalling down to Whitehall, and by smart women, trimly snooded and headed for lunch at the Berkeley, who wait nonchalantly in traffic blocks with a lorry snorting to starboard and a dray horse, looking thoughtfully at their fox neckties, on the port side. Shops close earlier to give their people a chance to get home before the blackout. No one can imagine what it will be like when winter really comes and it gets dark round about teatime.

October 29

The war continues to have a strange, somnambulistic quality in which the latest rumor that Hitler intends to try a 1066 invasion of British shores strikes just the right dreamy note. Lloyd's is laying odds that the war will be over by Christmas; others seem to feel that by the time the season of peace and good will is here this curious, trancelike period may have moved into the class of active nightmare. There is still an astonishingly general belief, or hope, or perhaps a mixture of both, that something will happen. What that something may be remains vague, but it is argued that enough things have happened already to confound anybody who imagined that this war was going to adhere to the rules.

The most persistent theory is that the light in the sky will arise from a conflagration inside Germany. However that may be, the fact that millions of people on both sides are apparently clinging to the conviction that a miracle may yet occur before it is too late emphasizes the world's detestation of war. The expected miracles differ in detail, but the desperate, unquenchable hope is the same in any language.

Food rationing is in the offing, though retailers do not seem to know the actual date when it is to come into force. Generous allowances are promised and the Minister of Food, Mr. W. S. Morrison, has issued the soothing statement that margarine is better for you in winter than home-produced butter. The *Express* is raising the cry "Why ration at all?," arguing that there is plenty of food for everyone and that the public should not be made to feel the pinch when there is no real need. Last month, the rush of careful housewives to

stock up their cupboards with homemade preserves and bot-
tled fruits made sugar hard to get, and this month imported
bacon and eggs have been so elusive that Britons had to give
up their favorite breakfast and eat more fish, which is again
fairly plentiful.

Apart from these deficiencies, now largely remedied, the
food supply seems to be abundant. One of the few staples
still unobtainable is ground almonds—so essential for the
concoction of Christmas goodies—but as a salesman at an
old-fashioned firm of grocers temperately remarked the other
day, "They were scarce even before this affair started."
Which was true, probably as a result of that other affair in
Spain.

The authorities promise that better lighting will shortly
be provided in trains at night. At the moment, nocturnal
travel is a glum procedure: the blue lights in the ceilings of
the carriages make reading an impossibility, which throws
the traveller rather heavily back for entertainment on his
own thoughts and on guesswork about his fellow-passengers,
whose noses he can see faintly through the encircling gloom.
Word has gone around that it is cozier to ride in the restaurant car, where the windows are blacked-out day and night
so that it is possible to provide a handsome inside light for
the customers. The result is a stampede of City gentlemen
and shopping matrons, with gas masks and parcels, into the
restaurant cars on the commuters' trains each evening. Since
it is necessary to order some kind of refreshment to justify
one's stopping in a restaurant car, the City gentlemen take
Guinness, and the shopping matrons space out a small sherry
over a long journey while the atmosphere slowly thickens
with smoke and with the passengers' snug satisfaction that
they are there reading their *Evening Standard*s like Chris-
tians.

Travel by day is bad enough, now that the timetables have
been further curtailed by wartime emergencies. Railroad
service seems to be even more erratic than it was during the
weeks when the big movement of men and materials to
France was under way. Every carriage window is pasted up
with a notice counselling people to lie down on the floor in

the event of an air raid, but with trains the way they are, often packed to standing room only at busy times of the day, it would be quite a problem to do so.

November 12

For the first time since the last war, there was no Cenotaph ceremony on Armistice Day and the pigeons in Trafalgar Square were not startled by the eleven-o'clock sirens—sirens would be too sensational for anybody these days. There were still, however, the poppies pinned to coats of people in the streets and tied to automobile radiators, and there were still the old sad thoughts, made sadder by the feeling that it may be going to happen all over again in spite of the men whose blood these poppies represent. For the first time in their memory, English tots had to get along without rockets and bonfires on Guy Fawkes Night. The necessity of substituting a few mild squibs indoors must have brought the war home to them, although toy departments have already helped readjust juveniles to new conditions with such topical pleasantries as miniature balloon-barrage sets and gas masks for dolls complete in smart cases. Children's gas-mask cases are now available, too—jolly affairs that soften the whole sorry business with colored pictures of Donald Duck and Bopeep. It is said that the new masks for children under five are to be pastel-tinted so that the dreary functional design may not obtrude too horrifically against some tender nursery color scheme.

The government white paper on Nazi concentration-camp atrocities was a best-seller here. Bookstalls were cleared out of copies as fast as they came in, and on the day of publication City men were reading the pamphlets on all the trains and taking them home so their wives could plod queasily through the indictment. There was a general feeling of satisfaction that the government had seen fit to release the evidence at last.

The first film to be inspired by the Allies' aims, which

Low of the *Standard* describes as "the best cause in the world, with the worst propaganda," has appeared. It is Korda's "The Lion Has Wings," which opened at the London Pavilion last week. Made in six weeks and starring Merle Oberon and Ralph Richardson as a man and woman who get caught up in the march of events, the real stars are the planes and the airmen, including those who raided Kiel, seen taking off and coming back after the job. Although the picture had to be passed by the Air Ministry, the War Office, the Ministry of Information, and the regular film censor, enough remains from the cutting to make it a stirring document.

The luxury shops, having boarded themselves up so that the Bond Street stroller has to squint at pigskin and emeralds framed as though they were peepshows, are now beginning to think up ways of getting back the custom that in many cases is still in rural retreat. Elizabeth Arden has circularized the various women's organizations, inviting them to use her salon as a place where Wats (Women's Auxiliary Territorial Service) and Waafs (Women's Auxiliary Air Force) can meet their friends, take a shower, and telephone. So far, Miss Arden has sacked no employees and her prices remain stationary. She was one of an enterprising combine which included Digby Morton, the young dress designer, and Aage Thaarup, the milliner, who decided that if women couldn't come to their clothes the clothes must go to the women, and, acting upon that premise, staged a show at Bristol this week. Morton did the suits, including a neat number for bicycling, Thaarup designed the hats, and Arden took care of the faces under them. The audience ordered new tweeds and complexions, briskly taking note that burnt sugar is the color Miss Arden boosts to go with khaki.

Officially, makeup is frowned on in the Services, but a good deal of bootleg lipsticking is done; Englishwomen have never looked prettier than they do these days when they are dressing more simply, often going hatless, and working so hard that sleep comes easy at night, bombers or no bombers.

The weather has been wet and mild, to the relief of people in the country who are patriotically trying to do without central heating as long as possible. Allowances on coke and coal were first cut to seventy-five per cent of what each household had used last year, then restored to a full one-hundred-per-cent basis—but with requests to be economical. The hardy English sit around their houses wearing sheep-skin-lined bootees, and women's shops report a tremendous run on good old-fashioned Viyella pajamas by chilly wives whose husbands have gone to France.

The attempted assassination of Hitler caused great excite-ment here and some disappointment, which is being summed up in a calm British "Bad luck," as though some-one had missed a pheasant. Everyone thinks that They will try again and that They may easily be a little quicker on the trigger next time. It is felt that some sort of big crisis is approaching and that the next few days may set the jugger-naut properly in motion, or switch it over to different tracks altogether. Whichever way it goes, England is ready to meet it with resolution and good humor.

November 24

The mining of the Dutch vessel *Simon Bolivar* has clouded the past week and roused public opinion more than any-thing that has so far happened in this war. The *Athenia* was at least a British ship; the *Simon Bolivar,* being a neu-tral, was different. People bought papers and stood at street corners, reading with, for the first time, unconcealed feelings of rage and bitterness the mounting death roll and the horri-fying tales of survivors. After his second radio talk of the war, Mr. Churchill had been a good deal criticized for a snorted reference to "Hitler and his Huns," but now the old epithet has been taken out of the mental lumber room, dusted off, and found to be as good for the atrocities of 1939 as it was for those of 1914. Mr. Chamberlain's announcement of immediate economic reprisals was greeted with satisfaction, although, ironically enough, it is the Dutch, through whose ports Germany has been shipping, who will suffer as much as anyone from the threatened seizure of German exports.

In view of the Minister of Agriculture's advice to dig for victory, everyone is thinking in terms of rotating crops as much as of color schemes for flower gardens, although an official pamphlet warns the overzealous against sacrificing rare plants and shrubs that may be difficult to replace after the war. More than a quarter of a million bulbs are now being planted as usual in the London parks, and the usual display is promised for the flower beds in front of Buckingham Palace, where crowds stroll in the summer admiring the perfect match of the scarlet geraniums and the sentries' coats. (It will be more difficult to match the new battle dress.) A short time ago, the Horticultural Society held its delayed autumn show, at which garden-lovers—and that in England takes in pretty nearly everybody—were able to view the newest floral aristocrats and find as much spirited solace as music-lovers have derived from the lunchtime concerts at the National Gallery.

The Queen, by the way, has been twice to those concerts. People pack into them daily, sitting on chairs if they are lucky and on the floor if they are not. Sandwiches can be bought for threepence each, but most of the office workers bring lunch with them and munch dreamily while listening to Bach and Schubert, taking no notice of the cameramen who suddenly pop from behind pillars to shoot pictures of Myra Hess at her piano or of some celebrity in the audience. Most of the paintings have been evacuated to country hideouts, but the regular National Gallery uniformed attendants are still there, hovering in the background, having a perfectly elegant time listening to the music, and keeping a practiced eye open in case someone tries to lift a Steinway and smuggle it out under his coat. The applause at the end of the programs is tremendous and moving. People hurry out into Trafalgar Square, shouldering their gas masks and looking all the better for having been lifted for an hour to a plane where boredom and fear seem irrelevant.

Probably the most notable feature of the wartime landscape is the absence of children and nannies in the parks,
which seem lifeless these days without the morning caval-
cades of prams and Scotch terriers. Sandbags and the strips
of adhesive paper gummed over windows are now accepted
as part of the scene. The sandbags have been brightened up
with color. Prunier's sandbags are the same shade of blue as
the paint on the building, which thus won the distinction of
having the most chic frontage in town, and a Westminster
antique shop has had its blackout shutters decorated by a
well-known artist with a mural painting of antique furniture, the owner, and her Pekinese dog, together with an invitation to step inside and view all three.

People are not staying at home nights. Places like the Café
Royal are packed each evening with customers drinking beer
and talking endlessly—talking about the war. Although notices are up in most places warning one not to discuss
matters of national importance (startled country vicars were
rebuked the other day for imparting what was called valuable information to the enemy in some innocent parish-maga-
zine chatter about old Mrs. Brown's son Alfred's being at
Scapa Flow and Farmer Green's hired man Charlie's serving
with the anti-aircraft in Kent), no one discusses anything
else.

Everyone agrees that Hitler doesn't know what to do next,
that the Turks should have been on the Allies' side in the
last war, that the Italians may again be on their side in this
one, and that the Germans may be in the next one, which
some say will be against Russia and will be the genuine Ar-
mageddon.

Coming out into the blackout after these evenings is like
falling into an inky well; the only lights are the changing
green and red crosses of the masked traffic signals and the
tiny flashing torches of pedestrians feeling their way like
Braille readers around the murky puzzle of Piccadilly Circus. A hawker with a tray of torches does a roaring trade
there these dark nights. So great has been the demand for
batteries that spares are now unobtainable, and exasperated
Londoners whose torches fail find that they either have to

buy a complete new one or risk breaking a leg when they sally out of doors. Everyone echoes Bottom in "A Midsummer Night's Dream": "A calendar, a calendar! look in the almanack; find out moonshine, find out moonshine." It is felt that moonlit nights may be an invitation to bombers, but at least they're more friendly.

On these fine mornings, London bus-drivers hail each other sardonically by saying, "Nice day for the *Blitzkrieg,* Bill," but so far nothing has happened. Anti-aircraft fire has been heard, and an enemy plane flew over Deal while thousands peered. Meanwhile, an advertisement in the *Times* suggests stocking up with "Nature's syren, the pheasant." It announces that an aviary of these birds in your garden will give audible warning of bombers long before the human ear can detect them, and offers a cock and five hens, all smart as can be at hearing the bombs leave the racks, for £2, carriage paid, from the Cotswold Game Farm, Stroud.

December 8

For the past week, whenever anyone has asked if there was fresh news, he has probably been inquiring after November's war, not September's. The Soviet invasion of Finland has set back the Comrades' cause in this country to an extent succinctly expressed by a mob in Aberdeen which broke some windows of a building occupied by Communists, tore up the floor, and burned Stalin's portrait in the street. People felt right up to the last, as they did about Hitler and Poland, that Stalin would not drop the handkerchief. Since he has done so, the campaign is being watched with breathless attention as a sort of test for the enormous Soviet war machine. Now that it has an imperialistic philosophy back of it, many people think it may turn toward Asia Minor and someday toward the Khyber Pass and the task of converting Mother India into Comrade India. Kipling readers have been brushing up on "The Man Who Was," that echo of the old dream of Russia's imperial ambitions. Members of the Finnish colony in London, many of them in national dress, went to church to pray for their countrymen, who at the moment of writing don't seem to be doing too badly, thanks to the snow, which they need (and have) as much as the Poles needed (and didn't get) mud.

Christmas shopping is starting, though the public was slightly intimidated by Sir John Simon's speech warning everyone to put his money away, as it would certainly be needed before long to help win the war. This raised a tremendous outcry from the shopkeepers, who now, at least, have been promised they will be allowed to use special shaded lights for their windows, so that shoppers can stroll and look at the Christmas displays after blackout hours. (An architect has just submitted to the Home Office plans for turning the whole of Oxford Street into a roofed-in market for the duration of the war.)

The toy fair at Harrods, usually a high spot, is a dismal sight this year. The toys are there all right, but the children are missing. Only occasional groups wander up to shake hands with Father Christmas, chivied along by anxious parents who have sneaked them up for the day from the country and are sandwiching the fair between a haircut and a visit to the dentist.

At this and other stores of its kind, business does not seem to be especially brisk as yet. To see the real crowds one has to look in at a Woolworth's (the young Princesses recently did a bit of Christmas shopping in one of them in Scotland). Merchants have been wailing about the stubborn refusal of the women to change into evening dress these nights—a refusal which is having a disastrous effect on the British fashions trade. There seems to be a general impression that it's better to be bombed in a high neck than a low one, and theatre audiences have a sober look about them, what with the khaki and blue of soldiers and aviators on leave and the dark dresses of the women.

Last Sunday, the first group of mothers and fathers was sent down from London to see their evacuated children in the country, with their expenses paid by the government. The railway stations looked much as they did during the evacuation itself, only this time the crowds waiting on the platforms were adults dressed in their best, happily clutching Christmas bundles for the children they probably hadn't seen in three months. Bringing the children home for the holidays is being frowned upon by the authorities, who cynically figure out that the season of peace and good will won't stop the Nazis from making an air raid if they feel like one.

In most of the reception areas, the hard-working women's voluntary services are organizing Christmas parties for the evacuees, with trees, crackers, and more fun than the kids have probably ever had in their lives. Some of the parents show their gratitude in touching ways. In one village, a Jewish tailor from the East End, charmed by the hospitality his family was receiving, wrote commanding his son to measure the man of the house for a suit. The boy clambered around the farmer with a tape measure and three days later the suit arrived with the father's compliments—slick as anything and the last word from Aldgate. Everybody was tickled to death.

The grade schools are not the only ones to be reshuffled by the march of events; public schools, too, have done a sort of general post—Dulwich, for instance, has gone to double up with Tonbridge. There is even a story of two schools' simply swapping premises, with satisfaction to all concerned. Eton and Harrow are carrying on as usual, having built air-raid shelters expensive and expansive enough to satisfy the most fidgety mother. Harrow thinks that it won't be bombed anyway, since the Harrow church steeple was said to be a grand landmark to German aviators in the last war. Eton has made a stately concession to current happenings by partially abolishing top hats, which are tricky things to wear with gas masks.

At Oxford and Cambridge, the remaining undergraduates are either foreigners or under military age, but the population of both universities has been augmented by various transplanted government departments. Oxford, in addition, now houses the Royal Institute of International Affairs, which has roosted at Balliol. The nineteen-year-olds are taking an abridged course, which can be completed after the war if they feel like it. No one seems to know what has happened to the young men who voted a few years back that under no circumstances would they fight for King and Country.

December 22

This is by a long shot the queerest Christmas season anyone remembers. Three months have brought about an unprecedented revolution in the cozy institution of British family life. The mass migration of big business concerns to the safety areas means that thousands of their employees will be sitting down to eat Christmas dinner in somebody else's home—a real hardship to the fireside-loving Briton, who likes to turn sentimental once a year. Thousands more Englishmen, abandoning their traditional reserve, will be tacking up stockings for strangers' children. Carol singers have been told that they will be permitted to sing how glory shone around so long as their lanterns don't shine around too conspicuously, but they must not ring bells, which might be confused with an air-raid signal.

The hotels and restaurants are arranging gala evenings as usual, banking on the fact that there's going to be a full moon, which, if the skies are clear, will help people find their way around. The shops report that people have been going in for the good old reindeer and snowy coaching scenes on Christmas cards rather than for pleasantries about gas masks and suchlike. Most of the churches have cancelled plans for midnight services because of the difficulties of blacking out large stained-glass windows, and Westminster Abbey has had to put off its annual carol service because all the choirboys have been evacuated to the country. Incidentally, it has been pointed out here that the Holy Family's flight into Egypt was one of the earliest examples of evacuation from the consequences of a dictator's power politics; what's more, that They stayed there until the danger was over, which points a seasonable moral to parents who are bringing their children back to the cities in spite of government warnings.

The *Graf Spee* was the Royal Navy's Christmas present to the British public. Naturally, nothing much else was discussed last week and everyone listened in on Monday to Mr. Winston Churchill, who abruptly let a cat out of the official bag by informing listeners that the first Canadian contingent had been escorted safely to a British port—news which the censor had told the papers must not be revealed until Wednesday morning. Mr. Churchill was rapped over the knuckles by the *Times* in a dignified leader headed "An Uncensored Broadcast" and jubilantly thanked by the *Daily Express,* which pointed out that anyhow Tuesday's Court Circular got away with an item about General Sir Charles Grant's representing His Majesty at the arrival of the Canadian troops. On the whole, the man in the street agrees with the *Express* and likes Churchill's bluff broadcasts, which seem to clear the air after the B.B.C.'s coy announcements about something that sounded like gunfire having been heard early in the morning by residents of a southeast coast town.

Music and the theatre have already revived gamely from the anesthetic administered to them in September. Now art is showing signs of stirring—and just in time, too, for artists are in a bad way. The Royal Academy, which has sponsored so many shows of international masterpieces, is remembering the cause of art at home and planning to open a United Artists Exhibition next month, to help the Red Cross and the Artists Benevolent Institute. Another Red Cross benefit is a show of drawings by the eight-year-old Plato Chan, which was formally opened at Cooling's by a slightly older artist— Sabu, the Indian boy actor of "Elephant Boy." Tooth's Galleries say they are giving no outstanding one-man shows until March, when they plan an exhibition of paintings by Augustus John, in which the high spot will be a portrait of Queen Elizabeth that John started work on last week.

Since the sea is such an unhealthy place these days, air travel has received a great fillip. Not only passenger but freight traffic is going that way, and there are a good many hush-hush rumors about new air lines to the Balkans. Imperial Airways, which has moved part of its personnel to Bristol, says it is running its services more or less as usual. Every week, two flying boats leave for Australia; one goes to Durban, South Africa; and two land planes take off for Calcutta. Traffic is heavy; some planes are booked right up to April and the regular London-Paris service is so crowded that flights frequently have to be run in two sections. War or no war, it is hoped that transatlantic passenger service will be in working order by about June, with a fleet of three flying boats—the Golden Hind, Golden Fleece, and Golden Horn. At the moment, an effort is being made to work out a tieup with the Pan American Clipper service at Lisbon; in fact, some of the papers announced the other day that such a tieup had already been made, but Imperial Airways says it hasn't, largely because of various diplomatic snarls, such as Franco's refusal to let planes fly over Spain. You can't fly to Helsinki now. You can't fly direct to Leningrad, either, but then you never could. Somehow the idea of an air service to the U.S.S.R. has always seemed a little tricky to the Imperial people.

1940

January 4

MOST PEOPLE chose to see the New Year in quietly, although the big London restaurants put on the usual shows in their main dining rooms, where nostalgic Scots could eat their Hogmanay haggis and soldiers home on leave could have a good time looking at the girls. The more soberly inclined sat by their firesides waiting for the chimes and wondering what 1940 was going to bring. One of the prophecies all Britons can make without the help of an almanac is that everyone is going to be considerably poorer this year. Thousands of car registrations won't be renewed, because petrol rationing makes it so difficult and expensive to run a private car. With the shadow of the government's budget, to be announced in April, hanging over them, families have had to cut their own budgets drastically. Small businesses, especially those connected with the luxury trades, have suffered terribly, and now the larger retail businesses, with their crushing overheads, are also taking a beating. Facing a new year sure to bring more and more demands on their bankbooks, their nerves, and their good humor, Britons had a right to be thoughtful.

The general mood seems to have toughened up a good deal in the past few weeks. People don't go around so much saying that someone's niece says that Halifax says that the war will be over by spring, and you hear fewer wishful-thinking stories about dissatisfaction inside Germany. There is a growing feeling that the war will be a long business, but,

[37

though no attempt is made to minimize the dangers of the actual and potential lineups against them, the English are, on the whole, confident. They worry, however, about what will happen in Europe after peace comes. Even quiet middle-aged ladies can now talk federation with the best of them and think the idea a fine one because it would end all that frontier-and-customs nonsense which fusses them on their annual sprees to Portofino and Annecy; entire families are frequently made miserable, because Grandmother puts the present tragedy down to the harshness of the terms of the Versailles Treaty and Grandfather thinks that by God, sir, they weren't nearly harsh enough.

The Citizens Advice Bureaus are among the most valuable of the social services brought into being by the abnormal life that everyone is living. There are a hundred and eighty of these in the London area and about eight hundred in other parts of the country, staffed by experienced advisers ready to straighten out personal problems arising from the war. People go to them for legal advice about houses and furniture for which they have been paying on the installment plan and which they have had to leave behind in the evacuation reshuffle. Old men and women call to find out if they can be evacuated to safe areas and the bureaus try to find billets for them, but it isn't easy. "Old and infirm people take a good deal of looking after and people grow tired of them" is the official explanation—a full-length tragedy in seventeen words. More cheering is the success the bureaus have had in transmitting messages from refugees in this country to relatives still in Germany; the charge is sevenpence for twenty words, and you mustn't mention the war. The bureaus, working with the Red Cross, have sent more than six thousand of these messages so far, routing them through Geneva.

Pantomime, London's traditional holiday-time entertainment, is here again, no less traditional because of the references to A.R.P. wardens and blackouts slipped in with all the old comic business about the Widow Twankey and the Baron. Troops who didn't receive Christmas leave amused themselves by getting up their own pantomimes, bawdy as

Elizabethan comedy and bristling with cozy personal gags that would have meant nothing to anyone outside the selected audiences, who loved them. A politer offering may be "Heil Cinderella," with book by Cecil Beaton and John Sutro, which is billed for production in Wiltshire this week before an audience of troops, who will be edified by the sight of titled thighs in tights and by Mr. Beaton himself as one of the ugly sisters.

Ordinarily at this season, the Victoria Station platform from which trains leave for Channel boats is jammed with people and luggage and bundles of skis, all heading for snow and sunshine. This winter, the golden age of the Swiss hotel-keepers seems to have come temporarily to an end as far as British visitors are concerned; after a recent snowfall, people merely waxed their skis and took them out to do a few wistful turns on the mild English slopes. Even in the face of such a depressing business outlook, the clerks in Thomas Cook's Berkeley Square travel office are successfully preserving that air of polite detachment which they have cultivated so carefully for years. A young woman who had somehow contrived to scare up a permit to leave the country went in there the other day and broke the cathedral hush of the place by asking, in as casual a voice as she could manage, how to get to the Swiss skiing country. The clerk simply nodded, reached for the proper travel folders, and said, "Certainly, madam. May I suggest that you go via Paris?"

One of the nicest sights in London has always been the little horsedrawn delivery van of Scotts, the hatters. This spick-and-span varnished turnout with a liveried coachman and footman on the box is frequently seen spanking sedately around the West End. The other day it turned up in St. James's Street, still elegant and just the same as usual except that the coachman and footman had left off their cockaded toppers and were wearing nicely brushed tin hats.

January 12

Hore-Belisha's fall has made a noise here compared to which the Eden and Duff Cooper affairs were just mild tinkles in the Cabinet china cupboard. The recent crash set everything swaying and caused the gloomier observers to prophesy that it might easily bring the cupboard down, too. Although informed circles had heard the warning cracks for some time, the public got the shock of its life when it picked up the paper last Saturday morning and saw the headlines. To most people, H.-B. seemed to be a competent man doing a difficult job; those in closer contact with him perhaps might have said that he was a difficult man doing a competent job. Even those who disliked him have never denied that he has produced results in his two and half years at the War Office. How much came from his own reforms and how much from the spadework of others is now a matter for interested speculation.

Over the weekend, photographers were allowed to go and snap the ex-War Secretary relaxing as a country gentleman on his estate in Wimbledon, looking at ease in an open-necked shirt and affably patting a bull terrier. The man in the street had come to think of H.-B. as being a good deal like a bull terrier himself—no beauty but a dandy fighter, snapping energetically at festoons of dusty red tape and through it all remaining the comedian who never forgot to grin broadly, usually toward the cameras, before nipping another august shin. However much that beaming talent for publicity annoyed some people, there is no doubt that H.-B. was satisfactory to the public, who had no access to the interdepartmental goings on, and his removal has let loose a shindy of a magnitude which presumably Chamberlain never expected.

The reaction of the Army, or anyway of the high-up staff officers, seems to be one of satisfaction; they feel the fellow

was a nuisance and a bit of an outsider too. The Jewish issue
possibly meant more than foreign observers who see England
as the welcoming haven of the non-Aryan refugee realize.
The English have their share of anti-Semitism, less violent
than the totalitarian article but still pretty strong, especially
in the upper classes. On the other hand, a typical cockney
comment, heard in a bus, was " 'Is nose 'appens to be the
wrong shape, that's all." Dailies like the *Express* and the
News Chronicle simplified the issue into a feud between the
perhaps over-impatient War Secretary and the blimpish
brass hats at the head of the fighting services and screamed
shrilly for someone's blood.

About the most plausible of the many rumors floating
around the town at the moment is that H.-B., in some of his
public and semi-public utterances, didn't practice the discretion necessary in his position. Perhaps that's what the *Times*
was referring to when it suggested that a perfectly simple explanation would present itself "to those who have been
brought into daily contact with the late War Secretary's expansive nature." In the general din of the battle, little has
been said or written about H.-B.'s successor, Oliver Stanley,
partly because there is little to say or write—baffled Britons
cling to the fact that he's Lord Derby's son, for the noble
lord is a good fellow—and partly because he is in bed suffering from influenza.

People now find it difficult to remember that only four
months ago it seemed possible that Londoners would go on
leading a troglodyte existence for the rest of their lives. In a
way, London has settled down to a wartime routine in which
people don't look up—much—when a plane flies over the
houses, and no one bothers to carry a gas mask except country cousins up for a gape at the balloon barrage. Maybe, as
the Premier warned everyone in his Mansion House speech,
it's the calm before the storm, but calm of a kind it certainly
is. Women crowd into the January sales and placidly buy
blankets shown in windows on which stickers say that there's
an air-raid shelter for fifty persons below. Friends mislaid in
September are drifting back to London again, looking rubi-

cund and somewhat sheepish in tweeds bought for a prolonged rustic retreat. Restaurants are doing marvellous business, even though you get only one lump of sugar with your coffee and the waiter is likely to point out that the little pat is butter and the big pat is margarine. If it weren't for the fact that you never stop talking about it and that the Premier's speech made the public uneasily certain that they'd never stop paying for it, you'd hardly know that a war was on.

January 27

For the past week, the principal topic of conversation has been burst water pipes. Londoners who evacuated their households in September and forgot to turn off the water at the main have come back to find their homes awash and plumbers as eagerly sought after as butter.

A committee headed by Sir Kenneth Clark has named the first four or five of a group of artists whose job it will be to record the wartime scene at home and abroad; the results are to be exhibited from time to time and will eventually be housed in the Imperial War Museum. The late Sir William Orpen did much of his best work in just such a capacity during the last war. The present selections are interesting because they belong to the progressive Left Wing of art and not to the conventional, academic Right. The results of the new group's trips to the front lines ought to be worth waiting for. Three of the first chosen—Rushbury, Kennington, and Roberts—were in on World War I, doing the same job. Kennington and Roberts were the illustrators of Lawrence's *Seven Pillars of Wisdom* and Kennington recently completed an impressive full-length recumbent marble figure of Lawrence in Arab robes which is to be a permanent memorial in the little country church in Dorset where that complex and fascinating genius lies buried, ever-recurring myths of resurrection to the contrary.

Sir Kenneth is a busy man these days. In appearance rather like a young and diffident Oxford don, he is a director of the National Gallery, a great art expert himself, and has just been appointed official adviser on film propaganda.

Quite a number of well-known artists are doing camouflage work in various parts of the British Isles. The other day, one of them asked for permission from the Air Ministry to go up in a plane and take a peek at his handiwork, remarking that it was impossible to get any idea of its efficacy from the ground, and after a good deal of waiting about, the request was granted. The camouflage artist hurried aloft with a pilot, but before he even had time to pop his head over the side, so the story goes, there was a roar of shrapnel bursting around the plane and the two men found themselves making a hasty forced landing, badly scared and quite a bit damaged, in a field in Essex. No one, it seems, had passed on word of the flight to the men in charge of a nearby anti-aircraft battery, who gleefully scampered to gun stations and let fly when spotters reported an unidentified plane approaching. Anti-aircraft people have been on the job guarding London since August, and most of them would probably sob with delight at the sight of a few Heinkels.

Lord Hawhaw, as the man who broadcasts from Hamburg in an English voice telling of supposed British losses in the war is known here, now has a revue named after him and has made the book counters with an "autobiography," told, or so it is pretended, to Jonah Barrington, who invented His Lordship's name in the *Daily Express*. Lord Hawhaw is good for a laugh anywhere. B.B.C. comedians, when short of a gag, simply ask in the familiar, slow, only slightly accented voice of the Hamburg broadcaster, "Where is the Isle of Wight?," and answer themselves by saying that the Isle of Wight has been sunk. But though Britons laugh at Lord Hawhaw, they listen to him; as a radio personality, he's far more dynamic than the majority of the suave young men the B.B.C. puts on the air.

February 16

It's a tough outlook for the debs of 1940. Not only will they have to sidle into society without any preliminary shouting and without being peeped at eating sandwiches in a queue of Daimlers outside Buckingham Palace on a June evening, but they won't be able to include Ascot in their first season. The Jockey Club brought out its new list of races not long ago, calling for fifty-three days of racing up to June 1st instead of the usual ninety-two, and cutting out several important meetings, including Epsom, Ascot, and Sandown. There will probably be substitute races for the Derby and the Ascot Gold Cup elsewhere, but they won't be quite the same thing—the one without the gipsies and the thrills of Tattenham Corner; the other without the dearly loved traditions of the arrival in state of the King and Queen, of Queen Mary's toque blooming above the hydrangeas of the Royal Box, and of débutantes tripping over their trailing chiffons on the lawns.

The weather, which is once again a permitted topic in the papers, has been responsible for postponing several race meetings in the last week or two. Those that are run on schedule are attracting big crowds in which it's not unusual to see an owner in the battle dress of a private smartly saluting his trainer and superior officer. Jockeys, by the way, have been demonstrating their sympathy for Finland by subscribing toward a luxurious ambulance, which will be presented to the Finnish Minister by Gordon Richards, a well-known jockey, early next month. The donors' names are inscribed inside it and it will be driven by Stapleton Martin, a trainer, who is taking a couple of his stablehands along to Finland with him as orderlies.

All sorts of presents, as well as money, keep coming in for the Finnish and other relief funds now getting under way in London. The recent arctic spell seems to have brought home

events on the Karelian Isthmus to women, who have peeled
the fur coats off their backs and rushed round to dump them
at the Finnish headquarters here. Somebody gave a fire engine to the Turkish relief people, and a day or two later the
Finns were presented with enough fire-fighting equipment
to outfit an entire brigade.

The Polish Relief Fund has been made £500 richer
through the efforts of John Gielgud, who gave a benefit series of afternoon lectures on "Shakespearean Peace and War"
at the Globe Theatre, where he has been appearing in a
short revival of the delightfully staged and acted "The Importance of Being Earnest." Even on one of the coldest days
so far this year, Gielgud fans turned up, blue-nosed but
loyal, to dote upon their idol as he stood, looking pale and
sombre, at an immense lectern in the middle of the stage
and battled his way through a Hamlet soliloquy in the teeth
of an unprecedented gale of coughs and sneezes from the auditorium. The lecture gave Mr. Gielgud a chance to run
through his and the audience's favorite speeches and to fill
in with one or two cozy personal anecdotes, all of which had
fine results for the Polish Fund when well-known actresses
took the hat round at the intermission. Mr. Gielgud's pro-
jected tour of the neutral countries at the head of a Shakespearean company has been temporarily delayed by some diplomatic snarl. He's going back to the Old Vic for a season,
which should please Bernard Shaw, who has been publicly
lamenting the calling to arms of male ballet dancers and
hoping that the theatre won't sink to the deplorably devital-
ized state it did in the last war.

Every day, another bit of life joggles back to something
near normal. One by one, the museums are opening again.
You can wander once more through the fish and reptile galleries at the National History Museum, but only if you bring
along your gas mask, for they don't intend to have any phos-
gened Londoners left lying around among the cobras. The
Victoria and Albert has reopened and so has the Imperial
War Museum, where ironically inclined visitors can take a
look at Hitler's and Chamberlain's signatures on the famous

peace-in-our-time document. Another interesting exhibit there is a drawing of a celebration held here in July, 1918— a meeting at which Mr. Churchill declared, "Germany must be beaten, must know she is beaten, must feel she is beaten." The Museum officials add a note to the effect that until re- cently delicacy has prevented them from showing the drawing, but that they are doing so now because "the sentiments ex- pressed in Mr. Churchill's speech have once more become appropriate and seasonable."

Rationing has made it perfectly in order for the weekend guest to arrive with his own little parcel of butter, which he places in the hand of the butler who takes his suitcase. If the guest wants to express lyrical appreciation of the visit, his hostess would much rather he said it not with orchids but with something like a pound of Demerara sugar or a few pe- trol coupons. The coupons are supposed to be non-transfera- ble, but a certain amount of juggling goes on continually, and one hears all the time about garages where they whisper that they can slip you a tankful of petrol if you want it, but somehow such places seem to be in parts of the country to which one never goes.

Meat is to be rationed next month, and is being unofficially rationed at the moment, owing to a breakdown in distribu- tion, which has meant that many butchers have had great difficulty in supplying their customers. A new order issued last week helpfully extended the pheasant-shooting season for another month. The real reason for this was to protect crops from the unusually large numbers of birds left in cer- tain districts because so many shoots had been called off. "The order," said the *Observer* kindly, "need not have an adverse effect upon the pheasants' domestic arrangements," but it's had a cheering effect upon British housewives, who like their Sunday roast and who are going to need a lot of education before they really take an egg and that substitute called macon to their conservative bosoms.

March 2

Mr. Churchill hit off the mood of these last few days exactly when he ended his speech at the lunch to the officers and men of the *Exeter* and *Ajax* in the Guildhall with the now famous phrase "The Navy is here." The Navy is here all right, bang in the centre of the spotlight, which excellent showmanship has focussed on it at precisely the psychological moment. The march through London of the men who helped do in the *Graf Spee* was one of those things that are managed superlatively well in these parts. The police, forgetting for the day their wartime regulation that crowds must be kept moving, good-humoredly tried to keep the excited crowds stationary. Everybody told everybody else sentimentally that it was just like dear old King George's Silver Jubilee all over again.

Recruiting of volunteers to go to Finland is going ahead briskly. Some of them are already over there and a skiing battalion is now being formed under the auspices of Captain Hubert Martineau, well known to St. Moritz regulars, who had the crack skiing pro, Bill Bracken, help him get up a list of names of likely recruits. It must have seemed like old Suvretta Week to the crowd who went down to Hampshire last week to start training. After a short course there, the volunteers are going to a French winter-sports resort to polish up a bit on ski soldiering.

A good deal of speculation has been aroused by the questionnaire which has been sent around to each volunteer and which, after the usual questions about physical fitness and so on, asks whether the individual is thoroughly experienced in mountain and glacier work. There being hardly any mountains and no glaciers in Finland, it's a nice point whether this is somebody's geographical slipup or whether it means that the battalions are eventually destined for a terrain where mountains and glaciers are plentiful. Again, it may be just the official way of making the recruits hazy as to where they're likely to end up, since people will talk in spite of the amusing new Fougasse posters that tell them not to.

The first directory of emergency addresses has just been issued and makes fascinating browsing. One or two firms give alternative addresses to be used only "if London is rendered uninhabitable," but the majority appear to be already installed elsewhere, with new telegraphic addresses and everything. Among the film companies, Columbia is rusticating in Kent and United Artists in Bucks, while the Manufacturers Life Insurance Company of Canada has moved to the Barrie-ish address of The House in the Wood, Hindhead. It's ironical to note that the Royal Society of Arts moved for safety to a Georgian mansion at Uckfield, Sussex, which burned to the ground the other day.

A great many of the firms listed have probably brought their staffs back to London by now, although spring is only just around the corner and spring is when everyone seems to expect that "something will happen." It's a fine state of affairs when a primrose by the river's brim isn't a simple primrose any more but simply a reminder to keep the gas mask handy and make sure you're spry at beating it across the road to an air-raid shelter.

March 30

Londoners were determined to enjoy Easter this year, Hitler or no Hitler. In normal years, people who are driving out of town try to get away on the Thursday before Easter, because by Friday, all the main highways are jammed with cars full of family parties hurrying to the sea or country. It was nothing like that this Easter, naturally, although a surprising number of motorists did seem to have saved up their petrol for one glorious holiday bust. Automobile Association observers stationed on the Brighton Road reported that Easter traffic, mostly small cars, was about seventy per cent of what it used to be in peacetime. Cyclists in shorts fresh from the mothballs invaded the country like flocks of returning migratory birds. The railways did an absolutely record business, what with B.E.F. men returning home on leave, parents going to the country to see evacuated children, and evacuated white-collar workers coming from the country to spend a weekend in town. The traffic toward London has never been heavier. Flat racing broke a twenty-seven-year tradition by opening at Hurst Park instead of at Lincoln, and cheerful crowds of Britons, irrepressible lovers of a bet, put their money on the dogs at White City and Wembley.

Hampstead Heath had its traditional Easter bank-holiday fair, though the merry-go-round organs had to be silenced for fear some nervous customer might think the brass notes were sirens. However, there was music, provided by amplified phonograph records played at a central point there they could be replaced by air-raid instructions if the real sirens sounded. Instead of blaring and tooting away till all hours, the fair had to close down at dusk, but that didn't stop the Tommies and their girls from having a swell time riding on the swings, eating winkles on pins, and knocking Hitler's block off for three shies a penny.

The more serious-minded went to Queen's Hall to hear Handel's "Messiah" sung by a choir dotted with khaki, or strolled in Hyde Park, where they discovered that the excavations made in September, when hundreds of tons of earth were removed to stuff sandbags, have now nearly been filled in again with earth carted from the site of the new Ministry of Food buildings on Horseferry Road.

Britons felt that they needed a holiday both to buck them up for whatever unpleasant budget shocks Sir John Simon may have in the bag for them in April (an income tax of ten shillings in the pound is gloomily predicted by some) and to distract them from the dizzy job of trying to figure out just what is going on inside Europe right now. The Brenner meeting and the possibility of a Rome-Berlin-Moscow axis left people surprisingly calm—an interesting attitude when you recollect the shindy that was raised over the Nazi-Soviet hitchup—but maybe they're more hardened to ideological acrobatics by now. An eleven-point "peace plan," put forward mysteriously by someone, has faded out of the news without making much of a stir, everybody being as busy disowning it as though it were some embarrassing bundle left on a respectable doorstep.

What did make a stir was the Prime Minister's Finland speech, perhaps the most critical of his career and certainly one of the most able. It effectually silenced much of the nonsense talked by armchair strategists who had rushed Allied divisions hither and yon in a proposed Scandinavian campaign and made everything work out fine, which is not at all the way military experts here think such an adventure would have worked out. The debate on Finland had been expected to produce some fireworks, perhaps even a crisis such as the corresponding debate caused in the French government, but it developed into a personal triumph for the Prime Minister, who built up such an impressive case that he received an ovation from both sides of the House when he sat down. Even his enemies couldn't deny that the speech was a tour de force, and the sudden announcement at the end of the debate that British bombers were at the very moment attacking Sylt came with tremendous dramatic effect. Everyone felt a good deal better after that.

It has relieved many people to know that something is finally being done about the thousands of aliens who last autumn were declared to be friendly by tribunals which in some cases had only the most sketchy credentials from employers or well-meaning guarantors to go on. The situation has received a public airing through the arrest and internment of a good-looking young German called Zolf. A small cockney, evacuated to a country community, spotted him taking photographs of a wrecked airplane with a movie camera owned by the local rector's daughter. The rector's daughter and various influential friends came to Zolf's defence, but the Home Secretary decided to intern him and to look into the cases of all aliens who were put on the B List in

September; that is, all those who were told that they must not own a camera or go more than five miles from their place of residence without informing the police.

The order has taken a big load off the minds of nervous ladies who have been talking silly about the numbers of German maids in officers' families around Aldershot and about the really surprising amount of German which one still hears spoken in London, especially in West Hampstead, where bus conductors enjoy tinkling their bells and bawling "Alight here for Finchley Strasse!" Although the spy mania has reached nothing like the hysterical proportions it did in the last war, and probably never will, you do see the "no German" clause sprinkled fairly liberally through the domestic-help-wanted columns—this despite the fact that foreign servants have long been the answer to the mistress's prayer in country districts where the British article won't stay.

Everywhere, you meet people who tell you virtuously that of course they don't want to hoard and then go on to say that they're prudently laying aside a bit of this and that. The announcement the other day that wool for luxury purposes would probably be rationed sent women rushing to buy lengths of tweeds which they're tucking away for their 1942 suits.

April 21

[*April 9, Germany invades Denmark and Norway.*]

The events of this last tremendous week, by far the most tense of the war, have certainly achieved one thing: they have given the British public just that shot in the arm which it needed after the long, stale winter, which saw far more of a war of nerves than the period preceding it. Once the first shock of the invasion of Scandinavia was over, people became fighting mad. The rape of Poland didn't stir up half so much feeling, because to most Englishmen Poland was just a name on the map, and that kept the tragedy impersonal. Britishers, however, have always had a warm spot in their hearts for the Scandinavian countries, perhaps not least because it was nice to know that a particularly sane and serene way of living was still going on there in the middle of everyone else's insanity.

Norway especially had seemed to be part of the family because of the marriage of its King to the English Princess Maud—a cozy royal relationship such as English ladies enjoy tracing over tea and crumpets. The fact that King Haakon is related in some way to King George has made it all seem very much worse to a nation which has a simple reverence for monarchs and doesn't like to think of them being harassed by Heinkels and taking cat naps in their boots.

For the first day or two, the clampdown on all genuine news from Norway—as opposed to the rumors that the Norwegians were negotiating for peace, that the *Bremen* was sunk, that the Allies had taken Bergen, and so on—made people gloomy and uneasy. London was suddenly a city of stay-at-homes, as it was in the early days of the war. Cinema box-office managers estimated that they were losing £250,000 a night because everyone was sitting by the radio, listening to the jitters of neutrals and wondering fretfully where the hell the Renown was. Mr. Churchill's blunt statement that the Allies had not landed in Norway and the Navy was doing nicely, although information must necessarily be scarce, made people feel better, but it was hardly the smashing victory they needed.

For that they had to wait until the first Saturday night after the invasion, when an announcer, in a voice trembling with excitement, asked everyone to stand by for an important announcement which hadn't yet "come down," as he put it, as though suggesting that the Almighty and B.B.C. officials were busy hatching it on some celestial top floor in Portland Place. Until it did come down, the announcer filled in, for what seemed like an interminable period, by playing records of English dances and Gilbert and Sullivan to the point where most of his listeners were reaching for their hats and starting out to round up a lynching party. However, the news that British troops had landed at Narvik was worth waiting for, and as it swept around town, beaming strangers congratulated each other and wrung each other's hands in an excitable and shockingly un-British manner. The much criticized B.B.C., by the way, has been right on the spot with its broadcasts in Norwegian, which are much appreciated by the sad little local colony of Norsemen. The Norwegian Minister to England has been on the air several times, telling his people back home what their countrymen here are feeling, and it makes Norwegians in London happier to think that they and their families may be listening in at the same moment. Queues of anxious relatives form daily at the legations of the invaded countries, and all sorts of people keep turning up and asking how they can help—blonde nursemaids, and angry retired English colonels who've fished the same stretch of Norwegian river for twenty years and don't intend to let Hitler spoil the season now.

After the Narvik announcement, there was so much excitement over rumors originating in Stockholm about the activities of British troops in Norway that when reliable word of B.E.F. landings elsewhere on that country's coast finally arrived, it was soberly received. Maps of Scandinavia and *Jane's Fighting Ships* were best-sellers all last week. Normally, such an expeditionary force would take months to equip and assemble, but this one got off to a prompt start, presumably picking up the fur caps and other paraphernalia of northern warfare where the troops that didn't start for Finland had laid them down.

The general feeling about this new phase of the war is optimistic. People are delighted that Hitler has finally come out in the open, and say that if this is really the overture to his much heralded *Blitzkrieg,* so much the better. They discuss the possible entry of Italy as a belligerent, but it's difficult for Britishers to take Italians seriously as enemies. People here are apt to grin as they read Signor Gayda's current martial howls in the papers, though the *Times* did go so far as to rebuke the Italian press for its presentation of news which was described restrainedly as "grossly tendentious."

One of the direct results of events in Scandinavia is the diminished girth of that same august journal, the *Times*. From being a paper which only a strong man could manage on a crowded train, it has shrunk to svelte proportions. The cutting off of Scandinavian pulp supplies hit the paper trade hard last week, and American buyers were ahead of the British in the Canadian and Newfoundland markets, which might have helped to ease the situation. All the dailies dwindled, and are likely to dwindle still more; it is even rumored that if things get much worse, the government may take control and issue one official bulletin of factual news, but Britons feel that the situation would have to be pretty bad for things to come to that.

May 12

[*May 10, Germany invades the Lowlands.*]

It is difficult to remember that this is Whitsun, the long weekend on which Londoners usually acquire the tan that must last them until their August vacation, and nothing has impressed them more as an indication that the government is really getting a move on than the decision to cut out the sacred holiday. People say that it feels like September all over again—same sort of weather, same sort of posters, same sort of empty sensation as the news came through of the bombing of Brussels, Calais, and Louvain—and the bus changing gear at the corner sounds ridiculously like a siren for a second, as it used to do in the first edgy days of the war.

On the Friday which began with the invasion of Holland, Belgium, and Luxembourg and ended with the resignation of Mr. Chamberlain, London itself seemed much the same as usual except that everyone carried a paper and most people for the first time in months carried a gas mask (ladies who felt like taking in a Whit Saturday matinée were warned by the radio that they would probably be refused admittance to the theatres without one). Air Raid Precautions workers, who have spent the last seven months playing darts and making themselves endless cups of tea, stood ready. Householders checked up on their blackout facilities and ran through the instructions for dealing with an incendiary bomb: you shovel sand over it and rush it out of the house in a bucket, after which, as the Ministry of Home Security cheerfully adds, "you will then have to deal with the fire which the bomb has started."

This being notoriously an inarticulate nation which likes to express its feelings at home and not in public at a café table, there were no excited crowds in the streets, and the only place where voices were raised above the average British monotone was Soho, where unemployed Italian waiters stood at the street corners or crowded into their favorite bar on Frith Street, vigorously arguing as to whether Mussolini is coming off the fence now, in which case they will be on the wrong side of an internment camp's barbed wire, or will wait for his friend to give him fresh proof of military prowess in the Low Countries.

Events are moving so fast that England acquired a new Premier almost absent-mindedly, without any excessive jubilation from Winston Churchill's supporters, who had been fearful that even at the last moment Mr. Chamberlain would hang onto the office, since he was said to feel, in his mystical Berchtesgaden manner, that it was his sacred duty to lead the nation to ultimate victory. Those who still believed him capable of doing so were mostly to be found in the middle class, for the aristocrats and the working people, who frequently plump on the same side in matters of policy, had long been resentful of his habit of surrounding himself with loyal but fumbling yes-men, and of the inflexible provincial caution which caused M. Osusky, the late Czech Minister to Paris, to observe, *"Monsieur Chamberlain n'est pas un homme d'état; il est un businessman de Birmingham."*

In Winston Churchill, people feel that they have a leader who understands exactly what risks should be taken and what kind of adversary they are up against; the iron of appeasement had burned too deeply into British souls for them ever to be quite sure again of Chamberlain on that second point. Diehard Tories, who once looked on Mr. Churchill as "a dangerous fellow," now passionately proclaim that he is just what the country needs. It's paradoxical but true that the British, for all their suspicious dislike of brilliance, are beginning to think that they'd be safer with a bit of dynamite around.

In the country, bus services have been suddenly cut to a skeleton schedule, because buses have been commandeered to serve as emergency ambulances. The hard-working ladies of the Women's Voluntary Services are standing by for a new evacuation of London, which may start at any moment; this time, only children of school age are to be sent, but it is thought that if the ports are bombed first, which many think probable, there may be a frantic unofficial evacuation of people of all ages from them, with which it will be extremely difficult to deal.

Since the public has been asked to look out for parachute troops at dawn and dusk, there has been a great deal of argument as to what a person should do who suddenly sees a German soldier tumbling from the clouds. One publication urged its golfing readers to carry a rifle in their golf bags, but this was not recommended by the *Times,* which observed, "It would not be correct for country gentlemen to carry their guns with them on their walks, and take flying or running shots as opportunity is offered. Such action would put them into the position of francs-tireurs and should therefore be avoided." The proper procedure, said the *Times,* in case you're worrying, is to telephone the police as calmly as possible.

Britons are certainly calm in the present crisis. They are neither excessively pessimistic nor optimistic over the news as it comes in, because they remember the initial optimism over what turned out to be the Norwegian reverse. It is probable that good will come out of this reverse in the long run, if only because it has stopped people from chirping,

"Ah well, we always start badly" or "We English always lose every battle but the last." There's a feeling now that in this war the last battle may not be recognized until it is over, and anyway, after Chamberlain's unfortunate colloquial remark about Hitler's having missed the bus, snappy slogans aren't so popular as they were.

It takes a good, stiff dose of adversity to release the formidable strength in what Harold Nicolson has called "the slow-grinding will power of the British people." To that has been added for the first time the quickening realization that they are fighting for their lives.

May 19

The last week has been a bad one. The calmness and cheerfulness of the ordinary citizen aren't in themselves new or surprising, for to be long on both those qualities is part of the national character. Unless it is stiffened by a realistic comprehension of what it may be required to face, such an attitude is possibly as irritating to objective observers as the blithe unconcern of someone taking his usual constitutional along a cliff which everyone else knows is in danger of falling. What is new here is that last week many Britons for the first time felt the ground shake underfoot, and still remained calm and cheerful.

It is now clear to the man in the street, reading his paper as he goes home to the neat suburban villa which may soon be matchwood, like the villas near Rotterdam and Brussels, that Hitler is out to win in the next six or eight weeks by any means he can, several of which will be bad for the population of this island. Even the hitherto unbelievable fact that it really isn't an island any more and that invasion from the air is quite in the cards wasn't unbelievable after a bit. The fact has been accepted, along with the realization that Hitler will bomb London when it suits him, without worrying over the certainty that Allied bombers will immediately take off for Berlin. From the cold-blooded way in which parachute troops have been employed in Holland, it is suspected that the Führer must long ago have conquered his emotional distaste for the thought of dead Germans—a distaste which so interested Sir Nevile Henderson.

For the first day or two after the invasion of the Netherlands and Belgium, many people expected raids to start right away—possibly on London, certainly on English ports and airdromes. Now it is thought that the German fliers will wait until they have consolidated themselves cozily in their new Dutch bases, or until the full moon wanes, although, as a matter of fact, they have already shown a pronounced dislike of night flying.

Whatever people believe, they do not expect to be left in peace much longer; neither do they cherish any comfortable illusions about the situation at the moment. There is only one thing of which they are certain and that is that they and France mean to hang on and to win, even though it will take, as Mr. Churchill has warned them and as they are beginning to believe, "many, many long months of struggle and suffering." If they are able to check Hitler's notion that a German victory can be accomplished in a few brilliant weeks, this dogged long-term way of thinking may turn out to be their best bet. The Prime Minister's short and trenchant speech, in which he told Britons that he had nothing to offer them but blood, toil, tears, and sweat, struck the right note with the public because it was the kind of rough talk they wanted to hear after months of woolly optimism.

On the whole, Mr. Churchill's appointments have been popular, not the least being that of Lord Beaverbrook to the newly formed Ministry of Aircraft Production. It is hoped that the Puckish-looking little peer and publisher will make the figures of bomber production rise as successfully as he has the circulation of the *Express*. The appointment of Anthony Eden as Secretary of State for War pleased his supporters, who have clung to him loyally through a period of temporary political eclipse; his appointment, and that of Duff Cooper to the Ministry of Information, roused the German wireless to a fury of denunciation against the "British war-mongers." Possibly the Eden promotion was no less unpopular in Rome, a thought which doesn't trouble the British nowadays, since they are convinced that Italy will be in the war before long anyway, possibly by next weekend, so as to make a neat tieup for historians with the date of her entry into the first World War—May 24, 1915.

One of the results of the Churchill government's new energetic prosecution of the war—or so people like to think —was the sudden announcement that all German and Austrian men between the ages of sixteen and sixty were to be interned: a precaution which most Britons feel should have been taken long ago. Another order has restricted the movements of all aliens, enemy or otherwise, living in certain districts—mostly the East Coast counties, where Fifth Column saboteurs might be most useful in the event of invasion. Although people are sorry for respectable Scandinavian, say, or French residents who have probably lived here for years and suddenly find themselves forbidden to drive a car, ride a bicycle, or go out after eight in the evening, there's a general feeling that the government hasn't gone far enough with its internment of enemy aliens, inasmuch as it's possible that a man of sixty-one may be a perfectly effective agent. There are, moreover, even one or two people who remember a lady spy named Mata Hari.

It didn't take long to get the machinery for receiving refugees going again; in the last few years, there have been such terribly frequent opportunities for practice. When the trains came in last week, the loads of homeless people were sorted out in centres that had been used for the reception of Jewish children from the Third Reich. The newcomers were labelled, fed, advised, and taken to temporary billets by workers who had been through all the heartrending routine before with unhappy people from Austria, Czechoslovakia, and Poland.

There's deep sympathy here for Holland and Belgium in their desperate plight, but, with the new realistic facing of the facts, people can't help remembering how Mr. Churchill's speech of a few months back, warning neutrals to take action before it was too late, was received with screams of anger and virtuous protest by those he was talking to. It is felt that if Belgium and Holland had had the moral courage to throw in their lot with the Allies right away, Brussels might not be in German hands or Queen Wilhelmina in London at this minute.

Perhaps it's worth recording that the British attitude toward the hope of American intervention is now one of weary but complete resignation to the belief that in this war the Yanks will not be coming. "Nothing will bring them in this time," people say cynically, and they are apt to grin as they read the latest solemn protest from the White House against German violence. To Britons living close to the facts of existence in Europe today, such protests sound like a note sent over by the neighbors complaining of the way a homicidal lunatic is carrying on in someone's garden, when it's obvious that a band of men with good stout ropes would be understood by the killer better than any amount of elegant phraseology.

May 24

While the greatest battle in history is being fought on the other side of the Channel, which has suddenly shrunk in most people's minds to something no bigger than the Thames, an equally great revolution has been taking place here. In a single day so much constitutional ballast was heaved overboard in order to lighten the unwieldy ship for this swift and deadly new warfare that a number of revered statesmen must have positively writhed in their graves. If the British people had their way, several more—who were once revered but are now revealed in all their heavy guilt of responsibility for placing the country in its present critical peril—would shortly be joining them.

Even the slowest minds in a race not famed for lightning

perceptions have grasped at last, with anger and bitterness, the exact extent of that peril to which the years of complacent leadership have brought them, and they are ready emotionally for the most drastic measures Mr. Churchill may choose to take. On the day the act was passed empowering the government to require all persons "to place themselves, their services, and their property at the disposal of His Majesty," a coster on a donkey cart possibly summed up the universal comment on the announcement of Britain's total mobilization when he shouted to a crony, "That's right! All in it together to knock 'is bleedin' block off!"

All in it they certainly are, donkey cart and Rolls-Royce alike. "There must be no laggards," warned Mr. Attlee. "Victory is our goal. We must and shall attain it." Nobody doubts that to do so the government will use its new powers, more complete than any government has held since Cromwell's time, to the utmost. The Englishman's home is no longer his castle but a place that can be commandeered at a moment's notice if the state needs it. Landowners must be prepared to give up their land; employers to close down their businesses or to carry on under government control, and perhaps at a loss; employees to change their jobs as they may be directed by the Ministry of Labour. It's the stiffest dose of totalitarian principles that a democracy has ever had to swallow in order to save the democratic ideal from total extinction, but there's a feeling of relief that the country is now united under a fighting leader who is not afraid to tell hard truths and to call for hard deeds when circumstances require them. Britons suspect that the present situation must be just as critical as it can be, because the King is to broadcast to them tonight and they have come to associate royal broadcasts with solemn national moments, such as abdications, the beginning of a reign, or the beginning of a war.

London has been a tense place in these last days of waiting, though the morale has been excellent. The first thing that strikes one is the unusual absence of khaki on the streets; the soldiers seem to have melted away, and with them has gone the booming prosperity of the theatres and restaurants, both of which are suffering badly. It's a fine time to shop in the big stores, for they're practically empty; the salesgirls huddle together, chatting in the middle of the departments and eyeing a potential customer as a group of mermaids might eye a deep-sea diver.

Barbed-wire entanglements have been erected around government buildings in Whitehall, and other barricades are halting road traffic into London for inspection at various key points. One beautiful spring evening recently, troops in their shirtsleeves were to be seen setting up sandbagged machine-gun and observation posts near the Houses of Parliament, watched by the usual expressionless group of loiterers, who might have been watching them erect gala flag standards for some bit of royal pageantry.

It's ironical that this summer looks as though it were going to be the best, as far as weather and growing things go, that England has had in years. The displays of tulips in the parks have been so magnificent that it's too bad the garden-loving Britons haven't had more heart to go and see them; the tulips in the big beds outside Buckingham Palace are exactly the color of blood. People have no heart for reading, either, unless it's the papers, which as yet have contained only one list of casualties—possibly incurred in the Norwegian campaign. Since they can't settle down to read a book or sit through a movie, they have to talk.

Atrocity stories that everyone over thirty remembers from the last war have turned up again, as good as new but with different details. They produce, together with the photographs of refugees pushing heaped perambulators along Belgian roads, a horrifying sense of living the same old nightmare all over again.

In the country, farm laborers and gentlemen with estates are flocking to enlist in the local defence corps formed to deal with what a B.B.C. announcer referred to in an absent-minded moment as American, instead of enemy, parachutists. A quarter of a million such recruits have been given rifles as well as uniforms or armlets, without which they're liable to be shot out of hand as francs-tireurs, and the job of patrolling lonely spots looking for an air armada. Rifles must be left with the authorities and not carried home, lest they fall into the hands of local Quislings.

The Fifth Column menace is taken very seriously here, as well it might be. Motorists have been warned to remove not only the ignition key but also the distributor from their cars if they intend to leave them for any length of time unattended, and it is particularly requested that garage doors be carefully locked at night.

Since many people believe that Eire is on the Nazi map as a jumping-off place for the attack on England, those who evacuated their families to the west in September are wondering if they picked on such a safe spot after all. Many more believe that with even the sleepiest hamlet not a stone's throw, as the bomber flies, from some camp, airdrome, ammunition dump, or aircraft factory, the beautiful word "safety" has temporarily gone out of circulation. In the south of England, the guns can be plainly heard pounding away all through the day, and at night the nightingales are drowned out by the drone of planes on patrol or coming back from a bombing raid.

June 2

[*May 28, Leopold III surrenders the Belgian army. British troops evacuated from Dunkirk May 26–June 4.*]

For the space of a day, Hitler had to give up his title of most-hated man to Leopold III of the Belgians. The restrained tone of the Prime Minister's speech (one wondered what blasting broadside Mr. Churchill would have delivered if he were still First Lord of the Admiralty) was not echoed by the press or the public, which were in no mood to await more facts after hearing the immediate, heartbreaking one that the British and French forces, treacherously abandoned, were fighting their way desperately toward the sea and evacuation.

The shock of Leopold's action was intense in this country,

where he has always been a popular and romantic, if somewhat pokerlike, figure, admired as much by those who had only read of his personal sorrows as by those who had actually come into contact with him. When the Dutch Royalty arrived in London and the papers were full of pictures of Juliana pushing her baby's pram like any chubby suburban matron, people said that it was no doubt all right for women to clear out, but you wouldn't catch Leopold doing it, no matter how bad things looked. In the dismay of finding that he would rather be a live Nazi than a dead Belgian, about the kindest thing anyone found to say of him was that the sudden and unprecedentedly savage attack on his people had finally unhinged a mind clouded by relentless tragedy.

Sir Robert Clive, who was Ambassador to Belgium from 1937 to 1939, has said of Leopold that "he was starved of friendship—both of men and of women; the loss of his wife was irreparable," and has traced the increasing influence on him of his evil genius, General van Overstraeten, who encouraged the Belgian King's tragically shortsighted obsession of neutrality at any price. All the papers suddenly remembered that Leopold had always been anti-French and fond of staying with his mother's Bavarian relations; most of them dug up the famous 1914 *Punch* cartoon in which King Albert, taunted by the Kaiser with having lost everything, replied proudly that he still had his soul.

When news of Leopold's surrender came through on Tuesday morning and ruined Englishmen's luncheon appetites, it was Mr. Duff Cooper, the new Minister of Information, who made a radio statement telling people to keep calm and promising a fuller report that evening. As the danger grows, Mr. Duff Cooper seems to be in increasing demand to make the kind of speeches that the public previously expected from Mr. Churchill, and he does the job excellently. He inspires confidence because he tells his listeners without any nonsense that they're in for an extremely unpleasant time, in which he knows they're going to behave well. On Tuesday, he reminded Englishmen that their country had been through unpleasant times before and had sur-

vived them, as it would certainly survive this one, and people went to bed feeling happier for having heard him voice a
belief that no one, in his heart of hearts, does not hold,
however black the news may be.

The calmness of the average non-military citizen is magnificent. Although, on the day of Leopold's capitulation, a German wireless commentator painted a colorful picture of London as a panic-stricken city, the truth was considerably less
picturesque. Once over the shock, Londoners sensibly forgot
Leopold and thought only of the men he'd left behind him,
fighting an heroic rear-guard action to cover the retreating
troops' movements. Then, after a seemingly interminable period of suspense, it was learned that the first war-stained, exhausted contingent had arrived safely on British shores, and
the relief and enthusiasm were terrific.

No one seems to think much beyond those arrivals at the
moment. It isn't yet known how many didn't come back, for
the long rolls of honor that one remembers as horrors of the
last war haven't made their appearance. The casualties
which the War Office has announced so far have been unobtrusively printed in the same higgledy-piggledy small type
used for harmless public notices, and a study of the regi-
ments involved makes it appear probable that most of the
losses listed were incurred in Norway, which already seems
incredibly remote.

Although these are anxious days and likely to become
more so, judging by the government's injunction to the stub-
bornly garden-proud masses to put up their air-raid shelters
even if it means spoiling the lobelias, and to have their res-
pirators fitted as speedily as possible with new filters to handle smoke gases, the public remains amazingly cheerful. Confidence in the French army and in Britain's own air force is
expressed everywhere, and the success of the new Defiant
fighting planes, a squadron of which shot down thirty-seven
enemy planes last Wednesday, has raised everyone's spirits
considerably. So has the energy of the new government,
which has got so much done in the last three weeks that people groan when they think of how much might have been

done in the last eight months if they'd started out under the right leadership.

Among the most novel and encouraging innovations of the Churchill regime are the care that is now being taken to fit the right man to the right job—typified by the selection of Sir Stafford Cripps for the Moscow mission—and a determination to rid this country, as far as possible at such a late last moment, of the Fifth Column menace. Various foreign-inspired organizations, which had counted on the well-known British combination of warm heart and wooden head to leave them sitting pretty for the duration, woke up to find themselves in Brixton Prison, while women aliens were suddenly rounded up and dumped on the inappropriately named Isle of Man. Britons with cars must now drive as best they can around a countryside from which all signposts have been whisked away in order to baffle an invading army that will presumably have left its maps on the mantelpiece.

Evidence that such precautions have sunk in was supplied by a man who reported that, travelling through Sussex the other day, he had received a dirty look from a cottage housewife of whom he had asked the way. Only after he had produced indisputable credentials, he said, had she unbent enough to indicate cautiously that he wouldn't be far off the mark if he turned to the right, past the next pub.

June 15

The fall of Paris [June 14] was the culmination of a tragic week for the British people. Stunned by the brilliant speed and organization of the German drive, and bewildered by the press, which alternately warned them against undue pessimism and easy optimism, they took refuge in the classic national formula for disaster: calmness, and an increasingly dogged determination to hold back for bitter months —or years, if necessary—a juggernaut which everyone now knows is out to annihilate the nation in weeks. "Our turn will come," said a man grimly one morning this week, as he watched the newspaper-seller on a pitch on St. James's Street chalking up "Germans Enter Paris" on the boards which have taken the place of posters.

One hears nothing but admiration for the heroic French resistance, and no kind of criticism of Weygand's command; the feeling seems to be that a magnificent fighting weapon has been crushed by a steam roller. All the criticism is reserved for the criminal complacency of former leaders on both sides of the Channel who refused to see that this war would be one of steam rollers, not of gentlemen's weapons, and prepared only to fight the last war over again in spite of the helpful hints of things to come given out by German armored divisions in Poland and by Italian dive bombers in Spain. There's a growing tendency here to ask the un-British and healthily pugnacious question "Why?" Why, for instance, the munitions and aircraft factories waited until three weeks ago to double and treble their output, and why the maximum effort was not called for in the early days of September.

There are so many more urgent and frightening problems to think of at the moment (such as how to induce stubborn East End mothers to evacuate their children, so that the defence of England will not be delayed by tragic fleeing hordes like those which blocked the roads out of Brussels and Paris) that these and similar questions must wait to be answered. However, the slow but formidable British anger, roused by the thought of young Englishmen firing rifles at oncoming tanks, makes it certain that there will have to be a pretty comprehensive answer someday. It's also certain that the end of the war will find a changed—perhaps a better, possibly a less pleasant—England, in which Englishmen will no longer be able to give their loving and undivided attention to the cultivation of their gardens.

On the night that the Germans entered Paris, Queen Elizabeth broadcast to the women of France, and at the close of her touching little speech, which was made in careful, schoolgirlish French and was followed by the "Marseillaise"

and the sober swell of "God Save the King," many people
were unashamedly weeping. It has been a week of historic
broadcasts, starting with Mr. Duff Cooper's on Monday evening after Italy's entry into the war. Next day, there were
protests from some members of Parliament who deprecated
Mr. Duff Cooper's bellicose tone and his impolite references
to Caporetto, and who deplored the fact that such bluster-
ings would only unify whatever split factions there may be
in Italy when an appeal to religious conscience might have
divided them further. To this, Mr. Duff Cooper replied
briskly, indicating that Englishmen had heard a great deal
too much in the same strain directed toward the German
people at the beginning of the war, and that if the honorable
gentlemen wanted someone to be kind and sympathetic to
the Italians, they could go elsewhere—sentiments with
which the majority of the public heartily agreed.

No serious-minded citizen would deny that Italy's entrance into the war at such a juncture was likely to have
highly dangerous and unpleasant results for the Allies, but
the average simple Briton believes that all the possibilities of
the genteel approach were tried out only too patiently in
September, '39. The reminiscent ring of the announcement
that pamphlets had been dropped on Rome caused a good
deal less satisfaction than the news that oil tanks had been
destroyed near Venice, which was hailed with delight by
many people who, a short time back, would have blanched
at the very thought of a bomb anywhere near a Giorgione.

On the evening of Mussolini's declaration, windows of
macaroni joints in Soho were broken by excitable crowds.
Italian restaurant owners elsewhere pasted notices in their
windows to the effect that they were one-hundred-per-cent
British. In spite of this loyal enthusiasm, many arrests were
made and the ranks of Mayfair's restaurateurs were noticeably thinned, the Quaglino Brothers and Ferraro, the popular
maître d'hôtel at the Berkeley, being among those removed.

People who had listened to Mr. Duff Cooper sat up until
quarter past twelve to hear President Roosevelt's great
speech, which came through perfectly and for millions of

Britons provided the one gleam of light in a dark and menacing week. The answer that anxious Britons make to the
new universal question, "Will the Americans come in?," is
by no means as hopelessly negative as it would have been a
short while ago. There is an increasingly trusting belief in
American assistance—first with guns and planes, and eventually with men. People simply cannot believe that the
great power whose chief representative spoke to them so
nobly on Monday night can continue to contemplate these
horrors unmoved. Time, however, is the principal factor, as
André Maurois said in his recent heartbreaking appeal for
France, in which he observed that one division then, even if
badly equipped, would be worth more than several divisions, magnificently equipped, in two months. Time, which
was once said to be on the side of the Allies, has turned out
to be, after all, Hitler's man.

June 22

On Monday, June 17th—the tragic day on which Britain
lost the ally with whom she had expected to fight to the bitter end—London was as quiet as a village. You could have
heard a pin drop in the curious, watchful hush. At places
where normally there is a noisy bustle of comings and
goings, such as the big railway stations, there was the same
extraordinary preoccupied silence. People stood about reading the papers; when a man finished one, he would hand it
over to anybody who hadn't been lucky enough to get a
copy, and walk soberly away.

For once the cheerful cockney comeback of the average
Londoner simply wasn't there. The boy who sold you the
fateful paper did it in silence; the bus conductor punched
your ticket in silence. The public seemed to react to the
staggering news like people in a dream, who go through the
most fantastic actions without a sound. There was little discussion of events, because they were too bad for that. With

the house next door well ablaze and the flames coming
closer, it was no time to discuss who or what was the cause
and whether more valuables couldn't have been saved from
the conflagration.

Similarly, people were more reassured by the half-dozen
sentences which the Prime Minister barked into the microphone that Monday evening than they would have been by
any lengthy, prepared oration. Mr. Churchill's statement the
next day was less stirring than sensible—a carefully reasoned
balance sheet of the chances for a British victory, well suited
to the grimly sane public mood.

Tuesday afternoon the newspaper-sellers were chalking
"French Army Still Fighting" on their signs, to which one or
two had added "Vive la France!" In the almost deserted residential streets, cars full of luggage and people moved away
from newly shuttered houses and turned into the traffic
going toward the big roads out of London.

Few people remembered that Tuesday was the anniversary
of the Battle of Waterloo, another occasion when disaster
trod very close on the heels of this country, and when it
seemed impossible that the British squares could stand up to
the assault of the greatest military machine in the world, led
by the greatest commander. "Hard pounding, this, gentlemen," said Wellington to his staff at one stage of that battle.
"Let's see who will pound the longest."

It's possible that the anniversary of Waterloo was celebrated unconsciously this year, after all. The determination
to keep pounding the longest is the only thing that people
have been able to see clearly in the past dark and bewildering week. News from France has been scarce. Rumors about
the French Navy and Air Force continue to get around, and
every other person claims to have seen a strange-looking
squadron flying with Gallic lack of formation in the direction of some British air field.

It would be difficult for an impartial observer to decide
today whether the British are the bravest or merely the most
stupid people in the world. The way they are acting in the
present situation could be used to support either claim. The

individual Englishman seems to be singularly unimpressed by the fact that there is now nothing between him and the undivided attention of a war machine such as the world has never seen before. Possibly it's lack of imagination; possibly again it's the same species of dogged resolution which occasionally produces an epic like Dunkirk. Millions of British families, sitting at their well-stocked breakfast tables eating excellent British eggs and bacon, can still talk calmly of the horrors across the Channel, perhaps without fully comprehending even now that anything like that could ever happen in England's green and pleasant land.

The authorities are certainly doing their best to drive the idea that it could deeply into the public consciousness. From now on, ringing of church bells for any reason except to warn of approaching invaders will be forbidden—a nice throwback to Napoleonic England which fits in well with squires watching the skies from the hill tops and peasants cleaning old shotguns in the villages. A movement to provide parashots with hand grenades is afoot, sponsored by Beaverbrook's *Express,* which manufactured the slogan "A hand-grenade dump by each village pump" and opened a whole new vista of horrible possibilities by insisting that every schoolboy who could throw a cricket ball was perfectly capable of throwing a grenade.

One morning this week, postmen slipped official pamphlets in with the mail, telling householders just what to do if Britain is invaded. Official advice is to stay at home unless told by the proper authorities to leave, "because, if you run away, you will be machine-gunned from the air, as were civilians in Holland and Belgium." People were also warned not to believe rumors, not to supply any German with food, petrol, or maps, and to overcome their natural inclination to mind their own business sufficiently to go to the police if they see anything at all suspicious.

June 28

The French acceptance of the crushing armistice terms came as a profound shock to the majority of the public, which had been simple enough to believe Marshal Pétain when he declared that France would make no shameful surrender. Many people had thought it possible that Germany would treat her fallen adversary with comparative generosity in the hope of dividing English opinion before putting out peace offers. When the full text of the terms was published, there was widespread anger, bitterness, and bewilderment in England, for the average uninformed citizen found it difficult to believe that anything could be more shameful than an agreement which handed over weapons of war, airfields, munition works, and industrial areas to be used unconditionally against a former ally.

Experts here have sorrowfully computed that the amount of undamaged material which has fallen into Nazi hands is "without precedent in the history of nations." Although it's not known how many industrial plants were destroyed before being evacuated, it seems possible that such measures were largely neglected, through the haste, carelessness, or inability to face tragic facts of the people concerned. Any Englishman with a map of France and a list of France's mineral resources before him can now grimly calculate exactly what help the Pétain government has extended to Hitler to carry on the war against Britain—precious iron ore from Lorraine, coal from the north, potash from Alsace—while memories of Continental holidays supply only too clear a picture of the smiling French countryside which is doomed to become the No. 1 Nazi granary and larder.

Because of those popular Continental holidays which in recent years had sent millions of English people of all classes across the Channel to explore France as a playground, the Entente had never been in better shape than it was when the

war started, and lovers of France were overjoyed at the indi-
cations that the two countries were going to work in ever
closer collaboration and with increasing good will. Today,
those same lovers of France feel that the most heartbreaking
of all the heartbreaking consequences of the French surrender is the possibility of so much good work being undone
that contempt here for a frail government may cause the
magnificent spirit of a people to be overlooked.

Meanwhile, the anxious hopes of all France's friends in
this country are centred on General de Gaulle, the gallant
and romantic figure whose abilities as a brilliant officer, with
more vision than his contemporaries, were known a week
ago to comparatively few, and who has since emerged as a pa-
triot whose voice speaks for the true France, now, alas, tragically silent. His statement that he had reason to believe the
French Navy would not surrender started all sorts of rumors
circulating. These stories were the only near-cheerful things
that anyone could discover in a sad week—these and the unexpected and briskly successful land raids at various undis-
closed points on the enemy coastline.

The immediate result of the focussing of German attention on this country was the start of nightly air raids, which
continued all the week. On Monday night, London heard
the sirens for the first time since September. The A.R.P.
services went into action smoothly and efficiently, and people who were walking home after visiting friends found
themselves politely but implacably headed off into public
shelters and kept there until the all-clear sounded, which it
didn't until four hours later. An unidentified plane droned
high overhead and the searchlights were in action, but nothing happened, and the only unusual sign next day was the
universal snappishness of the public temper.

Rural areas have had far more alarms and actual bombings than the cities, and it's ironical that many people who
fled to country retreats when war broke out have been in the
thick of it, as they wouldn't have been if they'd stayed put in
peaceful Chelsea or Hampstead. The German raiders have
turned up in all sorts of places where they weren't expected.

A boys' school which migrated from a danger area on the east coast to a supposedly quiet spot in the southwest came in for quite a spectacular raid the night the boys arrived—to the delight of the pupils and the consternation of the staff.

The general feeling after a week of broken nights seems to be that a move to copy the Germans and cut out night sirens altogether would be popular, since the damage the alarms do to the workers' output next day is inestimable and a civil population with jumpy nerves is one of the things which would suit Hitler best. There is also considerable criticism of the press and the B.B.C. for giving so much prominence to descriptions of raids and of civilian casualties, which so far have been infinitesimal compared to street casualties among pedestrians in peacetime; it's felt that it would be better to train the public to regard these risks as an unavoidable part of everyday life and no more remarkable than an accident on the Kingston Bypass on a fine Sunday.

London is remarkably quiet at the moment. What gaiety it has is being circulated by warriors in need of a little hard-earned relaxation and by the young things who are happily always there to provide it. For their benefit, nine or ten musical shows are still going strong, but the events in France did in all but two straight plays—Gielgud's "King Lear" and the ripsnorting melodrama "Rebecca." Various eminent actors and actresses have delivered lectures to the public on the necessity of keeping the serious theatre alive in wartime, but unfortunately what is happening on the stage of history is so tremendous that most thinking people find it difficult to take their eyes off the real thing and concentrate on manufactured drama. One act ended at Compiègne the other day, and the last and most important act is due to start at any moment. Indeed, it may have seemed to many, as they sat in their private air-raid shelters this week, that the footlights were already up and the orchestra was swinging into the sombre and terrible overture.

July 14

Now that the divorce between England and Pétain's France seems tragically final, there are all the unpleasant sequels that ordinarily turn up in such a situation: the recriminations, the comments of outsiders who saw it coming, and the danger of forgetting old loyalties and affections in the heat of argument. It's a saddening period of readjustment, with inevitable bitterness on both sides. The break was almost a certainty even before the naval action at Oran. Since then, the shape and color of the new French constitution have emerged more clearly from the meeting of the National Assembly at Vichy, a town which, the London *Times* acidly remarked, was an appropriate seat for the Pétain government, being a favorite resort of valetudinarians. It's a bewildering period for most people, too. French politics have never been very comprehensively reported in this country, and what the average simple Englishman believes about the character of the average simple Frenchman has only made the recent events more difficult to understand. On Sunday evenings, the B.B.C. always plays the national anthems of the Allies before the nine-o'clock news broadcast. Last Sunday, there was speculation as to whether the "Marseillaise" would be cut out, but it was played as usual, presumably in honor of General de Gaulle and his French Volunteer Legion, whose headquarters are now at Olympia, normally associated in Londoners' minds with Christmas circuses and Ideal Home exhibitions.

This week, more British refugees from France arrived, including a number of elderly and delicate people who had made their homes on the Riviera for many years and had been forced to escape, under conditions of acute horror, on colliers which took anything up to three weeks for the journey from Cannes to England. Every day, the "Information Wanted" column of the *Times* is packed with items inserted by anxious friends and relatives asking for news of Britons "last seen in Paris June 10th" or "last heard of in Beaulieu May 30th." The fate of those who didn't run in time remains problematical.

Perhaps in a reaction to so much tragedy, London in the past few days has seemed more cheerful and crowded than it has for some time past. The population has been increased by Australian and New Zealand soldiers, looking at the sights, and by hotel and other business people who have had to give up their establishments in the rapidly emptying seaside districts. The summer sales brought women up from the country determined to get the last lot of bargains at prewar prices, even if it meant getting sirens, too. Acquaintances one meets in the street say jokingly that they've come to town for a good night's sleep, since London at the moment is quieter than many a village which hears the Heinkels nightly.

The general atmosphere of the city is tense but by no means unhopeful, and the only really despondent people are parents who had wanted to get their children off to safety overseas—under the government scheme, now abandoned—before anything appalling should happen. Quite enough has happened already to make it obvious that even in the so-called safe areas there's no guarantee that terror won't drop in one dark night, when accurate bombing is difficult. Although a shortage of convoy ships is responsible for the scheme's breakdown, there were other snarls, such as immigration-quota restrictions and the criticism that preference had been given to children of the well-to-do—a charge which was vigorously denied by Mr. Justin Weddell, chairman of the American Committee here.

The response to the plan from parents of all classes had been enormous, to the surprise of those who a while back had come up against the resistance of London mothers to the notion of evacuating their children even to the distance of a two-hour railway journey. Certain folk, however, took the Spartan view that to send adolescent children out of the country at this critical juncture would be to implant in them the dangerous seeds of easy escapism. There was an immense amount of correspondence in the press. One boy of eleven wrote a letter declaring stoutly, "I would rather be bombed to fragments than leave England." A gentleman at Chester College implored parents not to be deterred by pictures of American family life as presented by Hollywood. "It is little realized in England," he wrote, "that the outlook of provincial American homes such as are likely to receive children is at bottom slightly more rigid and Victorian, if anything, than that of the corresponding homes in England."

Unmoved by Spartan theories or thoughts of Hollywood, seven thousand parents a day went right ahead with their applications, acting on the simple idea that it would be best to get their most precious possessions out of the way before all hell broke loose. The big Berkeley Street office of Thomas Cook's suddenly became one of the busiest places in London, with clerks working overtime to answer the queries of mothers and fathers who waited patiently in a queue which sometimes stretched into the street. Now that the scheme has been withdrawn, with a statement that the future dispatch of children must be at the parents' own risk, a cruel dilemma is presented to those who remember with equal clarity the shambles of French homes and the sinking of the *Arandora Star*. The one hope these worried people hang onto is that the overwhelmingly generous offers of hospitality from America may be followed up by the sending of American ships to fetch the children. Britons still have an immense faith in America and the workings of her national conscience, but they hope that any such gestures will not be delayed much longer. Over here, one gets a new conception of time. It doesn't march on; it hurtles, like a dive bomber.

July 21

President Roosevelt's speech of acceptance heartened people here enormously and was hailed as "a mighty wind dispersing the noxious fog" of calculated ambiguities and political trimmings which has obscured the drafting of the Party programs. The speech was cheering both for what it said and for what it didn't say—words which, however, the average Briton was gratefully certain he could read between the lines: that so long as Roosevelt was in the White House help would be forthcoming. People felt as relieved as though a public-spirited and kindly neighbor had decided that perhaps he wouldn't move out of the district after all. The President's personal popularity and the trust which millions of English place in him are immense. His plain speaking effectually drowned out the second oration of the day, Hitler's address to the Reichstag, which to most listeners sounded like the old, old story cooked up again—the denunciation of democratic warmongers, the last appeal to Britain to stop an unnecessary war, and the familiar attack on Mr. Churchill. It was observed here that Hitler made no mention of America, and that the possibilities of a long war were emphasized without any further reference to the previously promised dictation of peace terms in London on August 15th. This omission, however, did not alter the general opinion that the Battle of Britain is due to start soon. There are always plenty of people ready to predict the exact date. In spite of the self-elected Silent Column suggested by Mr. Duff Cooper to help check the idle spreading of rumors, the incorrigible unofficial prophets talked knowingly of July 15th as a date to keep your eye on. July 15th passed quietly. It's difficult to check up on the sources of such rumors, which are as fishy as the stories that whenever the German wireless announced such-and-such a town, factory, or airfield would be visited by bombers, the bombers turned up on the dot. No one ever seems to have heard these broadcasts first-hand.

Strangely, the idea of stopping the war at this juncture is one to which nobody gives a second thought. If this is, as it looks to be, the usual lull granted to the victim—a period in which German psychologists count upon fear and propaganda to do their disintegrating jobs on public morale—the first round has certainly gone to the British people. Their mood remains steady and cheerful, with a big increase in confidence traceable to the German pilots' evident reluctance to face up to British Hurricanes in the air battles of the past fortnight. The B.B.C. broadcast an eyewitness account of one of these fights off the Straits of Dover the other day and came in for sharp criticism from some listeners, who complained that the commentator's racy treatment of a life-and-death affair as though it were "an account of the Grand National or a Cup final" must surely have been "revolting to all decent citizens." The majority of decent citizens, possibly less squeamish, sat by their radios, hanging onto their seats and cheering. Another reason for increased confidence is the fairly unimpressive showing made by the German raiders in many of their attacks, which have certainly been comparatively unambitious and isolated up to date and seem to show that the pilots are often not so good as they might be. People believe that the R.A.F.'s nightly raids on enemy territory are a lot more effective. The skill and audacity of the R.A.F. youngsters have so captured the public imagination that the fliers are spoken of with almost poetical admiration, as though they were knights on wings.

More practically, the public determination to see that the pilots get the planes they deserve sent housewives trotting off to the aluminum dumps with their most cherished pots and pans in answer to Lord Beaverbrook's appeal last week. Belatedly, this country appears to be asking and getting the self-sacrificing gestures of everyday life which the totalitarian governments have enforced upon their people for years. On Tuesday, when the supplementary budget is made public, Britons expect to be asked to shell out more than their aluminum; they are gloomily but resignedly certain that Sir Kingsley Wood intends to take the shirts off their backs.

The House of Commons staged two lively debates this week, one on the postponement of the evacuation of children, the other on the closing of the Burma Road. Parents are still hoping that the scheme for the evacuation may be revived, possibly with the help of American boats. Labour members made much of the fact that the children of the wealthier classes seemed to have been sent away first—an impression given by the publicity these children received when they reached America. Actually, large numbers of poorer children, with less news value but equally vulnerable bodies, have reached safety in the last few weeks. As for the Burma Road agreement, the attitude among ordinary people appeared to be that the less said the better, but the little said was bitterly resentful. Many of them thought that in the announcement of the closing they were listening once more to what President Roosevelt termed the false lullaby of appeasement. Less prettily, it was felt that the dead rat under the boards was smelling up the house again. The average Englishman understands that there is nothing to be done about it, and understands also that the situation is a legacy from the past bad years of complacent leadership. To ensure that there will be no return to such years is for most people the clearest part of the immense program of spring cleaning and refurnishing which will face this old empire when the lights come on again in Europe.

July 28

Except for isolated air raids and attacks on convoys round the coast, this has been a quiet week. The results of the air battles have confirmed the general impression that the British pilots are outflying the Germans, man for man and plane for plane. On Friday afternoon, newspaper-sellers were chalking up on their boards "Twenty-three Planes Down Yesterday"—a new record which was later corrected to twenty-eight and which greatly encouraged people who had already been heartened a night or two earlier by Lord Beaverbrook's broadcast announcement that arrangements had just been made for the production in the United States of three thousand planes a month for this country. Skeptical listeners were even more impressed by Mr. Morgenthau's subsequent statement that the United States Government had agreed to give the British "every possible facility to place their orders and secure delivery." That, the doubters agreed, means something, though the date of the first of these precious deliveries must necessarily be far distant and time is a factor which may be heartbreakingly decisive.

President Roosevelt, Mr. Hearst, and Miss Dorothy Thompson also made important news here with varying pronouncements this past week. The President's statement on the possibility of sending American vessels to fetch children to the States brought hope to many anxious parents, but his insistence that there should be "reasonable assurances" of immunity from submarine and air attack didn't sound very good, for the recent example of the *Meknès* is in everybody's mind. Although most Britons believe that the sinking of one child-refugee ship would have the same galvanizing effect on American public opinion that the *Lusitania* outrage had, there are plenty of people who think that the Germans might be clumsy or callous enough to risk it. Mr. Hearst's resigned (so far as could be judged from the way it was reported here) forecast of the United States' entry into the war created considerable interest, for the average British newspaper reader thinks of Hearst as an unamiable ogre who has persistently roared fee fi fo fum over the blood of all Englishmen while shipping disembowelled English castles to California. Miss Thompson's radio eulogy of Mr. Churchill was also given respectful attention, although modest Englishmen blushed when she referred to "this incredibly delicate and exquisite mechanism, this remarkable and artistic thing —the British Empire."

In such a relatively peaceful week, people had time to grumble about the budget, which displeased practically everybody, as usual—this time for the novel reason that it was not severe enough. Sir Kingsley Wood was generally expected to stand or fall on the success of the supplementary measures that he had to introduce on Tuesday to bolster up Sir John Simon's earlier and disappointingly feeble effort. First reactions indicated that he had fallen. The old screws of estate and income taxes and duties on beer and tobacco were given a few more twists, but the feeling seemed to be that inflation had come a terrifying step or two nearer and that this budget had caught the man with a large income and the small wage earner, leaving the possessor of a medium income in a comparatively favorable position, especially if he happens to be unmarried or to have no children. The increase on beer and tobacco will make the fighting men glum, while the new book tax and the heavier entertainment duty caused Mr. A. P. Herbert to fume that although Bibles were to be taxed and Handel and Shakespeare were to become luxuries, betting was not taxed at all. Altogether, it was felt that the issue had been shirked once more and that these were not the bold and drastic demands for which the nation is ready after its rough awakening from those nearly fatal months when it was lulled into the belief that everything was lovely. The national capacity for self-sacrifice has so far been only timidly and experimentally tested; the British see far more clearly than the authorities realize that in this war it is neck or nothing.

Although London may not be precisely comfortable, it is at the moment one of the most exhilarating cities in the world in which to find oneself. It can't be comfortable to anyone who hasn't a morbid affection for danger, since, as people say simply, however good the defences are, some of those waves of dive bombers which may momentarily be sent against them will certainly get through. Horror may glide down suddenly and noiselessly out of the summer sky as it did on Barcelona, but all the same it's stimulating to be here, as one of the remaining Americans remarked, because of a new vitality which seems to have been injected into the staid British atmosphere. Possibly the feeling of increased confidence and purpose one gets from everybody is due to the fact that the British people are now not trusting in anybody or anything—not in the French Army or even in the American promise of planes—except the British people. After the bitterness and bewilderment of the last few tragic weeks, there's relief in finding that faith can be so simplified.

The everyday things of life that were thrown out of gear

by events are in order again; theatres and restaurants which were doing terrible business are packed once more. Although the city looks normal enough on the surface, there's always the underlying knowledge that at any instant this state of affairs may be violently ended. Mr. Malcolm Mac-Donald probably spoke for millions of ordinary and quite unheroic men and women when he said in a speech the other day that if he could choose the moment in which he most wanted to be alive, he would choose a few days or a few weeks hence, or whenever the enemy would strike with his maximum force against this island.

August 4

For the past week, foreign correspondents have been sitting at strategic points on the English coastline, waiting to get a scoop on the invasion, which, German propaganda to the contrary, many informed observers think will start at any minute. To Vincent Sheean and other professional trouble-chasers who have followed the long and tragic tale of violence through blood-soaked Europe, this period of calm and orderly living—perhaps the last that this country will know for some time—must seem gloomily reminiscent. The suburban housewife, setting out with a shopping basket or picking the runner beans that now twine over air-raid shelters in even the sootiest backyards, is no more or less placid than were housewives performing the last little chores of day-to-day existence in Barcelona or Warsaw just before hell broke loose in those cities. The ordinary Englishman, as though unaware that the attention of the whole world is on him at the moment, continues to get on quietly with his ordinary job and to find as much pleasure as this breathing space of civilization can offer.

There's no doubt in most minds that it's only a breathing space. All last week, the rumor went round that something would happen this weekend—a prophecy apparently based

on the coinciding of the anniversary of the outbreak of the
first World War (a moment which might appeal to Hitler's
fondness for the melodramatic gesture) with the more practical omen of a bright moon and high tides. Experts here
think that Germany will almost certainly make a gigantic effort to win before the winter and before the numerical supe-
riority of her air fleet is overcome by the combined efforts of
the aircraft industries of Great Britain and the United
States. Many people, however, believe that the Blitzpeace is
not yet over, and that the German leaflets dropped over Britain for the first time on Friday were the opening shots of an
intensified propaganda offensive.

Meanwhile, the success of the R.A.F. raids on Germany
continues to do excellent things to public morale. There is
some surprise that the raids on this country have been so
slight in comparison, but the supposition is that the German
Air Force is being refitted and reorganized for the big attack. It also seems certain that the British flyers' night navi-
gation is better than the Germans' and that it's easier for
bombers to find their objectives on the Continent, where
roads are long and straight and where rivers and big towns
are unmistakable landmarks, than in England, where the
crooked, ambling roads, the straggling towns, and the jum-
ble of absolutely identical little fields and hedgerows are a
navigator's headache. For once, the national talent for muddled planning looks like a good thing.

That this talent is not yet eradicated from all government
departments was unhappily evident in last week's House of
Commons rumpus over the policy of the Ministry of Information, the unwieldy and expensive organization headed by
Mr. Duff Cooper and responsible for censorship, propaganda, and the distribution of news. In the opinion of most
thinking citizens, the Ministry has failed miserably in its
present form. Certainly nowadays British propaganda isn't a
patch on what it was in the last war. The machine which
functioned so successfully and inexpensively twenty-five
years ago became the model upon which the Germans based
their own system. Foreign broadcasts in particular have been

criticized as being polite Foreign Office English, correctly translated but hardly calculated to fire oppressed people into action; the enormously important problem of broadcasts to the French has not yet been successfully tackled.

These were not the defects which were attacked in Thursday's debate and Friday's press, unfortunately. Instead, the discussion had to do with the far less serious question of the Ministry's house-to-house quiz on what people are thinking about the war. To a nation which likes to keep itself to itself, this seemed an unwarranted intrusion into the people's private lives. Householders were urged by the press to shut their doors in the faces of the investigators, who were promptly named "Cooper's snoopers," and members of Parliament declared that "it is no part of the duties of the Ministry of Information to go spying round the homes of ordinary citizens already sufficiently harassed and perturbed, though exceedingly courageous." This stung Mr. Duff Cooper into a bitter attack on the newspapers, which he claimed were keeping the agitation alive as a stunt to make up for a shortage of news.

It was possibly an inauspicious moment to try out such an innovation. The recent unsuccessful venture of the Silent Column, designed to prevent the leakage of information to the enemy, had only just perished—with the assistance of a characteristic kick in the pants from Mr. Churchill, who has won Britons' admiration and confidence by a persistent policy of treating them as sensible adults whom it is possible to trust. Large sums of money were expended in trying to put over the Silent Column idea, which gave a magnificent free hand to busybodies and came perilously close to tampering with the precious democratic possession of free speech. One of the few happy achievements of the movement was the upsetting of an important government official. At dinner in a restaurant, he was telling a friend a perfectly harmless anecdote, perhaps well studded with Ministerial names, when the waiter handed him a note from the next table suggesting that he was talking far too loudly and too much.

As for the Ministry of Information's latest proposal, it's

not hard for anyone with a nose for such things to find out what people are thinking and saying without going to the trouble of a doorstep canvass. Everyone is reading *Guilty Men,* an anonymous survey of the rotten heritage which Chamberlain took over from his predecessors. The great, unmoneyed masses and the immensely powerful middle classes believe and intend that England will win the war. There are still people with property who think they believe the same thing but consciously or unconsciously add the stipulation that they expect to go on living in the same old England, under the same old bad peacetime conditions. This section of the community corresponds to the French group that was responsible for that country's collapse and for the Pétain government, and there is widespread determination among ordinary people to crush any such ideas here. Finally, all classes seem to feel that the United States is already spiritually in the war, and that Japan, without firing a shot at England, has declared for the Axis combination.

August 12

[*The beginning of the Battle of Britain. In August the German air force attacked British coastal defenses and shipping; in the last week of the month the main thrust was directed against aircraft factories and Royal Air Force bases. On September 7 the Germans began the night bombing of London.*]

The Prime Minister came out a short while ago with a grave warning that the dangers of invasion had not in the least abated, just in case these days should be lulling anyone into forgetting what may well turn out to be a terrible August holiday program. This is the time of year when people ordinarily pack their bags and go off to pick up a tan which will last the winter; this year, most of them are staying put in their homes while the homes are still there to stay put in. There is now a feeling in informed circles that the next two weeks will be the critical ones, developments being possibly timed to coincide with an intensified Italian push in northeast Africa. Certainly last Thursday's and yesterday's mass air raids over the Channel, in which on each occasion the R.A.F. made a magnificent showing by accounting for sixty planes, seem to indicate that the phase of softening-up operations is over and that any future attacks are likely to be part of the real thing. Many observers think that the Germans lost a chance by not launching their big attack in the bewildered period immediately after the collapse of France, when the defences of this country had not been effectively coördinated and stiffened, as they have now.

Speaking in the House of Commons last week, Mr. Arthur Greenwood mentioned the great strides that have been made in the production of war materials when he gave his analysis of the government's present economic policy. The ordinary Briton found the speech reassuring, and Mr. Ernest Bevin's vigorous interpolation even more so, for the queer reason that both speeches emphasized that in spite of what progress has been made, there are still difficulties to overcome before the situation can be described as satisfactory. It was probably indicative of the public temper, as well as that of the House, that the portions of Mr. Greenwood's speech which speculated on Hitler's possible difficulties with the oppressed and starving peoples of his new possessions were not so favorably received as the warning that the power of the enemy must not be underestimated.

The appallingly dangerous phase during which people still thought that Hitler was a bit of a joke, that the German populace was not behind him, and that dud bombs would prove to be full of love and kisses from disgruntled Skoda workers is happily something which everyone wants to forget as quickly as possible. Underestimating the enemy, England now knows, is one of the first milestones on the road which leads to Vichy.

The tragic problem of the oppressed and starving people

of Europe was, however, in the minds of all sober men and women this week. Mr. John Cudahy's statement that Belgium would have a famine by October, though undoubtedly sincere, seemed to most people to bristle with dangerous potentialities. The general view here is that there need be no food shortage in Europe this winter if Germany fairly and conscientiously divides the stocks available; at the end of June, the British recall, it was stated that Germany had not begun to tap her vast seven-million-ton grain reserve. The average Englishman fears that if the immense humane impulse in America is exploited to pour food into Europe, the food will find its way into Germany in spite of promises and international commissions. It has been suggested that the British government should make it clear that the blockade of enemy-occupied territories will be lifted the moment the Nazis evacuate them. It has also been suggested that a huge stock of food should be built up in America, Australia, and South Africa and a guarantee widely broadcast that it would be released to countries in need of relief just as soon as their populations showed signs of organizing a revolt against the Nazi rule. Whatever the results of the issue raised by Mr. Cudahy, Englishmen are sadly certain that bad blood between Britons and old friends must be one of them. Far less skillful propagandists than the Germans could find several fine ways of using hunger as a whip with which to touch up hatred.

It's hoped by all sensible men here that something will soon be done to remedy the mistakes of the wholesale internment of refugees which was put into force at the height of the Quisling scare. There has already been a good deal of agitation that has resulted in the appointment of an Aliens' Advisory Council, which met for the first time last week, and in a White Paper issued by the Home Office that lists eighteen categories of persons eligible for release, including "scientists, research workers, and persons of academic distinction for whom work of national importance in their special fields is available." At least one Nobel Prize-winner is among those kicking their heels behind barbed wire. Mr. H. G. Wells and Professor Gilbert Murray have registered strong protests against the indiscriminate internment of distinguished exiles. Mr. Augustus John now heads an Artists' Refugee Committee, which is working for the release of all artists who previous to the mass internment were regarded as friendly. The present unimaginative state of affairs seems to most Englishmen like an appalling waste of skilled manpower, time, and money, even if it doesn't show up in the still worse light of an insulting betrayal of men of good will.

The R.A.F.'s brilliantly successful week raised the public's spirits enormously. It was hoped that the number of German planes destroyed by the British fighters would be duly noted by a section of the American press which appears to people here to act as though mesmerized by the achievements of the *Luftwaffe*. Many astonished Britons, taking time off from the war to read how American editors think it's going, have felt like protesting, like Mark Twain, that the reports of their death have been greatly exaggerated. Even the New York *Times* came out recently with the surprising statement that "over the island kingdom flew scores of German planes dropping tons of bombs that ripped apart English towns and farmsteads." This read to people living in the supposedly ripped-apart towns like something the Hamburg radio commentator might have thought up.

August 25

London has accepted its sirens with the usual exciting British display of complete impassiveness. Inasmuch as everybody feels deep down in his bones, and in the uncomfortable area of the stomach, where most people keep their courage, that the first of the big raids are upon us at last, the universal calm has seemed almost ostentatious. People have queued up for the public shelters as quietly as if waiting to see a motion picture. When the first of the sirens went off early one evening, the lights went off, too, in the bar where a group of

us happened to be, but the barman continued to arrange
sprigs of mint in some drinks as though absorbed in this artistic effort. Running footsteps and blowing whistles
sounded from the street. It was instructive to watch the behavior of persons who turned up, panting slightly, to meet
their friends for a drink. "I ran all the way from Bond
Street," said a pretty, hatless girl to a young naval officer,
who seemed to take it for granted that pretty girls should
choose this form of exercise on a warm August evening. We
all went on chatting pleasantly while pretending that we
were not listening for the first crash of the bombardment or
calculating how long it would take to duck down to the basement. When the all-clear sounded after a period of eventless
waiting, there was a little stir of gaiety and most of the customers ordered another drink.

Since then, there have been plenty more sirens, but the
raiders have not got further than the outer suburbs, where
the gunfire was especially heavy in the night raid a week ago.
Every other person one meets can give exact details of damage and casualties—details which unfortunately never tally.
It was announced that a hundred and fifty girls had been
killed in the bombardment of the Coty factory, but the story
was denied next day by the Coty people themselves, who
said that the girls were not working at the time of the raid.
This is the kind of thing which starts rumors and makes the
public suspect that it is not being told all it should be, and
it was a relief to learn that from now on official lists of the
killed and injured will be posted as soon as possible outside
borough town halls. Monthly totals of casualties are to be announced in the press.

Failure to sound the sirens in one of last week's raids was
the subject of a question in the House of Commons which
drew from the Minister of Home Security the uncomfortably
insecure statement that citizens must be prepared not only
to be warned without being bombed but also occasionally to
be bombed without being warned. The problem is a difficult one, since to sound sirens in all towns within likely
range of the raiders' course would be to throw a spanner
into industrial output by day and into workers' precious

sleep by night. However sensible this argument seems, it is unfortunately only human nature to feel aggrieved when the first intimation one receives of hostile aircraft overhead is a bomb splinter landing at one's feet. Considering the terrible opportunities for practice that this country is likely to get in the near future, some more universally satisfactory system will probably be worked out before long.

Now that raids are obviously going to become part of the day-to-day routine for millions of people, there is a good deal of fervent discussion as to the best place to make for if one is unlucky enough to be caught out of doors when the sirens start. Shoppers prefer Harrods, where chairs are provided and first-aid workers unobtrusively but comfortingly hover about. In the public shelters, it is usually a case of standing room only, which becomes hard on the feet after an hour or so, but is less of a hardship to most than the ban on smoking.

On the whole, the general feeling seems to be one of relief that "it" has come at last, although there is no doubt in anyone's mind that the raids on the London area so far have been little more than reconnaissances. Still, the first round of the mass offensive in the air is over and the result has certainly been overwhelmingly in Britain's favor. The second round may bring some harder hitting, but the public is confident and cheerful. The ordinary individual is magnificent in a moment like this. Recently, the Ministry of Information launched a series of advertisements which, in the form of the soul-searchings of an unattractively smug and breezy citizen, gave the public the Ministry's notions of correct British behavior under every possible stress and strain: "What do I do in an air raid? I do not panic. I say to myself, our chaps are dealing with them, etc." The campaign would seem to be another of the Ministry's unfortunate bloomers, since under stress every charwoman reacts with the courage, restraint, and humor traditionally expected of aristocrats.

In spite of the alarms of the past week, London still looks a good deal safer than many a country district which has unexpectedly found itself right in the centre of the *Blitzkrieg*. A person living near a well-guarded military objective frequently discovers he has passed a less harassing night than his friend in some village on the other side of the county, where raiders, chased by the R.A.F., were jettisoning bombs all around.

In the beautiful fruit-growing country, over which in happier days the Paris airliners peacefully droned, fag ends of last week's raids upset the harvesting of the plum crop until exasperated farmers hit on the notion of digging trenches in their orchards so that the pickers could remain in the fields during dogfights overhead, snatching another bushel or so at every lull. Country people continue to be sturdily unimpressed by visitations from the enemy. ' I just turned over and went to sleep again," said one old man, relating how a bomb had fallen a hundred yards from his cottage gate.

The Prime Minister's most recent speech and the successful action against Italian ships raised everybody's spirits. Anthony Eden is curiously uninspiring. Alfred Duff Cooper, after one first-class broadcast, turned in a series of outbursts which set the teeth of even the not particularly sensitive on edge. Mr. Churchill is the only man in England today who consistently interprets the quiet but completely resolute national mood. The sinking of the Italian ships was a tonic chaser to the nasty taste that the evacuation of Somaliland had left in the public's mouth. For most Britons, one of the bitterest of the many bitter consequences of France's capitulation was that it has made operations against Italy vastly more difficult. The feeling of this country about Italy has an angry, personal quality, as though it were directed against someone who has been guilty not of crime on a heroic scale but of mean behavior, such as bilking at a race meeting or pinching the poorbox of a church.

August 30

The nightly nuisance raids of the past week continue. Since the damage they have done has been slight, their objects would seem to be reconnaissance and interference with the civilian population's sleep. Their immediate result has been a sudden display by Londoners of a talent for taking cat naps in all sorts of places. On Tuesday, the morning after the longest air-raid warning to date, which stranded hundreds of suburbanites in town without a toothbrush among them, matrons snoozed in buses and clerks devoted their lunch hour to dozing under trees in public squares and gardens. By the middle of the week, people were accepting the daily performances of what they now call the "Wailing Willie" as a dull routine instead of an alarming novelty. During a raid last Monday night, when some cinema managers interrupted their programs to give audiences the choice of leaving or of moving into greater safety at the back of the auditorium (a suggestion which brought to many of their hearers qualmish visions of being the meat in the sandwich between the balcony and the floor), most people stayed put, even if their enjoyment of the entertainment was understandably diminished. Pubs remained open and companionable parties gathered. At Queen's Hall, a Wagner concert ran to greater length than "Götterdämmerung," while the immortal Richard's compatriots droned somewhere in the vicinity; when Sir Henry Wood's official program ended, members of the symphony orchestra obliged with solos and the indefatigable audience filled in with community singing and amateur talent until the all-clear came, around three. "Was it [the air-raid siren] Siegfried's horn or Fafner's growl or both together?" asked the *Times* music critic in a facetious mood next day. Since experts agree that night raids are likely to become more numerous, Londoners are adapting themselves sensibly and courageously to this new phase of the war. On Wednesday, the manager of the Empire had only to walk out on the stage and say "I suppose you know why I'm here" to get the biggest laugh of the evening.

The damage of the most severe night raid was confined to that part of Pepys' London where the crooked, mazy lanes are dotted with blue plaques announcing the site of such-and-such a building which was destroyed in the Great Fire of 1666. After a good deal of coy hesitation, the censors revealed the fact that the affected area was Cripplegate, where a potential Great Fire of 1940 was put under control by the prompt action of the fire services. Strangely enough, the fire station, just a street's width away from where one of the bombs fell, was the only building in the block in which no windows were broken. The rest of the houses were a mass of staring desolation. For a couple of blocks, what had been office buildings were blackened shells inside which one could get glimpses of charred wreckage. If the bombs had fallen in the daytime, the casualties in this closely packed area would have been tragic.

By midweek, the work of reconstruction was already going ahead. Men were running up scaffolding around the damaged buildings, hurrying to and fro, like ants in a heap which someone had just kicked apart. What had been an ill wind for many people had blown good to the glaziers, from whose vans, backed against the pavement, hundreds of square feet of glass were being lifted out of straw packing. The danger from falling glass and odd bits of masonry was still considerable, and police barricaded the surrounding streets to anyone who couldn't show a pass or prove legitimate business there. Opposite St. Giles, the church where Milton is buried, the front had been blown out of a dark and Dickensian little eating house, and two men in bartenders' aprons sat together discussing events among the broken mahogany hatracks and scattered spittoons. A notice tacked up outside announced business as usual. Around the corner, in Aldersgate, a sign in front of a delicatessen shop which had suffered the same fate proclaimed cheerfully, "We are wide open." It was doing a good trade among customers who did not seem to be moved by the fact that they could leave by the conventional door or through the space where the window had been.

At St. Giles, a bomb had fallen slap on the sandbags protecting a stained-glass window, blowing a hole in the wall and toppling Milton off his plinth outside. On the vacant plinth were still inscribed Milton's own curiously appropriate lines: "O Spirit . . . what in me is dark illumine, what is low raise and support."

Naturally, there has been a good deal of hopeful talk this week about retaliatory raids on Berlin, but it is realized that such reprisals, though satisfactory, would do less good than the present devastating R.A.F. raids on Germany's centres of war production. A campaign of destruction of factories, power plants, and airdromes is more useful than the German policy of hitting and running where no possible military objective can exist. Incidentally, the announcements of the first air-raid deaths are beginning to appear in the obituary columns of the morning papers. No mention is made of the cause of death, but the conventional phrase "very suddenly" is always used. Thousands of men, women, and children are scheduled to die very suddenly, without any particular notice being taken of them in the obituary columns. To observers here, it sometimes seems that more than Milton has been toppled off his plinth. All that is best in the good life of civilized effort appears to be slowly and painfully keeling over in the chaos of man's inhumanity to man.

September 8

The air *Blitzkrieg* started in earnest yesterday—Saturday— with the first big raids on London. It is as yet too early to report on the full extent of the damage, which has certainly been considerable, especially in the dwelling-house sections of the East End. Observers of the Spanish War methods of terrorizing civilian populations have frequently remarked that in Spain the heaviest bombardments were directed on working-class districts—structurally more vulnerable and emotionally more prone to panic than less crowded areas of a city. The job of providing homeless and frightened people with shelter and food is one which workers have apparently tackled heroically. They are probably going to have increasingly and tragically frequent opportunities for practice. The

figure of four hundred killed, which has just been announced, may well mount higher in future bulletins, in the
same way that the figure of raiders brought down was given
as five in last evening's reports but by this morning, with
fuller information coming in all the time, had totalled eigh-
ty-eight.

Those who were weekending in the country guessed the
magnitude of the attack from the constant roar of aircraft
passing invisibly high up in a cloudless blue sky. At dusk, a
red glow could be seen in the direction of London, but it
died down as the stars and the searchlights came out, and
again waves of bombers passed overhead at intervals of about
ten minutes. In between waves, one could hear the distant
racket of the anti-aircraft guns picking up the raiders which
had just gone by, and at the same time one half heard, half
sensed the unmistakable throbbing of the next waves of engines coming nearer over the quiet woods and villages. This
morning it was difficult to get a call through to London,
probably because so many anxious people in the country
were ringing up to find out what had happened and to try to
get in touch with members of their families who were in
town. Further big attacks were expected today, but the attitude of those who were returning to the city was sensible
and courageous. "Let them send plenty. There will be more
for the boys to bring down" was a typical comment.

Up to yesterday, the raids on London had not been developed beyond a point which indicated that they were merely
reconnaissance or training flights to accustom enemy pilots
to night work over the capital. Sirens had become tiresome
interruptions which Londoners learned to expect at fairly
regular intervals during the day, roughly coinciding with the
morning and evening traffic rush and with the lunch hour.
Unless shooting accompanied the alarms, they were ignored,
as far as possible, except by especially nervous individuals.
The dislocation of office and factory work schedules was
more or less remedied by the posting of spotters on rooftops
to give the warning when things really become dangerous locally. Until that warning comes, workers have been getting

on with the job, sirens or no sirens. No part of the Premier's speech last week was better received, by the way, than his statement that the whole of the air-raid-warning system is to be drastically revised and a new ruling concerning it announced in the near future; what he described as "these prolonged banshee howlings" are apparently more alarming to a great many people than an actual bombardment.

Life in a bombed city means adapting oneself in all kinds of ways all the time. Londoners are now learning the lessons, long ago familiar to those living on the much-visited southeast coast, of getting to bed early and shifting their sleeping quarters down to the ground floor. (After recent raids on the suburbs it was noticeable that in all the little houses damaged by anything short of a direct hit people on the upper floors had suffered most, and that in surprisingly many cases those on the ground floor had escaped injury entirely.) Theatres are meeting the threat to their business by starting evening performances earlier, thus giving audiences a chance to get home before the big nighttime show warms up. The actual getting home is likely to be difficult, because the transportation services have not yet worked out a satisfactory formula for carrying on during raids. The busmen's union tells drivers to use their own discretion, and the London transportation board's orders are that buses are to go on running unless a raid develops "in the immediate vicinity." The drivers grumble that it would take a five-hundred-pounder in the immediate vicinity to be heard above the din of their own engines.

The calm behavior of the average individual continues to be amazing. Commuting suburbanites, who up to yesterday had experienced worse bombardments than people living in central London, placidly brag to fellow-passengers on the morning trains about the size of bomb craters in their neighborhoods, as in a more peaceful summer they would have bragged about their roses and squash.

Earlier in the week, the first anniversary of the declaration of war passed peacefully and found Britons in a state of encouragement which less than three months ago would have

seemed downright fantastic. The Anglo-American agreement
was a birthday present that was received with tremendous
satisfaction. Officially, it was greeted as "the most conspicu-
ous demonstration that has yet been given of the general
American desire to afford the utmost help, compatible with
neutrality, to a cause now recognized as vital to the future of
the United States." Ordinary comment was less solemn, but
no less grateful. The successful conclusion of the agreement,
combined with the superb work of the R.A.F. and the significant new spirit in the French colonies, has been responsible
for a big increase in public confidence which reacted favorably on that sensitive plant, the stock market. In spite of the
dark times ahead, it is believed that better things are coming
into sight beyond them.

September 14

For Londoners, there are no longer such things as good
nights; there are only bad nights, worse nights, and better
nights. Hardly anyone has slept at all in the past week. The
sirens go off at approximately the same time every evening,
and in the poorer districts, queues of people carrying blankets, thermos flasks, and babies begin to form quite early
outside the air-raid shelters. The *Blitzkrieg* continues to
be directed against such military objectives as the tired
shopgirl, the red-eyed clerk, and the thousands of dazed
and weary families patiently trundling their few belongings
in perambulators away from the wreckage of their homes.
After a few of these nights, sleep of a kind comes from
complete exhaustion. The amazing part of it is the cheerfulness and fortitude with which ordinary individuals are
doing their jobs under nerve-racking conditions. Girls who
have taken twice the usual time to get to work look worn
when they arrive, but their faces are nicely made up and
they bring you a cup of tea or sell you a hat as chirpily as
ever. Little shopkeepers whose windows have been blown

out paste up "Business as usual" stickers and exchange cracks with their customers.

On all sides, one hears the grim phrase "We shall get used to it." Everyone takes for granted that the program of wanton destruction, far from letting up, will be intensified when bad weather sets in and makes anything like accuracy in bombing impossible. Although people imagined early in the war that vicious bombardments would be followed by the panic-stricken departure of everybody who could leave the city, outward-going traffic on one of the major roads from London was only normal on the day after the worst of the raids. The government, however, has announced new plans for the evacuation of children who were not sent away under former schemes or whose mothers last week had the unhappy inspiration to bring them back to town for a holiday at home.

The East End suffered most in the night raids this week. Social workers who may have piously wished that slum areas could be razed had their wish horribly fulfilled when rows of mean dwellings were turned into shambles overnight. The Nazi attack bore down heaviest on badly nourished, poorly clothed people—the worst equipped of any to stand the appalling physical strain, if it were not for the stoutness of their cockney hearts. Relief workers sorted them out in schools and other centres to be fed, rested, and provided with billets. Subsequent raids killed many of the homeless as they waited.

The bombers, however, made no discrimination between the lowest and the highest homes in the city. The Queen was photographed against much the same sort of tangle of splintered wreckage that faced hundreds of humbler, anonymous housewives in this week's bitter dawns. The crowd that gathered outside Buckingham Palace the morning after the picture was published had come, it appeared on close inspection, less to gape at boarded windows than to listen to the cheering notes of the band, which tootled away imperturbably at the cherished ceremony of the Changing of the Guard. This was before the deliberate second try for the Palace, which has made people furious, but has also cheered them with the thought that the King and Queen are facing risks that are now common to all.

Broken windows are no longer a novelty in the West End, though the damage there so far has been slight. In getting about, one first learns that a bomb has fallen near at hand by coming upon barriers across roads and encountering policemen who point to yellow tin signs which read simply "Diversion," as though the blockage had been caused by workmen peacefully taking up drains ahead. The "diversion" in Regent Street, where a bomb fell just outside the Café Royal and did not explode for hours, cut off the surrounding streets and made the neighborhood as quiet as a hamlet. Crowds collected behind the ropes to gaze respectfully at the experts, who stood looking down into the crater and chatting as nonchalantly as plumbers discussing the best way of fixing a leaking tap. Police went around getting occupants out of the buildings in the vicinity and warning them to leave their windows open, but even with this precaution, when the bomb finally went off that evening there were not many panes of glass left.

The scene next morning was quite extraordinarily eerie. The great sweep of Regent Street, deserted by everyone except police and salvage workers, stared gauntly like a thoroughfare in a dead city. It would have been no surprise to see grass growing up out of the pavements, which were covered instead with a fine, frosty glitter of powdered glass. The noise of glass being hammered out of upper windows, swept into piles at street corners, and shovelled into municipal dust vans made a curious grinding tinkle, which went on most of the day. The happiest people there were two little boys who had discovered a sweet shop where most of the window display had been blown into the gutter, and who were doing a fine looting job among the debris. Around the corner, the florid façade of Burlington Arcade had been hit at one end, and an anxious jeweller was helping in the work of salvaging his precious stock from the heap of junk that a short while before had been a double row of luxury shops.

Scenes like these are new enough to seem both shocking and unreal; to come across a wrecked filling station with a couple of riddled cars standing dejectedly by its smashed pumps makes one feel that one must have strayed onto a Hollywood set, and it's good to get back to normality among the still snug houses in the next street.

Wednesday night's terrific, new-style anti-aircraft barrage reassured people, after scaring them badly. A.R.P. workers, who have been heroic all the week, were told to warn as many as possible that something special and noisy was going to be tried out that evening, but all over town persons who hadn't been tipped off thought that the really terrifying din was a particularly fierce bombardment. Houses shuddered unceasingly until the all-clear sounded in the dawn, when everyone felt better because, although Londoners had had a bad night, the raiders must have had a worse one. The behavior of all classes is so magnificent that no observer here could ever imagine these people following the French into captivity. As for breaking civilian morale, the high explosives that rained death and destruction on the capital this week were futile.

September 21

After a fortnight of savage nocturnal bombardments, Londoners are settling down with courage and resource to live by a completely new timetable. The big stores and many of the offices now close an hour earlier in order to give workers a chance to get home and have a meal before the uncomfortable evening program begins, which it does with unfailing regularity. Getting home is a tricky business for those who live in the suburbs, for bomb damage and rush hours at unexpected times of day have put a strain on the transport services. Lucky commuters have been cadging lifts from passing motorists and lorry-drivers; the not-so-lucky have been doggedly hiking rather than risk being caught out in the night air, ·which definitely isn't healthy just now, as much because of the terrific anti-aircraft barrages as because of bombs.

Families of modest means who have no cellars in their homes and perhaps don't care to trust to their Anderson shelters start queuing up outside the public shelters as early as six in the evening, with their bundles of bedding and their baskets of food. Thousands more turn the tube stations into vast dormitories every night—a kind of lie-down strike which at first perplexed the authorities, who could not think what to do with passengers who paid their three-hapence and then proceeded to encamp quietly on the platforms. Since these folk have given no trouble and haven't, as was feared, cluttered up the corridors to the inconvenience of passengers with a genuine urge to get somewhere, the latest semi-official ruling is that the practice can be continued. The Ministries of Transport and Home Security, however, have appealed to the public not to use the tube as a shelter except in cases of urgent necessity. The urgent necessity of many of the sleepers who doss down on the platforms nightly is that they no longer have homes to go to; each morning, more are leaving their underground sanctuary to go back and find a heap of rubble and splinters where their houses used to be. The bravery of these people has to be seen to be believed. They would be heart-rending to look at if they didn't so conspicuously refuse to appear heart-rending. Their reaction has taken the form of anger, and there is a good deal of hopeful talk about smashing reprisals on Berlin. Anger has probably been responsible for a recent rise in munitions production. Hundreds of men and women are working a bit faster as they think of those heaps of rubble.

Bombs of heavy calibre were dropped in some of this week's raids, and time bombs were also extensively used. A new headache for householders is the possibility of being evacuated with only a few minutes' warning, as they must be when a time bomb falls anywhere near. The most heroic among the millions of heroic workers in London these days are the Royal Engineers, who deal in squads with time bombs, going down into the craters and working with mathematical nicety. The squad which saved St. Paul's naturally came in for much deserved publicity, but there are plenty of equally courageous groups risking their lives daily with the same coolness, if under less spectacular circumstances. The auxilary fire services, too, have done magnificent work, and an announcement of civilian-service decorations which will be the equivalent of military honors is expected shortly. Firemen, wardens, Home Guards, and nurses alike were killed while on duty during this week's raids. Nurses have been under fire constantly, for several hospitals have been hit more than once. St. Thomas's, on the river opposite the Houses of Parliament (which presumably were the target), is a tragic sight, its wards ripped open by bombs.

The bombers have turned their attention to the West End for the last few nights and the big stores have suffered heavily. John Lewis & Co. and others were badly damaged, but one gutted building looks much like another, and Londoners, after a brief glance, go briskly on to work. Taxi-drivers grumble about the broken glass, which is hard on their tires, and about the difficulty of navigating in neighborhoods which they know like the backs of their hands but which may overnight become unrecognizable. All the same, their grumbles have the usual cockney pithiness and gaiety, and taxis get you home in spite of anything short of a raid right overhead. Gaiety does turn up even in such grim days. It was funny to see raw sirloins of beef being carried from one stately club, which was temporarily cut off from its gas supply, to another equally stately establishment, which had offered the hospitality of its old-fashioned coal ranges; it was funny to see a florist's beautifully arranged hot-house blossoms waving in a stiff breeze that blew through the shattered windows of his shop.

There are now more people who appear to believe that the invasion is imminent and that the increasing fury of the air attacks is the first stage of the German plan for it. A story has been widely circulated that some sort of attempt at invasion was made and failed a few weeks back. It's certain that the bulk of the population (and, one hears, of the Army, too) is now yearning for the invasion to be tried. With the land forces praying daily that the Germans will start, the R.A.F. goes over nightly and stops them from starting.

September 29

Adjusting daily life to the disruption of nightly raids is naturally what Londoners are thinking and talking most about. For people with jobs to hold down, loss of sleep continues to be as menacing as bombs. Those with enough money get away to the country on weekends and treat themselves to the luxury of a couple of nine-hour stretches. ("Fancy," said one of these weekenders dreamily, "going upstairs to bed instead of down.") It is for the alleviation of the distress of the millions who can't afford to do anything but stay patiently put that the government has announced the distribution of free rubber earplugs to deaden the really appalling racket of the barrages. Plans to improve accommodations in air-raid shelters by the addition of bunks, heating, and better sanitary arrangements were announced at the same time, to the relief of physicians who had been figuring out that if winter comes, a really first-class epidemic can't be far behind. This announcement was also welcome news to Londoners who use the shelters nightly and are ready with fight and staying power so long as the authorities do the right thing by them. In some boroughs, relief organization isn't so intelligent as it might be and homeless people have to wait interminably and needlessly at rest centres while billets are found for them. Often the billets are bombed the first night and the homeless are back at the rest centres the next day, angrier than ever. Relief workers report that anger is the first reaction of people who have lost everything, and that old people feel the loss worst of all.

Excellent unsentimental work is being done in rest centres of the hard-hit districts by women's voluntary services. Besides billets, new wardrobes are provided there, and money for current expenses is advanced by the public-assistance funds; the pitiful bundles of belongings salvaged from the wrecked homes are carefully checked and stored. Mothers who wish to be evacuated with their children are sent to out-of-town billets, and the authorities hope that twenty thousand children a day will shortly be leaving the city to which too many of them, alas, were brought back by parents when things looked quiet. The rest centres also deal with inquiries from soldiers and sailors who return on leave and find their homes gone and their families missing. An appeal was recently broadcast to relatives of servicemen asking them not to forget the daily or weekly letter that can save endless anxiety for those in uniform. It was also announced that an organization to trace missing relatives in bombed areas will be set up at once.

The courage, humor, and kindliness of ordinary people continue to be astonishing under conditions which possess many of the merry features of a nightmare. Nobody imagines that England has seen the worst tricks the Germans have up their sleeves. There is a good deal of talk about gas. People seem calmly certain that it will be used before long, if civilian morale shows no signs of cracking, and that with it will come a characteristically elaborate story about British fliers having used it first over Berlin. There was a strong feeling of confidence last week, in spite of Dakar.

The Battle of London, however, was naturally more important to those in the thick of it than anything happening on the coast of Africa. The morale on the home front certainly inspires confidence. East Enders, who had suffered most, stuck up paper Union Jacks in the heaps of rubble that used to be their homes. Women pottered placidly in and out of a big Oxford Street store which had been badly damaged but had the usual uniformed doormen standing outside its boarded-up windows, over which stickers had been pasted declaring that all departments were open.

Things are settling down into a recognizable routine. Daylight sirens are disregarded by everyone, unless they are ac-

companied by gunfire or bomb explosions that sound uncomfortably near. A lady who arrived at one of the railway
stations during a warning was asked politely by the porter
who carried her bag, "Air-raid shelter or taxi, madam?" As
anyone else here would have done, she took a taxi. To those
who live in apartments, a good night is now one in which
the whole block doesn't start swaying; if it merely shudders
gently, people remark that things are nice and quiet tonight.
It's dusty work getting around London these days. Objects
that feel like small rocks have a habit of lodging in one's eyes
and turn out to be grit from the debris of wrecked buildings.
Often the first intimation that a place of business has been
hit is a small notice in the *Times'* personal column saying
simply that Messrs. So-and-So are opening up in a day or two
at a new address. Gieves, the famous military tailor on Bond
Street, whose shop was completely gutted, ran a stately advertisement regretting that it was necessary to inconvenience
clients for a few days, as though the fuss had been caused by
a bit of spring redecorating.

Some of the damage has been curious. A section of one big
block of flats was taken out as neatly as a slice carved from a
cake. Homes on Dover Street were opened up like doll
houses, so that passers-by could see pictures still hanging on
a wall or some trivial little ornaments still arranged neatly
on a mantelpiece that was dangling in space; it seemed as
though people's lives as well as their inanimate possessions
were being dissected in public. The exact whereabouts of
bomb damage is concealed with irritating coyness by the censorship bureau, which yesterday admitted playfully that "a
church famed in a nursery rhyme" had been hit. Any child
who has played oranges and lemons will be glad to step up
and give you the answer, which is a sad one for those who
have loved the last bits of Wren's London all their lives.

October 6

Londoners have been encouraged during the past week by the very definite slackening of night raids over the city. The anti-aircraft barrage seemed to be fiercer on several nights, but the bombing of central London was noticeably less. The effect on the public of a whole string of comparatively good nights was a tonic one. Shopgirls who had been looking as good-tempered as ever but terribly tired around the eyes suddenly bloomed as though they had been given a beauty treatment. Taxi-drivers spoke knowingly of something new being tried out in the defences. Whatever the cause, the number of planes that got over the town was certainly smaller. The most likely theory advanced by the aeronautical experts is that as the gunners get more accustomed to the workings of some new equipment they've been given, the anti-aircraft fire is becoming far more accurate, with the result that many raiders are crippled so badly they have to go right back to their bases instead of cruising leisurely overhead until dawn. It is possible that bad weather has also helped, though people are skeptical that the Germans would let poor visibility interfere with a program of obviously indiscriminate destruction.

Suburbanites and country dwellers paid last week for London's better nights. Bombs which were probably intended for the city area were unloaded on rural districts, perhaps because the pilots didn't fancy getting any closer to the barrage, which can be seen over an astoundingly wide area and beats any Fourth of July display that ever gladdened a small boy's heart; everyone hopes that after the new evacuation of mothers and children gets going there will be few small boys left in London to be gladdened by it. As though to make up for this increased nocturnal peacefulness, during the day the sirens have gone mad on several occasions, giving such non-stop performances that people lost track of whether they

were listening to the end of an all-clear or the beginning of
the next warble. The din had little effect upon crowds in
the streets, for the system of posting roof spotters to warn pedestrians that enemy planes are approaching any given local-
ity has been found to be more sensible than an indiscriminate going to earth at every alarm. When the guns went off
the other afternoon, the spotters in one section of the city
could be heard shouting like muezzins overhead, and even
then there was little agitation in the streets, although a couple of passers-by did, as a great concession to the warnings,
break into a sort of stately trot. The reaction of the big
stores during a raid is unpredictable. Though some stay
open, many more either shut infuriated customers out or
shut them in for a prolonged and fuming stay in the bargain
basement.

Buses and tubes continue to run as usual. Buses came on
the streets last week with new anti-splinter nets spread over
their windows—an idea which may or may not be effective
but doubtless has a good psychological effect on the passengers. Certainly far more costly methods of counteracting
blasts didn't save the plate-glass windows of shops in the
West End, which were blown out as easily as those with
which no such prudent precautions had been taken. Shopping in Oxford Street now has all the charms of shopping in
an open-air market, with silk stockings and fragile under-
wear blowing in the breeze let in through paneless windows.
Some firms exhibit notices requesting the public to refrain
from handling goods in showcases whose glass has been shattered, adding the somewhat unnecessary explanation that the
lack of glass is "due to enemy action"—the same phrase
which has been adopted to explain civilian deaths in the
obituary columns of the morning papers.

The owners of property damaged in air raids are faced
with numberless problems, for the ins and outs of the "war-
damage" act of 1939 relating to landlords and tenants are so
involved that the only people who are likely to get any satisfaction are the solicitors. The extent of the tenant's responsibility and exactly how much and when the government is

going to pay in compensation are made uncertain by all the usual legal "inasmuches" and a few more besides.

The work of reconstruction goes forward briskly, however, whenever possible. The salvage firms and the little men in bowler hats with foot rules in their waistcoat pockets for measuring smashed windows were among the busiest people in London last week. In one West End street, racks of men's overcoats were being carried out of a wrecked tailoring establishment that looked like a surrealist nightmare, with bolts of tweed nestling beneath the collapsed ceiling. Salvage workers were carting dusty fragments of furniture out of the rubble that used to be a block of beautiful old houses in Berkeley Square. An ornate, painted, barely recognizable grand piano was standing in the street, and the men were assembling bits of a Georgian wrought-iron fanlight. The public has been warned not to pick up anything from the debris of a bombed house, since such an action might be misunderstood. Heavy sentences are being imposed for looting; quite often, though, cases of this kind are proved to be the result of someone's mistaken but perfectly innocent enthusiasm for saving belongings and handing them over to the police.

The Cabinet changes produced some surprises and a good deal of satisfaction. Mr. Chamberlain's resignation, long rumored, caused profound relief, though it was a disappointment to many that another member of the old firm, Lord Halifax, didn't go out at the same time. The rise of the energetic and dynamic Mr. Ernest Bevin, the new Minister of Labour, and the appointment of Sir Andrew Duncan as Minister of Supply were popular. There are hopes that other weak spots in the government will be stiffened before long. Mr. Churchill, as the *Times* remarked, "is still, in some respects, a solitary figure." That solitary figure continues to command the devotion and confidence of all classes in a way which has probably been equalled only by the great William Pitt in 1759, "the year of victories." England would seem to have found her man of destiny at a critical juncture, when her well-wishers were beginning to fear that destiny was taking the down, not the up, grade. An extraordinary leader and the determination of an extraordinary people have brought back hope and dignity to a scene that has long and humiliatingly lacked them.

October 27

Last week, Londoners had reason to be grateful for their famous climate. With the hunter's moon waning and what the laconic official communiqués describe as "unfavorable weather conditions" settling down over the capital, the raiders decided not to risk it en masse. One of the newspaper-sellers who chalk cheerful cockney footnotes to the day's events on their bulletin boards wrote on his: "Another quiet night? I hope so." The previous week, he had been chalking up defiantly: "Germans claim one thousand tons of bombs on London. So what?" Only a few hundred yards away from his pitch, the ruins of a little masterpiece of a Wren church gave mute answer.

In that week, London had taken punishment so vicious that a lesser fighter would have been knocked groggy. After a night officially described as the worst of the war and a preceding one of almost equal horror, the army of men and women office workers who are now Britain's front-line troops got to their jobs somehow, although new bomb damage had increased transportation difficulties. Many people arrived at business to find that their premises had been written off in the night. Ordinary getting about town was difficult enough, what with traffic being diverted by red signs warning of bombs that hadn't exploded and by craters in the pavement which were tragically eloquent of bombs that had exploded only too well. Every dawn found the army of homeless people increased. At one rest centre, accustomed to handle two or three hundred raid victims daily, breakfast was being provided for fourteen hundred. On the mornings after those two nightmare nights, it was saddening to walk around and see how much was down, but people who kept their sense of perspective and noted how much was still up were probably right. London is no Rotterdam yet, though there are areas where one can see in horrifying miniature what an undefended capital must look like after organized murderers get loose on it.

In these anxious days, an unnecessary refinement of torture is added by the Ministry of Information department responsible for releasing news of air-raid damage. Some of its references to "famous squares" and "well-known London stores" that have suffered sound like crossword-puzzle clues and cruelly agitate the thousands of people who have friends or relations living on squares or working in London stores. A reference to the bombing of "a famous public school" made countless parents jam the telephone system with frenzied inquiries as to whether Eton or Stowe or a dozen other possibilities had been the victim.

Another piece of gratuitous jarring of the nerves is the wording of the official communiqués, which are apt to sound offensive when read by one of the B.B.C.'s breezy young men at an hour when people are just struggling up from air-raid shelters. It is hardly consoling to those who have been through a terrifying night to hear an antiseptic voice assuring them briskly that enemy action was "on a smaller scale than on previous nights." To someone newly facing grief, the chirpy statement that "casualties were slight" has a way of sounding callous.

Recently, however, the censorship department released without any tinkering the news that London had lost another link with her historic past in the destruction of the Middle Temple Hall. In the Temple the next morning, people were wandering around looking at the wreckage and wearing a curiously uniform expression of anger. "And to think," said an elderly gentleman wrathfully, "that all this was caused by a house painter!" Lists posted up on the walls announced that the legal gentlemen whose chambers had been in the badly damaged buildings could now be found at other addresses. Workmen were busy in the debris, removing the hopeless rubble which covered still recognizable and beautiful carved stone bosses and splintered blue-and-gold woodwork. In Pump Court, elegant eighteenth-century doorways and windows had been smashed and brickwork that had taken a couple of centuries to mellow had been ripped away in a moment of wanton destruction, but typewriters were still clicking busily behind the gaping windows. The blast of the explosions had broken windows on the south side of the Temple Church and the custodian was indignantly dusting broken stained glass off the choir stalls. For some reason, the magnificent east window has not been removed to a place of safety; neither have the recumbent bronze figures of the Knights Templars.

If history is being torn up by the roots in London, history is also being made. The new race of tube dwellers is slipping a fresh page into the record; nothing has ever been seen like the concourse of humanity that camps underground every night. As early as eleven-thirty in the morning, people start going down to stake out the evening's claim with folded rugs, newspapers, or bundles of bedding. By five, when the homeward rush hour is on, one walks underground between double rows of men, women, and children—eating, drinking, sleeping, reading papers, and just sitting: all part of the most extraordinary mass picnic the world has ever known. The tubes are so much home to them now that they take off their shoes and stockings, loosen their collars, feed their babies, and carry on their personal quarrels without seeming to be any more aware of the tramp of passing feet than one is of traffic in a busy street. The authorities are working out a system of permanent canteens, and have also talked about compulsory inoculations and disinfectant sprays, as an epidemic of influenza—if nothing worse—would seem to be inevitable when the bad weather really sets in and people go straight down off the streets in their wet clothes.

With such urgent local problems on their minds, thinking citizens are also looking further afield and wondering what is going to happen to the French fleet and what America will do after the election. The recent moves of Laval and Franco seem to indicate that a new European lineup is being planned to coincide with the American election period. The press and public here devote considerable space and time to what America is saying, doing, and thinking. As men once watched the East for a portent, millions are now looking to the West with hope and confidence.

November 9

The interest taken over here in the recent Presidential election was greater than it has ever been before, and satisfaction with the result was general. Londoners beamed on Wednesday as they read their papers, in which the war was momentarily pushed into second place. A Roosevelt victory had been hoped for by nearly everybody, although some citizens had wondered whether they ought not to root for Willkie, too, since both candidates seemed to meet on common ground in their determination to help Britain as speedily and fully as possible. There is solid comfort in the assurance that the continuity of American policy is unbroken and that it remains the one distinct feature in the otherwise confused and menacing landscape of the next four years. Britons feel that in those four years they are going to need every friend they can get, and in the occupant of the White House they are certain they have one.

For most people, four years is now a pretty optimistic estimate of the possible length of the war, which seems to be opening out afresh in Italy's cold-blooded and unprovoked attack on Greece. The immediate repercussion of this has been to strengthen the general feeling against Italy. The Prime Minister stated in the House, amidst cheers, that British bombing attacks on military objectives in the Italian cities would be continued on an ever-growing scale. He was followed by Mr. Hore-Belisha, who observed that "nothing would rejoice the British public more than to learn that Italy was being given unstinted doses of that medicine which she was so ready callously to dispense to others," and by the

Honourable Member for Epsom, who suggested that the national slogan should be "Sock the Wop." Certainly there is widespread hope that the newly acquired air and sea bases of Greece will allow the relentless hammering of the Italians that was made geographically difficult by the defection of France.

About the spirited Greek resistance there is enthusiasm but no undue elation. The British are apt to learn lessons slowly and painfully, but they cannot very well forget the initial cheer which greeted the news that the Poles (for Poles, read Norwegians, Dutch, or Belgians) were fighting splendidly, and they remember how this news was followed by the first ominous official hints of "slight infiltrations" and of "falling back to prepared positions." It is true, as people say, that the Greeks are not fighting the Germans—not yet, anyway; it is true that the Italian move looks like a good thing strategically for British ships and aircraft, which have been brought four hundred miles nearer to the weakest point in the Axis. For the present, however, nobody needs the official warning not to place too much confidence in reports of Greek victories arriving from roundabout and dubious sources.

Although there are plenty of sarcastic jokers who remark in private, "Well, I suppose we can expect another magnificent evacuation in a fortnight or so," whatever nonchalance there is hides a good deal of anxiety, and events around Byron's beloved isles are being watched and waited for with strained attention by numbers of Englishmen who, like the poet, may find themselves dying in those parts. It was Byron, incidentally, who remarked that the Greeks disliked the French and mistrusted the Russians but "looked to the English for succor"—an instinct which hasn't altered in over a hundred years and which the English devoutly hope will remain sound.

Londoners have been reminded of an earlier Italian aggression by the presence of King Zog of Albania, who is staying here with his wife and child. When a bomb fell near his residence during one of the recent raids, people said knowingly that the Italian bombers, which had been reported over the capital, were obviously out to get Zog. Humbler establishments that weren't sheltering any royal Jonahs got hit just the same in the week's raids, which involved some long *alertes* but were less punishing than last month's. There was actually one completely calm night. This break in everybody's nightly rhythm was so upsetting that many lay awake counting the unnaturally silent hours instead of snoring peacefully, as they are accustomed to do through a barrage. There is a good deal of talk about the possibility that night raids will slacken off or even cease altogether during the coming months, when the weather around these shores is likely to settle down into its usual raw and sodden wintry form. This, however, is only unexpert surmise. More realistically, the authorities have announced the free distribution of antiseptic tablets, which may help to check an enemy that will certainly call at the shelters even if the bombers stay grounded at home—the influenza germ.

Meanwhile, the promptness with which air-raid damage is tackled continues to be the most encouraging recent development. Railwaymen get less publicity than workers in the more spectacular services, but they deserve quite as much for the efficiency with which they keep the lines open for the public. Tracks that are blown to glory overnight are somehow patched up sufficiently to be opened again in a surprisingly few days. Kipling would certainly have enjoyed seeing how romance, in the shape of squads of grimy men in tin hats, brings up the nine-fifteen more or less on time every morning. Repairs of damage to the essential services are also amazingly quick, although there are wails from the temporarily waterless and heatless.

It's obvious to any thinking citizen that, as the Premier emphasized, the war on the sea is at the moment far graver than the war in the air. Word that the staggering total of 198,000 tons of shipping had been lost in a single week a while back was a shock to the complacency of those who had fancied that the threat of U-boats had lessened. That was why Mr. de Valera's uncompromising attitude against letting

England use the vitally necessary Irish ports seemed to many to be the most significant and serious happening of the week.

November 24

Nothing has made the English happier than the resounding trouncing given to the Italians in Greece; nothing would make them happier than a second Taranto. After an initial period of wariness, in which people fought shy of placing too much credence in the reports of Greek victories, everyone now feels that there are really sound reasons for delight and are properly delighted. As someone remarked in slightly dazed tones, Britain has actually acquired an ally who not only has thrown the invading forces back on their ear but has carried the war well into enemy territory. Such a state of affairs is novel enough to make the British want to cheer as loudly as the M.P.'s did when the Prime Minister, in his opening-of-Parliament speech, spoke of the Italian adventure as "a felon's blow" and a piece of "pure unmitigated brigandage."

Although news of British help to Greece has been necessarily scanty, it is hoped that the actual aid was not, and that the Navy and the R.A.F. will hit hard at Italy and go on hitting. When word came through of Taranto—a spectacular triumph for that Cinderella of the services, the Fleet's air arm—cockney newsdealers chanted with lugubrious relish, "Eyetalian fleet done in! No more macaroni!" A minor local backwash of the great events in the Koritza sector has been a rush of business to an excellent little Greek restaurant on Charlotte Street where Londoners go to munch loyally at skewered lamb and bay leaf and to exchange complimentary toasts in the resinous *vin du pays* with the proprietor.

The queerest thing that has happened for a long time, and one of the most revealing bits of national psychology, is the revision of the public attitude toward Mr. Chamberlain's qualities and statesmanship now that his ashes have been duly laid under the paving stones of Westminster Abbey. The newspaper eulogies made strange reading to anyone with an inconveniently long memory who could remember some of the pungent phrases the identical newspapers had cooked up about the ex-Prime Minister back in April. The British weakness for old dogs, aging actresses, and veteran statesmen is incorrigible, however, and enough was said on the occasion of Chamberlain's death to make one feel that another woolly legend was in the process of being built up. In bars and buses, one heard people say mournfully, "Ar, 'e was too much of a gentleman to be up to their tricks, 'e was." An unlovable personality, he had to wait to be dead to be loved by the nation, for some of the strangest reasons that ever didn't get engraved on a memorial tablet.

[*November 14, the center of the city of Coventry was destroyed in an air raid.*]

It was perhaps unfortunate that the reprisal raids on Coventry should have coincided with the appearance in certain sections of the press of the cheerful statement that a defence against night raiders had been found. Citizens of Coventry, wandering among the ruins of their homes and public buildings, may well have felt that they might have been let in on the secret sooner. The premature optimism was hastily squelched by Air Marshal Sir Philip Joubert. He told the public that the problem of defeating the night raider was well in hand, but added that there was no single remedy for night bombing. Experts agree that the most effective remedy must be in the air—plentiful night fighters coördinated with guns and searchlights—and not on the ground, thereby dispelling the popular dream of some Wellsian or Jules Verneish machine that would intercept and cripple raiders by the pressing of a button.

All the same, official denials did not stop the totally unexpert but hopeful opinions that something was under way which would soon make evening sirens as relatively unalarming as day ones. That it was not already in existence was only too mournfully evidenced by the vicious full-moon attacks on the capital which were announced by the Nazis as a second reprisal for the bombing of Munich. Many people feel that this chat of reprisals is simply another way of saying that the air war is entering into a new and more bitter phase, in which Coventry may be only the first of many terrible chapters.

After a recent big raid on London, the desolation of damaged areas was intensified by a day of rain that helped to put out the fires but also turned dust and rubble into a vile mud in which the rescue squads skidded around as though on a skating rink. Owners of buildings with damaged roofs found themselves alive but damp, for tarpaulins were almost impossible to find.

December 7

The most important news of the past week locally was the Independent Labour Party's proposal for a peace conference, which Parliament soundly trounced by 341 votes to 4. Though, as Labour's Mr. Griffith remarked, there is not a man, woman, or child who would not welcome an end to the conflict if it meant a real peace for the stricken world, no one can see how such a peace could come about with National Socialism sitting in at the conference table. The British people are now in a better position than most to state that war is ruinous, uncomfortable, and deadly, and Mr. Churchill seems to have made one of his rare bloomers a short time back when, in his natural exuberance, he dug up the old saw about its being a grand life if you don't weaken. For an enormous number of people who are leading existences of unspeakable dreariness and privation, life can hardly be grand, but the voting of the House reflected pretty accurately the grim national realization that any sort of life is preferable to the travesty of honorable survival now being enacted on the other side of the Channel.

The very fact that the debate was allowed to be aired in public at all at such a time summed up more succinctly than words the way of living which House and people are resolved to defend at whatever terrible cost. All the same, there emerged from the debate the very strong general feeling that Britain's war aims ought to be given a good deal more coherence than they have been if they are to compete with the German alternative of a new European order. Early last summer, when France was crumbling under an attack that left all military tactics known to the Allies a couple of jumps behind, people slowly realized that they were up against a new way of making war; now it's also understood that there will have to be a new way of keeping peace if the war-sickened soul of this planet is even to begin to take heart in our lifetime.

The Greek successes and Badoglio's sudden exit made everyone feel a good deal better last week, although there was some disappointment that Britain's aerial attack on Italy was not of greater proportions. Technical difficulties are probably the explanation, but to the ordinary unexpert citizen, who knows nothing of these, it merely seems as though the High Command were lacking his own healthy appetite for socking Mussolini as often and as painfully as possible. This restraint on the part of the High Command was possibly the reason for a crop of rumors that Italy was already nibbling at peace negotiations, that Badoglio's resignation * was the sign of a split between the Army and the Fascist regime, and that Mussolini was faced with a dangerous crackup in civilian obedience. Most people, however, remembered only too clearly how last winter a press campaign tried to make them believe that something of the kind was happening in Germany—a pleasant fantasy from which they awoke to encounter a disastrous spring and a united Germany firmly bent on their extinction. Similar wishful thinking is discouraged on this occasion, although popular enthusiasm for the Greek successes is tremendous. Now Britons

* Field Marshall Pietro Badoglio resigned as chief of the Italian General Staff.

are waiting to see what form German aid to Italy is going to take; it is thought that this aid will more likely concentrate on keeping British sea and air defences busy at home than on the launching of a military campaign in the Balkans.

Certainly it has become clear in the past few weeks that the Nazi plan of attack has changed again. London has had comparatively quiet nights, while the provincial cities have suffered one after another in a series of raids which, as though agonizingly mocking some nursery game, keep the taut spectators in suspense about whom death is going to tag next. The names of the victims of these raids were released quicker than usual by the Ministry of Information (which is. said to be going to take over the running of the B.B.C.), but on one occasion, when it was announced that a "West Country town" had been bombed, people with friends in Bath went through some bad moments before it was revealed that the city was Bristol. Possibly the unusual celerity of the censorship department was brought about by the complaints of the American correspondents. It has been openly stated and deplored that their understandable irritation over official red tape has overflowed into their dispatches and made an unduly gloomy picture of damage done by raids on Britain's war-production facilities and of the possible rockiness of the nation's financial resources.

· The "off-the-record" observations of Mr. Joseph Kennedy have caused much interest here. He had been so boosted by the press that the public had become mesmerized into thinking that a man with nine children and such an expansive smile, not to mention an impressive golf handicap, must necessarily be a prince of good fellows and as pro-British as they come. When it was discovered that those much publicized teeth had actually bit the hand that patted him, resentment was general and acute. The *Times* acidly observed that what Mr. Kennedy was telling friends in the United States could not fairly be mentioned, owing to his trick of talking off the record, and then went on to remark that "he is said to be distilling the sort of gloom which he has apparently adopted as his second nature."

What was said of the former Ambassador around Britain's firesides and in her air-raid shelters was often blunter than that. Just as Mayfair was taken in by Ribbentrop, so those in the vast middle section of the populace now feel mournfully certain that the beaming paterfamilias from Washington has somehow managed to do them dirt.

December 20

[*December 9, British counterattack Italian forces in North Africa.*]

London has been a city of smiling faces and heart-warming headlines all week. The papers have solemnly warned the public against imbibing too freely of the "heady wine" of victory on land and pointed out that difficulties were sure to be encountered as the British lines of communication lengthened in Africa and Graziani's shortened. All the beaming average citizen knows is that the victory in the western desert has finally scotched the public's suspicion that, though the Air Force is magnificent and the Navy grand, the Army still thinks it's fighting some other war—the Crimean, say. What made people happiest was the perfect timing, slickness, and coördination of the attack, showing that the bitter lessons of France and Flanders have been well and truly learned. "Speed" and "brilliance" had been ruefully looked upon as exclusively Nazi nouns for so long that it was certainly heady to find them back in the British vocabulary again.

The Greek successes have also come in for their share of the general enthusiasm. Milliners have whipped up something known as the Evzones hat, which women are supposed to slap patriotically on their pates this winter, and distinguished correspondents have written to the *Times* suggesting that "to prove our admiration and gratitude to our Greek allies, it would be a just as well as a graceful act to return to

them the (so-called) Elgin marbles," which were removed by
the noble Lord Elgin from the Parthenon at the beginning
of the nineteenth century. Surely the British have been in
the mood to give the Greeks anything. One of the favorite
occupations for the long and momentarily quiet evenings has
been to tune in on the German news commentator and listen to him carefully skirting around the news of what has
been happening to the Axis partner. Many people think that
Hitler's aid to Italy may take the form of a move over the
Alps and that it's quite in the cards that German broadcasts
will soon be coming over the Rome wave length, too.

All the jubilation didn't lessen the shock and universal regret caused by the death of Lord Lothian. The public had
known him principally as a member of the famous Cliveden
set and had only lately awakened to the fact that it had a
great ambassador in Washington. The news of his death was
received as a national disaster. Some of the suggestions put
forward in the press as possible candidates for his successor
—Lord Beaverbrook and Mr. Lloyd George, for instance—
have been funny. At the moment, Sir Archibald Sinclair, the
Secretary of State for Air, looks like the best of the suggestions, having the charm, the brains, and the breeding necessary for what, after the Premiership, is Britain's No. 1 job
today.

Meanwhile, the big news locally is the sudden cessation of
all air activity, which has given London some of the quietest
nights since the blitz started. Although conditions frequently have seemed perfect for raids, the boys just haven't
been coming. Naturally, there has been plenty of speculation
as to the reasons for the lull, which were mostly felt to be
sinister ones. Although the Prime Minister has never ceased
his warnings that invasion is not necessarily something to be
put away till spring, the press is just now rediscovering the
danger and playing it up as hard as it can.

Figures of weekly shipping losses are also given great
prominence, apparently in a campaign to make the public
realize that Britain will have to pull in her belt a bit tighter
during the new year. They certainly have been a sobering

antidote, if one was needed, to possible undue elation over the Italian defeat. A chart of tonnage-loss averages brought out by one of the morning papers looked like a fever patient's graph, swooping dizzily up to the 200,000-ton mark in October and still hovering critically near the danger line. People are grimly convinced that it will swoop up again in the new year unless the knocking out of Italy can be accomplished by then, with the highly important result that the Mediterranean fleet would be released for convoying Canadian butter and New Zealand mutton to England's stomachs.

The abundance and variety of food stocks available are still amazing, but there have already been hints from Lord Woolton, the energetic and capable Minister for Food, that various commodities must be kissed a long good-bye for the duration. The Christmas shops have showed little shortage of the traditional delicacies, except turkeys, which are both scarce and expensive. The big stores came out valiantly with holly-and-cellophane-garlanded signs proclaiming that "There'll always be a Christmas," and did a rattling good trade in spite of the publicity campaign suggesting that a couple of National Savings Certificates in the toe of the stocking was all that any good citizen could need. Parents have taken advantage of the lull in the blitz to smuggle children up from the country for a brisk scurry through the toy bazaars, thereby brightening the lives of all the Santas, who had been drooping in their red flannelette and false whiskers among the childless acres of dolls and electric trains.

However unseasonably men may be behaving at this festival of peace on earth and mercy mild, the heavens are contributing a seasonable note. British astronomers are excited over what they call the triple conjunction of Jupiter and Saturn—a spectacle which was last seen in England when Charles II was on the throne and is recorded as one of the strange happenings preceding the birth of Christ. Londoners tacking up the holly in their Anderson shelters are hoping that this will be the only unusual display in the heavens when once more they celebrate that birth on the night of December 25th, 1940.

1941

January 4

L AST SUNDAY NIGHT'S BIG FIRE RAID may have produced some good results to balance tragic losses. The authorities and the public showed signs for the first time of realizing that arson was going to be used as a major weapon in the war. As usual, the British learned their lesson expensively, and it was poor consolation to be told that quite a bit of the damage could have been prevented if fire-watchers had been organized, as they now are, on a compulsory-service basis. Lord Beaverbrook's lively *Daily Express* has been saying for some time that fire-spotters ought to be thus organized and that every householder should be made responsible for preventing fire bombs from igniting his own premises. With the heart of the City still smoldering, Mr. Herbert Morrison, the Minister of Home Security, went on the air to ask that this be done. It was also announced that a census would shortly be taken of the entire able-bodied manpower in the shelters, which pleased many people who feel that too much has been said and written about the courage of the crowds that spend the nights down below and too little about the truly courageous men and women who remain above guarding other people's property.

Up to that Sunday night, incendiaries were looked upon as tiresome annoyances incidental to a raid. Now that the really serious gap in the air-raid precautions of the big cities has been seen, there is talk of possible hasty legislation providing for the imprisonment of owners of industrial plants that are destroyed by fires which spread because of neglect of proper precautions. Citizens also have been asked, and have shown a willingness, to form communal fire-fighting squads which are to take turns patrolling the streets, armed with the keys of absent neighbors so that fires in empty houses can be quickly reached and controlled. For the reserved and suspicious British, this represents a step forward not only in civic discipline but also in the un-English mateyness which is one of the few pleasant things to come out of the war so far.

Meanwhile, the debit side of the Sunday raid was heavy. Some years back, lovers of the antique raised a howl of protest when it was proposed that the scantily attended Wren churches in the business section be demolished. Now that so much of the demolition has been accomplished overnight, not only the lovers of the antique are horrified but also citizens who for a lifetime had been cozily conscious that the churches were there without ever feeling compelled to go inside them. Thousands have gone to mourn over St. Lawrence Jewry and the quaintly named St. Andrew by the Wardrobe—now that they are in ashes—who would hardly have been able to recognize one steeple from the other when those steeples were still elegantly vertical.

In the general lamentation over the national treasures which have been lost, there is a tendency to overlook the fact that a good deal that wasn't precious but only unhygienic, inconvenient, and an offence to civic pride has also gone down in the flames. Wren churches can be rebuilt (it is rumored that one wealthy young man has offered to duplicate the Guildhall as soon as the war is over), but there are also many dark and noisome spots which Londoners hope won't be restored when the time for planning a new town arrives. Already there are brisk discussions over the advisability of setting up all the old monuments again in precisely the same historic spots they used to occupy. One school of thought, headed by Clough Williams-Ellis, the architect, is all for resurrecting Wren churches with the exactness that meticulous records make possible, but wants them resurrected on more convenient sites, where millions instead of a few conscien-

tious tourists can admire and see them. The other school
deprecates slavish imitation and hopes that rebuilding will
strike out along bold contemporary lines, emphasizing the
point that Sir Christopher himself did not dig up the old
blueprints when he was commissioned to rebuild St. Paul's.
The St. Paul's assignment may yet again fall to someone or
other, for in the last raid the great dome was spared only by
a margin which a chance breeze, blowing sparks from nearby
blazing warehouses, might easily have narrowed to disaster.

Taking a walk through the damaged section at the beginning of the week, one had to pick one's way over the hoses
that lay coiled across the dark little alleys. Some of the fires
were still smoking and the firemen were hard at work in
their tin hats, thigh boots, and dirty uniforms, which they
probably hadn't scrambled out of since Sunday. Some of the
streets had been roped off so that the Royal Engineers could
blow up dangerous buildings, and the ropes were used as a
kind of necklace along which were strung flapping bits of
paper giving the temporary addresses of firms that had been
burned out. An enormous Union Jack flew from the Guildhall's one undamaged roof, but the main body of the building was a sad sight, with blackened statues looking down on
the mass of debris where the famous Gog and Magog have
disappeared in the ruins of the proudest link with the City's
history.

It was thought by many that the raid might be the first of
a devastating series leading up to an invasion, which is again
forecast for a variety of dates in the near future. Both the informed and the uninformed seem to feel that an attempt will
be made as soon as the screws have been tightened sufficiently in the Nazi air and submarine forces. Faced with
such a menacing new year, most Londoners celebrated their
parting with the tragic old one in a quiet fashion. In spite of
the good news from the Libyan front and the heartening effect of President Roosevelt's fireside talk, no one was inclined to underrate the dangers ahead in what may well be a
critical year not only for the British Empire but also for men
of good will everywhere.

January 18

The crackup of the Libyan seaport of Bardia was about the best news for the British in very many weeks. Perhaps the best news of all, though, was that before the thrilled and delighted public had got its breath back again, the boys were quietly sitting down outside Tobruk. The speed and perfect organization of the whole offensive made it seem deceptively easy—like watching a champion holing a long putt or sending down a winning forehand smash. It was certainly instructive later to find out what the Axis had to say about the Italian defeat. The British blinked when they heard from Rome that it would make no difference to the Italian people, "who are of yeoman stock quite different from the neurotic community found today in Britain." The neurotic community also got a wry grin or two from the German official comment that "while the British gain a military victory, the Italians' is a moral victory," a statement which brought back memories of the journalistic bunk that was dished out here at the time of the Battle of Norway and other disastrous incidents. It now seems to be a well-worn propaganda convention on both sides that good soldiers never lose; when they do, it's a moral victory, not a rout.

Students of Kipling were gratified by the promptness with which Sir Archibald Wavell, in the middle of the stress and strain of a campaign, came right back with a message full of *Jungle Book* references in answer to the Kipling Society's cabled congratulations on "Tabaqui's discomfiture." The General replied neatly, "Many thanks. Hope Shere Khan's skin will soon be on Council Rock." The *Times*, fastening gleefully upon this particularly juicy bit of bookish jocularity and interpreting it for its less cultured readers, explained that Tabaqui was, of course, Mussolini—"the dish-licker, one of the jackal tribe, a jungle gossip, talebearer, and mischief-maker"—and that Shere Khan, the man-eating tiger, was "Hitler and his German man-killers, who wish to destroy Mowgli, the man child." A correspondent then suggested that "Rikki-Tikki-Tavi would make a good type for Greece —little Greece, which has flown at the venomous aggressor." Even in the middle of the current enthusiasm and confidence, however, no sober Briton is likely to forget that the main struggle with Shere Khan is yet to come; that, as the Germans commented, without any literary trimmings, "Cyrenaica is not the scene of war upon which the fate of a powerful conflict can rest."

What has been taking place in Libya and on the Mediterranean hasn't distracted the public, especially the feminine half of it, from noticing the equally significant happenings in the food stores at home. Recently, many housewives, on getting to the butcher's, have found themselves in the position of Mother Hubbard and her dog. The cupboards were bare, so much so that a lot of harassed butchers put up their shutters and went home to listen to the B.B.C. explain that a jam in distribution was responsible for the meat rations of most people being cut in half or worse. The disquieting shipping losses—although, to the relief of everyone, the situation has looked a good deal healthier in the past fortnight —have probably been more to blame for the sudden shortages of this and that to which the ordinarily well-provisioned British are having to accustom themselves.

It is true, nevertheless, that distribution is not working as smoothly as it might be. While many London retailers have had plenty of food and a diminished number of customers to buy it, unhappy tradespeople in the country have had to contend with an enormously increased population and a supply of foodstuffs often unintelligently rationed on the basis of the local consumption before the war. Commuting businessmen are ordered by their wives to make forages on the meat markets in town in search of the elusive pork sausage or to send their clerks down to the East End, where an occasional vintage pot of now almost unobtainable marmalade may still be unearthed. It's possible that the conservative

British, who have always been excessive meat eaters since the days when Fielding's squires downed a leg of mutton for breakfast, may turn into a nation of simpler and healthier feeders if Lord Woolton, the extremely competent food controller, succeeds in his present efforts to make families conscious of oatmeal and raw carrots by publicizing them as antidotes for blackout blindness. Many people who want this war won as quickly as possible think that the controller might also take a crack at hotel and restaurant menus, which are still as generous as though there wasn't a U-boat afloat.

It seems to the same questioning minds that the war effort could be tightened up in other departments as well. Although there has been a big reduction in the number of occupations which exempt a man from war duty, it's still noticeable that there are altogether too many skilled mechanics in chauffeurs' uniforms and too many first-class horticulturists engaged in nursing along someone's prize rhododendrons instead of getting the land into shape to stop the U-boats from being the threat they are now. The latest lists of exempt occupations, by the way, make fascinating reading; in them one learns that no military service is required of tea tasters, underhand puddlers, twisters, strippers, dog whippers, tidal-water bargees, funeral directors, and pulpit men (who are concerned with the manufacture of steel and have nothing to do with the also-exempt evangelists).

It is thought that Mr. Bevin, in the statement expected from him next week, is at last going to make use of the drastic powers over manpower and industry which were given him so enthusiastically some months ago. Now that the period of gestation is nearly over, the nation is hoping to see something really lusty and kicking delivered.

February 9

The fall of Benghazi was naturally the big news of the week. Although the town had been expected to capitulate sooner or later, the brilliant speed of the operations took everyone here completely by surprise and the excitement was intense. Whatever the reaction in Europe, the effect on the British has been an enormous and welcome increase of confidence in the Army, on which they may soon have to depend for success much nearer home than Libya. One hears it said that history is again repeating itself and that the Eastern Theatre is probably producing the best general of this war, as it did of the last—in Allenby. With so many once much-boosted military leaders fading away into the twilight of the generals, Britons are hoping devoutly that one of the new men who are on their way to the top will turn out to be the Wavell of the Western Theatre when the curtain eventually goes up on it.

Both informed and uninformed opinion seems to be that the curtain may go up at any moment. Every few days, the press discovers some new and absolutely infallible date for the attempt to invade Britain: the third week of February and the middle of March are periods which apparently you ought to tick off on your calendar. Most people seem to think that though Hitler may not obligingly fit his actions in with the journalists' predictions, something will certainly be tried soon—a frame of mind which makes all small personal planning for the future seem futile. Not long ago the rumor got around that the German High Command was only waiting for three and a half days of good weather before giving the word to go. No one could explain the significance of the half-day, but the story had all sorts of Londoners solemnly counting the hours and scanning the stormy heavens, which remained reliably seasonable.

The reason for the general belief that something is going to happen this time is the government's sudden warning to housewives to stock their invasion larders and to everyone to carry a gas mask. Members of Parliament have been asked to set a good example to their constituents by remembering to bring their masks along to the House. Judging by the results of a census taken at a big railroad station in London, which showed that an amazingly small proportion of travellers had their masks with them, a surprise gas attack at any time in recent weeks might have had disastrous results.

It looks as though a serious attempt is now being made to impress upon the public the point that chemical warfare and even worse unpleasantness may be expected. In a local broadcast the other evening, a speaker brought many a family party up with a start by supposedly quoting from a German newspaper the outlines of Nazi plans for dealing with a conquered Britain, plans which included a yearly German baby for all healthy English females and the sterilization of all healthy English males. The indignation in British homes over this ungentlemanly notion was acute and from the official point of view probably satisfactory.

There has also been a lot of talk about the lull in the blitz, which gave Londoners a chance to dine out, see their friends, drop in at a pub, or simply take the dog for an evening amble around the block more peacefully than they had been able to for some time. While enjoying the holiday, people found all kinds of ingenious explanations of it, the most popular one being that German aviators and planes were resting and getting equipped for the really stupendous attack to be launched during a full moon. The quiet interval, whatever the cause, enabled London to get along with the job of removing a good deal of the mess and the city has been noticeably spruced up during the last fortnight, even to the extent of placing new sandbags around the pedestal of Eros.

February 15

Events are moving fast. The headlines of the last day or two have looked disquietingly like the headlines in previous periods of expectancy preceding a sudden Nazi swoop. Everyone appears to be taking advantage of what may be the last few weeks of comparative sanity to warn everyone else that complete chaos is approaching. Londoners rustling through their papers on their way home the other evening must have felt that they had seen something of the kind somewhere before as they read the ominous announcements that Turkey had warned Bulgaria, that the Australian government had warned its people, and that the United States government had warned its citizens in Japan. The fact that next day the Cassandras of the press hastened to say that they hadn't really meant to make anyone's flesh creep didn't alter the general conviction that the horizon couldn't very well look stormier.

The situation in the Balkans seems to people like the same old act which they watched last May—the familiar paralyzing propaganda, the usual accusations against the British, and the bleats of the prospective victims that they only want to keep on friendly terms with everybody. Confidence in Turkey's refusal to be intimidated is as universal as the regret that everything points to the Greeks' being in for a bad time. With their usual impassiveness, the English seem to be digesting the probability that their own bad time has been planned to coincide with the opening up of a new phase of warfare in the Balkans and on the Pacific.

The press continues to hammer away at the subject of invasion as hard as it can. Beaverbrook's *Evening Standard* has been running a series of articles, "written by a distinguished team of strategists," discussing various ways in which the Germans might attempt to invade the country. According to these writers, the land attack would probably be concentrated in the south and southeast, and the aim would be to take London quickly by using shock-troop tactics. The *Times'* expert has been far less specific but has said that landings would no doubt be attempted at various points, perhaps coinciding with one in Eire, and that the area involved would see "the largest-scale air fighting the world has ever known."

The experts may prognosticate, but this is a time when the ordinary man's guess is as good as theirs. All anyone can know is that events are moving swiftly and steadily toward the long-awaited spring offensive, which may begin here, experts and non-experts now think, with no more warning than a fierce one-night aerial blitz, on areas where landings are to be attempted. Naturally, these days of watchful waiting are anxious ones, but on the surface, at any rate, people remain remarkably sane. They say they will be glad when "it" comes, much as they did when they were waiting for the big air raids to start. They say they expect the going to be difficult and dangerous for a short time; that is, "until things have sorted themselves out," by which ten out of ten English mean the failure of the attempt. Without complacency or false optimism, the plain people, against whom the invasion's full violence will be directed, are grimly determined that there will be only one end to the story.

Meanwhile, it has relieved numbers of country dwellers to hear that rural district councils are at last prepared to feed village communities, which, in the event of an upset in food distribution, are in just as much danger of starving as cities. Communal kitchens are being organized all over the country to take care of people who can't afford to put away tinned goods for a prolonged siege. Civilians have been told that, should the worst happen, newspapers may cease to appear and even the radio may be silent for an indefinite period, thus throwing the country back into eighteenth-century ignorance, which won't be bliss but anguished wondering. In answer to a question in the House, which has been taking advantage of the lull to explore such topics as the number of aliens employed in London restaurants and the shortage of gold lace for naval officers' sleeves, the Prime Minister promised that he would certainly make some sort of address to the nation at the beginning of a state of emergency. His speeches at such critical moments, as the public confidently knows, are terse affairs, whittled down to the last blunt word but no less heartening than the magnificent prose of those made in retrospect.

People are still saying that the Prime Minister's broadcast last Sunday was his best to date. They always enjoy a chuckle over his deliberate Anglicizing of foreign names and the lip-smacking gusto with which he invariably introduces a reference to one or another of "those wicked men," but what they like most is his great gift for making them forget discomfort, danger, and loss and remember only that they are living history. These days, people find themselves looking at England with a new eye, almost as though they were seeing it for the first time, and discovering once again that deep, inarticulate love for it which is real even to Britons who have never set foot on its damp and overcrowded shores.

The passing of the lease-lend bill by the House in Washington was received with cheers in London.

March 22

[*March 11, President Roosevelt signed the Lend-Lease Act.*]

President Roosevelt's historic speech was recognized by the press as "a political event of the first order" and by grateful millions everywhere as an occasion for a small, private *Nunc Dimittis*. Simple Britons who had been inclined to fret at the stately wording of the lend-lease bill now found themselves listening to a language that they could understand and a promise that they could believe. "Thank God!" said someone only half jokingly. "The tanks are coming." To most people, the guarantee of food is at least as important as the guarantee of ships, planes, and guns, and the bridge of ships to get them here is the most important problem of all. It becomes increasingly evident to the women who buy the food and the men who eat it that the subjugated countries are not the only ones which are going to have empty cupboards unless a quick answer is found to the Atlantic menace.

The recent alarming jump in the figures of weekly shipping losses and the bombings of the big ports are creating a situation which people, even with the current confidence, can't fail to see as extremely serious. Its implications are evident in the complicated conjuring act that Lord Woolton, the resourceful Minister of Food, is frequently obliged to perform, such as diverting the attention of the public with an extra inch of cheese in the right hand while spiriting jam away with the left. It seems clear that a much more drastic system of rationing and a complete reorganization of the storage-and-distribution policy will be needed to carry the country through the next few months, during which the shipping losses may be expected to get worse instead of better. Although the relief and enthusiasm which followed the President's words were immense, no thinking Briton was likely to forget what the Prime Minister had said in his speech welcoming Ambassador Winant at the Pilgrims' luncheon. His remark that the Battle of the Atlantic must be regarded as one of the most momentous ever fought only bore out the grim, general conviction that the sea, not the air, is once again going to be the classic battlefield on which England will settle the question of her survival.

The German propaganda bureau has already announced that Wednesday's big raid on London officially opened the spring offensive, whose avowed intention is to bring Britain, through starvation, to her knees. The raid was the heaviest of the year and people looked a bit dark under the eyes when they turned up at work next morning. They may well have thought it a little tactless of the Air Ministry to choose that day to jubilantly release the news of a small but heavy attack on Cologne. After such a night, nothing but a large and heavy attack on Berlin would have sounded like what Mr. Churchill calls "delectable tidings." Rather tardily it was pointed out that weather conditions here had been unfavorable for a big takeoff, but it was doubtful whether this really consoled homeless Londoners, most of whom would lose their homes all over again for the pleasure of hearing that Berliners had caught just as big a packet of hell as their air force is giving.

It was in a raid ten days back that one of the West End night haunts got it, and those who sat enjoying a quiet, bed-time Scotch on a balcony there had the terrifying experience of seeing the ceiling come down on the dancers below while they themselves were left perched intact on the edge of chaos, their glasses freakishly unspilt in front of them. It was thought that the incident would cramp the style of restaurateurs, who have already had plenty to contend with, but when the big barrage opened on Wednesday evening, all the popular places were as full as ever.

If Ernest Bevin, the Minister of Labour, has his way, there soon won't be any young things to take dancing anyhow. The call-up of women of twenty and twenty-one, along with men of forty and forty-one, was announced for next month. The next women to register will be twenty-twos and twenty-threes, rather than eighteens and nineteens, because of the latters' "educational commitments." The whole thing has been handled very tenderly; the government has taken into consideration the rooted British antipathy to compulsion of any kind, even in the middle of a life-and-death struggle. There has been a busy press campaign to assure the young women that the yellow complexions munition workers acquired in the last war handling TNT are by no means unavoidable in this one, since science has developed a protective cream which works on all except possessors of ultra-sensitive skin. Nervous parents are also soothed by promises that the state will act as the most vigilant of guardians to youthful daughters far from home. Finally, if a woman is pregnant or has young children, she is not to be called up at all.

The beginning of the long-threatened drive to bring womanpower into the war effort resulted in a House of Commons debate which will produce, it is hoped, plain assurances that women will be given reasonable wages and working conditions and more responsible executive posts than they have at the moment. There are those who think that a general call-up of unoccupied women won't be necessary, and that Bevin is relying on a universal scuttle to get in on the good jobs early. Certainly the social pattern is already being affected by the new order. Domestic servants are soon going to be as extinct as the mammoth, and the advertising columns of the morning papers are filled daily with the wails of anguished ladies trying to tempt cooks with details of enormous wages, happy homes, and safe locales, where a bomb is guaranteed to be unknown. The snatching away of kitchen help in their prime has brought fresh life to ancient servitors, who have come creaking out of retirement to ask and get money that British mistresses think is fabulous.

There are also plenty of people who hope fervently that Bevin won't stop with what he has done and will show the kind of wholesale ruthlessness for which the nation is emotionally ready but which so many of those at the top still seem reluctant to use. It is indicative of something special in the way of national determination that the continuance of horse racing has just been hotly attacked by a number of angry critics who have figured out the nice mathematical problem of how many hens could be fed on the daily ration of one race horse. Among those who answered this criticism was the King's brother-in-law, Lord Harewood, who replied with dignity, "Those interested in racing have not pressed for the indulgence of their hobby when it conflicts with the national interest and all sections of the racing community have accepted the rulings of the stewards of the Jockey Club with not more grumbling than is the birthright of every Englishman."

April 6

This Sunday morning's news of Germany's aggression against Yugoslavia and Greece was the climax of a fortnight so bewildering that Britons have hardly known from one moment to another what emotions they were going to be called upon to register next. As the dazzlingly good news of a week or two ago from Yugoslavia, East Africa, and the Mediterranean was followed by an English attempt to overhaul a French convoy, the British withdrawal from Benghazi, and the mounting tension everywhere, the papers became just about as comfortable as a bomb lying on the breakfast table. It all culminated for most people at nine o'clock this morning, which is the belated hour when the B.B.C. news bulletin is given out on Sundays in deference to Sabbatical late sleeping. After taking in the announcement's main features, one might just as well have switched the radio off without troubling to wait for the familiar Nazi details—the notes to ministers telling them in polite diplomatic language that undiplomatic violence had already started, the early-dawn move against frontier troops, the statement that the step was necessary to counteract Machiavellian British schemings in the attacked countries.

For the past fortnight, Londoners have been listening to the unnatural silence at nights and wondering what was brewing. Now that they know, sympathy for the plain people of Greece, who must be in for a time that will tax even their remarkable courage, seems to be the predominating emotion. Anxiety as to where Turkey stands is probably the secondary one. The bare facts of the Russian agreement with Yugoslavia, which are all that are known at the moment, were also thoughtfully discussed over this morning's chilling coffee cups. Although Parliament decided only a few days back that the British Sabbath must be kept as a day of unbroken mental rest and refreshment, there was little of either for anyone today. What with discussions, arguments over strategy demonstrated on newly bought maps, and glances at the clock to see if it wasn't time for the next news bulletin, it felt too much like one of Hitler's old-fashioned Sundays.

The withdrawal from Benghazi was the powder coming at the end of a week of almost pure jam. Until that reversal, the news had been so good that the press forgot to warn the public against the intoxicating effects of victory and gave itself up to downright jubilation. Probably the Belgrade *coup d'état* caused the greatest excitement, because to the uninformed observer it was so entirely unexpected. The possibility that something might come of the last-minute broadcast in which Colonel Amery, Secretary of State for India, appealed to the Yugoslav people, first in Serbian and then in Croatian, to stand against the Nazis had been regarded with polite skepticism here, coupled with admiration for the speaker's thoroughly un-English lingual dexterity. Mr. Churchill's brief and dramatic announcement subsequently of "the great news" of Yugoslavia's decision was therefore electrifying. There was general satisfaction over the fortunate bit of timing by which Matsuoka's * Berlin stopover coincided with the Serbian revolt and his arrival in Rome with the crushing Italian defeat in *Mare Nostrum*. The fact that the visitor made all his compliments in English also tickled the British, who last week were ready to be tickled by anything.

Unhappily, there was less amusement over Mr. Matsuoka's return call at Berlin on his way to Moscow, for by that time Benghazi had been evacuated—a shock to public opinion which the *Times* described only as "disagreeable." This restrained adjective hardly summed up the universal disappointment and the angry feeling that someone must have been caught napping somewhere.

April 20

Nazi successes seem to have a way of coinciding with those rare and enchanting spells when England really does look like a demi-paradise and not a waterlogged island where nine-tenths of the population have colds in the head. Last year's climatically perfect June was soured for Britons by what was happening in France; this year's April is clouded in much the same way by what is happening in Greece and North Africa, especially Greece. There are other points of similarity, too, which are distracting the attention of the English from the announcement by daffodils in the London parks and cuckoos in Surrey woods that summer is icumen in—with what seasonable unpleasantness few are anxious to predict.

In the new mood of criticism that is the inevitable hang-

* Yosuke Matsuoka, Japanese Minister of Foreign Affairs.

over from the biggest optimistic jag the nation has had for many months, there has been a tendency to resent the supposedly soothing official formula, also dug up from last June's files, explaining that the rapid German advance (in North Africa, this time) would be braked very soon by difficulties of supply. Those with long memories weren't really surprised by the subsequent disclosure that *Panzer* divisions had romped to the Egyptian borders. Because there had to be a scapegoat for the deep public uneasiness and because most observers felt that Wavell didn't deserve to be it, the present machinery of news censorship has come in for a large share of the castigation. Not unnaturally, people feel that they are entitled to have the facts, however unpleasant, released with the swift professional competence displayed by the German propaganda machine. Although it is gratifying to know that the British press is free, unhappily it is often through the brisk statements of the notoriously shackled enemy that Londoners first get wind of some setback, which is announced here only after the sacred pause for official cud-chewing. There was grumbling, too, over the way the presence of a considerable German mechanized force in Libya was announced abruptly to a startled public, in the manner of someone who has just discovered a sinister-looking bundle under a gooseberry bush, and the result of cloaking it in polite mystery has been to strengthen a crop of rumors as to how it got there. If tanks and the full paraphernalia for mechanized warfare could be slipped so neatly across one bit of water, the British, looking at the Channel sparkling behind barbed-wire barricades, quite naturally ask themselves whether it couldn't be done just as neatly across another bit.

Altogether, the handling of the Libyan news has been as inept as the official air-raid statements, which still breezily announce that casualties caused by this bombardment or that were "not unduly heavy." No such phrase was used, however, to describe last Wednesday's casualties, which will probably make a new and tragic record when the tired rescue squads finally finish getting the bodies out of the wreckage. Official taciturnity about the names of victims (even obituary notices inserted by relatives in the newspapers cannot give the actual date of an air-raid victim's death but only the month in which it occurred) broke down to the queer extent of allowing the release of the news that two peers and a crooner had perished. Blind fatalism was probably as good a refuge as any on that night, in which death was democratically making no social distinctions. In many cases, well-built shelters deep down beneath expensive brick and concrete proved little better than the kitchen tables under which humble families stoically crouched and listened to hell breaking loose around them. Damage was so nearly universal that owners of premises with unbroken windows, though relieved, felt a trifle guilty as they explained to less fortunate neighbors that they couldn't imagine how they had escaped. The only inspiriting thing about the whole ghastly business was to see how people took up life again next day, performing such simple acts of faith as shopping, taking in a movie, struggling to work by buses that had to go on endless detours around torn-up streets, and buying spring flowers from hawkers who set up their defiantly gay barrows on pitches glittering with powdered glass.

It would be useless to minimize the fact that the past week has been a bad one for the British—probably the worst since the collapse of France. People say, "We got over it then. We shall get over it again," which isn't a hopeful statement but just a statement. Already the national talent for standing disappointment better than any other nation in the world is stiffening the public to meet further sharp losses, which seem to be regarded as practically inevitable. As a nation, the British wear disaster more gracefully than they do victory, and the thorny crown is only a little more uncomfortable this time because of the recent shouting over the laurels which the Libyan and Eritrean conquests were making so beguilingly familiar.

May 4

As far as could be judged last week, people here were feeling better, though not, alas, because the news looked better. Before the news could be expected to improve, Londoners seemed to feel grimly certain, it must first, like a dangerously ill patient, get a good deal worse. The reason for the slight lifting of the public spirits might have been put down to the reports of the evacuation of a large proportion of the Imperial forces from Greece. The relief this time was quiet; there was none of the emotional enthusiasm, none of the sense of having witnessed a stirring miracle, which was felt after Dunkirk. The reaction to the withdrawal from Greece was mostly mental, a silent realization of an appalling job ably carried out. "But then," as one pub-keeper wryly remarked, "we ought to be good at it by now. We've had enough practice."

Progression to the stage where such small jokes, however wry, are possible at all is probably the result not only of eased tension over the fate of the Imperial forces in Greece but of the way the popular imagination has for once outstripped the gravity of the news. Even not particularly pessimistic Britons are now looking quite openly ahead to a program of further sickening wallops, which will have to be endured more or less stoically until the day when they can be given back with interest. As a consequence of having envisaged worse to come, there has been a general relaxation of nervous strain which, with the resultant freedom from false hopes and wishful thinking, might almost be termed feeling better.

The only really cheerful bit of news in the last uncheerful fortnight has been the announcement that the United States has extended its Atlantic patrols. This was received with tremendous satisfaction here, and its importance rightly made it the central theme of Mr. Churchill's speech last Sunday.

The audience which sat down beside its radios to listen to him was probably the most critical one he has had to face since he took over last May. People felt confident that they would get, from the man who had told them "many mistakes and disappointments will surely be our lot," the truth about a major setback which was certainly the latter even if it wasn't the former. They got it, without any polite skirting around the uncomfortable word "defeat."

All the same, many listeners felt that there was a rather too summary dismissal by the Prime Minister of the public uneasiness over a situation which surely only a ninny could feel completely easy about. Mr. Churchill, in passing from a mention of this uneasiness to a eulogy of the morale of the bombed cities, gave some the impression that he thought the national anxiety was being caused by the increased German air attacks, whereas nine out of ten adult Britons who aren't ninnies are worried less about England's ability to take it, which is unquestionable, than about her ability to give it, which unhappily isn't. It is hoped by all these anxious people that several questions the Prime Minister didn't answer will be ventilated at the forthcoming debate in Parliament on the progress of the war.

Why couldn't more of the three million men under arms in Britain have been sent to Greece instead of weakening the defence of Egypt by taking troops from there? Why are the Rumanian oil fields still unbombed? Why has the public here been left in complete darkness concerning developments which, if made known, could hardly have helped the enemy, since press and radio elsewhere had already freely reported them? Why wasn't the successful bombardment of Tripoli carried out weeks earlier, when it might have made a vital difference in the trend of subsequent events? It is this sort of thing that is being asked, in no spirit of disloyalty to a leader who has always been himself a doughty critic, by ordinary people everywhere—over tea tables, bars, and workbenches, in trains, clubs, and air-raid shelters.

One couldn't pretend that there is absolute confidence in the progress on the home front, either. Among the most common causes of concern is the fact that this is still a one-man government. When things go wrong anywhere, it is the public's trusting habit to expect Mr. Churchill to put them right, which would be fine if one overworked man could only cut himself into a hundred pieces. Since he can't, people would like to see a second in command who could in any way measure up to that solitary figure. (There is also talk of the advisability of including Dominion statesmen, such as General Smuts of South Africa, in a new Imperial Cabinet. Englishmen, with their ears still burning after what the Nazi propaganda department made of Australian comments on the use of the Anzacs in Greece, feel that anything which would bring the Dominions closer to the government would be a tactful move.)

The appointment of Lord Beaverbrook as Minister of State was probably the official forestalling of a public demand for a trouble-shooter to assist Mr. Churchill, and it has had a popular reception. In past discussions as to who could be found in the government with anything like the dynamic Churchillian qualities, someone has always been pretty sure to say, "Well, of course, there's that fellow Beaverbrook." If the someone has happened to be elderly and Tory and suspicious of Fleet Street methods, a Canadian accent, and the face of an irreverent street urchin, the remark has been made with groans, but it has been made. People who are none of those things, but only anxious to see the war won as quickly as possible, are hoping that the newly resurrected title of Minister of State carries with it a roving commission to kick inefficiency and departmental dawdling hard wherever it is encountered. The appointment was received with cheers.

May 17

[*May 10, Rudolf Hess parachutes onto Scottish soil.*]

A Nazi leader, catapulting down onto a Scottish moor, succeeded for several days last week in shifting the war into the

key in which war rightly belongs—that of large-scale lunacy.
The debt which the nation owed to Herr Hess showed in relaxed, smiling faces everywhere. After the strain and anxiety
of recent events, people were glad to open their morning papers and find headlines that weren't tragedy but pure comic
opera, with a libretto which might have been better if it
hadn't been a trifle farfetched. The subsequent twist, the report that the unexpected visitor had hoped to tumble in on
a duke, amused everyone—except, presumably, the duke in
question, whose picture, snapped by the photographers,
showed him shielding his face with a newspaper. A column-
ist in the *Express* told his readers, "Your Hess guess is as
good as mine," and put forward one to the effect that Hess, a
sick man, had come over because he knew that all the best
German doctors were in this country as refugees. A London
cinema audience roared when a newsreel commentator, anticipating further Nazi monkey business, said that even the
arrival of Göring wouldn't surprise anyone, and added, "But
I hope he brings his ration card."

Although the press spoke solemnly about maggots in ap-
ples, handwriting on the wall, and cracks in the rotten Nazi
façade, the simple and wholehearted reaction of the public
was enjoyment of the first good laugh that had come its way
in weeks. The erudite readers of the *Times* contributed
their own bit of scholarly merriment, one lady writing in to
say that a passage from "Hamlet"—Act V, Scene I—might
be pretty apt just now. (First Clown: "He that is mad, and
sent into England." Hamlet: "Ay, marry; why was he sent to
England?") Another reader, in a slightly more sinister vein,
pointed out that Vergil, Herodotus, and Ovid all tell of classic and warning counterparts of "the devoted servant of the
besieging leader who gets himself made prisoner in order to
betray the beleaguered city from within."

On the whole, the devoted-servant theory led among people who have come around to the sound and skeptical way of
thinking that any apple proffered on a Nazi platter usually
has the maggot in the British bite. To these people, Mr. Ernest Bevin's voice had a refreshing ring when he declared

roundly at a public luncheon that Nazism remained Nazism
to him, however charmingly it spoke to flustered Scottish
housewives, and that, as far as he was concerned, Hess was a
murderer. This was a pleasant antidote to all those papers
which had gone to town on Hess's looks, ideals, clean living,
and devotion to the wife and child whom he had inexplicably elected to leave behind in Germany. After a couple of
days of such stuff, the public was justly a bit muzzy as to
whether it was reading about Hitler's right-hand man or
Gary Cooper.

Naturally, there were endless theories between the ex-
tremes of seeing the adventure as a dark piece of Nazi diplo-
macy and as the beginning of the end in Germany. It was
variously held that Hess's flight was a link in an invasion attempt which hadn't jelled, that Hess had been taking a look
at the big Saturday-night raid on London, that it wasn't Hess
at all, and that it wasn't anybody but only a violent and unprecedented brainstorm on the part of the British propaganda department, which had seized the opportunity offered
by early stories from Berlin of the Nazi leader's disappearance. Incidentally, the singular ineptness of the German
handling of the story is taken here as proof, depending on
how you look at it, either of genuine Nazi discomfiture or of
Hitler's having been in the know all the time. People who
hold the second view reason that Dr. Goebbels' department
is usually so efficient that such elaborate confusion, contra-
diction, and general flat-footedness must be part of the gag.
Probably the only view to hold until further facts are available is the simple one that this flight into fantasy has provided the best mental holiday anyone has had since the hair
of most thinking adults over thirty started to turn gray.

After such a pleasant little excursion into unreality, the
weekend news of the capitulation of Vichy and of the subsequent German move into Syria made an unpleasantly realistic impression. The English suddenly woke up to the harsh
fact that if they weren't actually at war with their old ally,
they were only a couple of jumps from it. On the basis of the
resulting bitterness and anger against Vichy that one hears

expressed on all sides, it would seem that the Englishman's traditional mistrust of the French has been alive under the surface all these years, waiting only to be scratched into open antagonism again; what German propaganda has for so long attempted, the men of Vichy have at last accomplished. For lovers of France, these are sad, bad days.

Although Dakar isn't a name that the English remember with pleasure, owing to de Gaulle's abortive expedition there, most of this weekend's discussion centred around it. To millions of Britons, that remote dot on the African coastline has become real and tremendously important. They had already read with intense interest President Roosevelt's stern message to French listeners. Every pronouncement he makes is scanned by the press and the public alike in these anxious times, not only for its obvious meanings but for two or three oblique ones as well. Naturally, there is hopeful speculation as to what he is going to say on May 27th, if by that time actions have not spoken louder than words. In ten days quite a lot of history can be made—enough, possibly, to change the world for some time to come.

June 1

[*May 27, President Roosevelt broadcast the announcement that the American patrol of the North and South Atlantic was to be extended, and declared an "unlimited national emergency."*]

At four-thirty last Wednesday morning, lots of Londoners broke off the beauty sleep of yet another uncannily blitz-free night and got up to join the world at President Roosevelt's fireside. His speech had been more eagerly awaited than any other pronouncement since the war began; when the President was through talking, its implications were as eagerly discussed. Those who made the early-rising effort were able to feel superior to those who didn't, for the morning papers carried the address only in condensed, stop-press form. When the full text was published later in the day, the general impression seemed to be one of keen satisfaction over a piece of speaking plain enough to leave no one, friend or enemy, in any possible doubt. The minority, which still likes its declarations of war cut and dried in the old, now demoded way, was disappointed that the President had not announced a definite, immediate program involving convoys. The vast majority, however, believed that reassurance on this point could be read into his firm promise to get the goods here by any means and in spite of any intimidation. British admiration is profound for the Roosevelt sense of strategic timing, which the people here regard as second to none, not barring Hitler's. Hearing the words of the great proclamation ringing out on the unusual stillness of the London night was a moving experience—as moving as hearing George VI haltingly Godspeed his people into war on a beautiful September evening long ago.

Maybe the enthusiasm over the President's address was sober because of the realization of the solemnity of the step taken, or maybe it was because all the wild superlatives had been used up over the *Bismarck* the day before. That news appeared in time for beaming Londoners to celebrate with a quick one in the lunch interval. The excitement was tremendous, for everyone had been holding his breath, and not daring to hope, ever since word came that the hunt was on. In the view of the experts, the destruction of the *Bismarck* more than cancelled out the loss of the *Hood,* though this perhaps was not altogether the view of the faithful public, to whom the elderly *Hood* had always seemed a special and practically indestructible bit of national property. There was considerable criticism of the reference to luck in the official communiqués, although Lord Chatfield corroborated them to the extent of saying that any hit at such a range must be a matter of luck rather than of skill. The fact that the *Hood* was lost in exactly the same way as three ships at Jutland also raised a lot of questions as to whether all the knowledge gained in that engagement had been embodied in her construction.

Questions, in fact, have been running all through the past week's news. Events in Crete look on the verge of supplying a bitter solution to the major poser—whether a combatant fighting with an army and air force but without a navy can get the better of one fighting with an army and navy but without an air force. As the news from Iraq has improved, the news of the desperately important battle of Crete has grown more serious, until it now seems that the press is cautiously coaching the public to expect the worst. The worst being exactly what every Briton equipped with eyesight and a good map has expected for the last week, no developments in that direction are likely to come as a shock, though that doesn't lessen the dreary agonies of waiting, wondering, and somehow living until the next news bulletin. As a rehearsal for invasion, the campaign off the Grecian mainland has probably provided valuable lessons for both sides, but at the moment all that Britons are thinking about is the men being dive-bombed on Cretan beaches, just as a year ago they were thinking of the same thing happening on the beaches of Dunkirk. The miracle that occurred then doesn't seem possible now, either geographically or in view of Mr. Churchill's recent sombre promise that Crete would be defended "to the death."

With this ever-present anxiety weighing on people's minds, it's not surprising that the Whitsun weekend doesn't seem much like a holiday, although banks will be closed as usual on Monday, unless, in the stately official phrase, "anything unforeseen occurs." Actually, something unforeseen to the public was sprung this morning when the President of the Board of Trade came on the air to announce the imminent rationing of clothes, thereby ruining the Sunday-breakfast appetites of millions of women who regretted not having bought that little outfit they'd dithered about the other day. Sixty-six coupons are to be the basic ration for twelve months, no matter where you shop, which sounds all right until you realize that you must fork out, for example, seven coupons just for a washable frock and five for a sweater. To get a pair of pants, a man will have to turn in eight; if he's a Scot and fancies a kilt, he need part with only six. It was prosaically announced that the spare page of margarine coupons in the Englishman's food-ration book is to be used for clothing until the authorities get around to issuing separate clothing books, which should give couturiers an elegant shudder. No one quite knows how this is going to work out or how the officials plan to prevent a bootleg smock or two from changing hands quietly under the counter, but it is certain that this new step will mean the writing off of hundreds of small businesses which have bravely struggled along against the blitz and the disappearance of their best clients to the country.

The country is where millions of unmoneyed as well as moneyed Londoners usually count on going for an annual Whitmonday excursion, but this year a stroll to look at the sheepshearing now giving a bucolic air to Hyde Park is probably the nearest most will get to it. The usual jaunts to the seaside are impossible, even for those who can take the time off, because most accessible bits of ocean are in defence areas prohibited to casual tripper traffic, which, anyway, has been severely curtailed by the recent further cut in the gasoline ration. It is hoped by aggrieved civilians that something equally tough is going to be done about Army gasoline, which apparently isn't stinted, judging by the sorties of lorries sent on unessential journeys that a dispatch rider on a motorcycle could perform just as well at a fraction of the expense for fuel.

Motorists, gloomily counting their diminished gasoline coupons this month, were cheered by finding a memorandum from the Ministry of Transport tucked inside the book. It gives instructions for the immobilization of cars in the event of invasion. The magneto and the fuel-injection pump must be smashed with a hammer, and in case non-mechanical owners should stand gaping and wondering which of the silly-looking things to smash first, the pamphlet recommends gently that "they should go to the nearest garage at once to find out."

June 15

The long and puzzling lull in heavy air attacks is one reason it is thought that something big and especially unpleasant must be cooking. When and if invasion starts, there's reason for hoping that civilian defence to meet it will be considerably better organized than it is just now. Any number of questions concerning this subject have been under discussion lately—the quite literally burning one, for instance, of the present system of fire-watching and fire-fighting, which is said to be still far from perfect. It has been suggested that all branches of home defence should be directed by a separate ministry, with the unenviable but necessary job of coördinating the lamentably uncoördinated local authorities, who occasionally act as if they thought that though other cities may get blitzed, some divine umbrella will save them from the same fate.

The Minister of Health brought more concrete comfort this week when he gave details of the organization of mobile teams of A.R.P. officials, which will be ready to go instantly to the assistance of any heavily attacked town. A system to care for bombed-out people by establishing them in camps and hostels away from probable danger areas is also to be set up; this should solve the problem of homeless families who have been trudging nightly into the country to sleep in damp but peaceful woods. Another suggested reform is based on a sound psychological knowledge of the English character. The Minister of Health has advised the appointment of paid billeting officers—brutal souls better able to tell the lady of the manor to prepare for ten évacués right away than

a gentle local spinster wobbling up the drive on a bicycle between the immemorial elms.

June 29

[*June 22, Germany invades Russia.*]

Since last weekend, the English have been facing up to a
tough job of readjustment. Having in the past decided to
regard Russia as the great imponderable who would continue to sit shrewdly on the fence until the moment when
she could come off it and dictate terms to a war-exhausted
world, they realized suddenly that the fence was deserted
and its former occupant was right there on the firing line
beside them. The first shock was as great as though a grizzly
had dropped in for afternoon tea. As far as could be gathered, most people—not only those who learn what's going
on by reading the newspapers but those who should be well
informed—hadn't expected it to happen. The rumors of
some such development, with which the town had been
buzzing all the previous week, had been viewed with caution as being either the buildup for a super-bluff that would
end in concessions by Stalin or a bit of wishful thinking on
the part of those who had often spoken hopefully of the possibility of Russia and Germany flying at each other's throats.

When that possibility was confirmed as an actuality on the
most dramatic Sunday morning of the war, some of the gallant attempts to digest the startling new idea looked queer
and others plain funny. Vicars leading their flocks in prayer
for the Allies may have faltered a trifle at the notion that
they were now imploring divine protection for the godless
hordes of Soviet Russia. The young and merry looked forward (in vain, as it turned out) to hearing the "Internationale" played by the B.B.C. before the nine-o'clock news,
along with the customary national anthems of the Ethiopians
and other Christian folk. All the doubts and questions, and

many of the jokes, were dissipated later in the day, however, by the firm tone of Mr. Churchill's speech, which must have been one of the trickiest to prepare of any he has made and which couldn't have been better done. As Englishmen were saying admiringly the next morning, "He always bats best on a sticky wicket."

This particular batting performance effectually knocked the fears of the landed gentry and the possible murmurs of upper-class near-Quislings right out of sight over the pavilion. Its effect was immediate and excellent. The press still seemed a bit shy of the word "ally" but enthusiastically discovered "partner," emphasizing that the new lineup was to be strictly a business arrangement, with Britain tactfully closing an eye to the Hammer and Sickle and the Soviet presumably doing ditto to the Cope and Crown. The Communist Party suddenly decided that this wasn't an imperialist war after all, while prominent White Russians, such as Prince Vsevolode, announced that in such a situation the color of anyone's politics mattered less than his love of country. In case there should be fears that disturbing doctrines might be imported from the new partner, Mr. Wang, president of the London Chinese Association, pointed out reassuringly that in spite of Soviet coöperation with his country, China isn't even pink. The Soviet Ambassador, M. Maisky, was photographed being benevolently beamed upon by a lord at a lunch party where the toast to Russia was proposed and received with as much acclaim as the toast to Finland had roused at a similar lunch, not attended by M. Maisky, about sixteen months ago. Mme. Maisky was written up by the press as a keen gardener who kept the Embassy flower bowls full of Old World cottage roses, this being a sure short cut to any British hearts which might still be feeling a bit doubtful.

Whatever doubts remained in most sensible minds were concerned not with ideological twisters but with the question of Russian resistance, about which the experts are not particularly comforting. It is known that the Soviet transportation system was in a pretty bad snarl just recently and people fear that the Nazis' best points—organization and communications—may turn out to be Russia's worst. All that anyone seems certain about is that the invasion of Britain has been shelved until the outcome of the new struggle has been determined.

Meanwhile, the respite is seen as the best opportunity that has come Britain's way for some time. The stepping up of the R.A.F. bombing program and the daytime fighter-patrol successes over northern France have been taken as encouraging signs that Britain is going to use its chance well. Londoners hope that the new situation will be exploited to the full to raise the workers' production level, which has got to reach a superhuman new high in the next few precious weeks, and to encourage the suppressed Communist element in the Reich. People wouldn't say no, either, to a few more raids on occupied territory, like the Lofoten one, only on a bigger scale; with Germany so formidably engaged, they argue, there couldn't be a better time. There's no doubt that lots of Britons also believe this is the moment for full American intervention. One of the first responses to the Russian news was anxiety as to what the American reaction would be, and there was a good deal of relief when the official offer of all possible aid to the Soviet Union was announced.

With so much importance being placed by Britain on the slightest move in Washington and with so much anxious glancing at the United States barometer, naturally any gestures of amity between the two English-speaking countries are much encouraged. As the result of an idea thought up by the *Daily Express,* many London rooftops will courteously flaunt the Stars and Stripes on the Fourth of July. Another extension of hands across the sea was made recently by the Board of Education, which disclosed with horror the sad fact that less American history is taught in English schools than British history is taught in American schools. In the future, English tots will learn all about Bunker Hill and Saratoga, so that they will have the right background for telling *their* children about Anglo-American coöperation, which by then, ninety-nine per cent of the British now seem firmly to believe, will have written a vital and invigorating chapter in the world's history.

July 13

For all their caution, Londoners seemed to be in a bullish mood last week. There was excitement and relief over the news of the American occupation of Iceland, which was regarded as the most important move yet made toward the winning of the Battle of the Atlantic. The increasing weight of the R.A.F.—in bombing attacks on German war-production centres and in daylight sweeps over France, with the satisfactory result of withdrawing Nazi fighter planes from the Russian campaign—was another reason for increasing confidence, although it is widely hoped that the opportunities of this critical moment aren't going to be entirely limited to the air. The world-shaking din of events on the Eastern Front only accentuates the sad fact that things are all too quiet on the Western Front, though most Britons would give their back teeth to see a series of brisk harassing operations up and down the length of the enemy-occupied coastline. They seem to feel that such a move, in addition to having a healthy effect on the sit-here-and-wait-to-be-invaded jinx which has been perched on many English shoulders since last summer, is the very least that a grateful nation can do to relieve a bit of the pressure on Russia, for whom admiration is steadily increasing.

It is comic to see the somersaults turned in the last fortnight by all sorts of people who used to blanch at the sight of a hammer anywhere near a sickle. The discovery of Russia is the most exciting thing that has happened here for years and one that is bound, after the war, to make necessary some sort of modern remodelling of England's old-fashioned silhouette. Right now, it seems that something new and vital has been injected into the air. The announcement in the Court Circular that His Excellency Dr. Vi Kyuin Wellington Koo had been received in audience by the King and had presented his letters of credence as Ambassador Extraordinary and Plenipotentiary from the Republic of China to the Court of St. James came in the same week as the arrival of the Russian military mission. Together with the Iceland news, it looked to lots of thinking Britons as though the first rough draft of what Lord Cecil has termed "the quadrilateral of freedom"—the British Empire, the United States, the Soviet Union, and the Republic of China—was already on paper.

Londoners turned out in force to take a look at the Russians when they arrived at the railway station. Many people felt that they ought to pinch themselves sharply as they read the list of the bigwigs who were lined up at salute as the train steamed in. They felt still more that way the next morning when they saw the photograph of the occasion which the *Times* carried in its austere columns. What an earlier paper, printing a slightly muzzy picture, had described in its caption as "an enthusiastic crowd waving at the newly arrived Russian mission" was here clearly revealed as a group of enthusiastic Party members greeting the Comrades with homely clenched fists.

Twenty-four hours later, the great daily didn't record in its obituary columns any sudden deaths from heart failure of its more diehard Tory readers, but it did record a denial from the War Office of a report that photographers at the station had been ordered not to catch British and Soviet officers in the unprecedented act of shaking hands, presumably because the Intelligence Department thought a stately bow from the waist was all that was necessary between business partners. Whatever the facts, the indignant shouting over the reported insult to the Russians and the confused official explanations that some officious junior must have been responsible for the trouble were all in the best Gilbert-and-Sullivan traditions of muddled chivalry. Meanwhile, the mission continued to stop traffic as it moved about London. The crowds that gathered outside the War Office and other places to see its members seemed to feel that they were about to witness visitors from Mars and were startled to find that General Golikoff, Colonel Pugachoff, and the rest were a smart, quiet-looking lot, so far from being exotic that, as one disappointed lady remarked, "they might almost be English."

After the rumpus over the photographers had subsided, newspapers of all shades of political opinion joined in castigating the B.B.C. for omitting to include the "Internationale" in its Sunday-evening rendering of the Allied national anthems. Some writers thought that a tricky problem could be evaded with dignity by substituting a Russian national folk air for the "Internationale," which is criticized as a purely revolutionary song bound to give offence to many. Such a description apparently doesn't apply to a little number called the "Marseillaise," to which Britons are allowed to listen quite placidly every Sunday. The aforementioned great daily was all for abolishing the weekly anthems altogether, on the ground that "it is to be hoped and believed that we have not yet exhausted the number of nations to be enrolled at some time as belligerents in the same cause" and that too many anthems will exhaust the listeners. The most ingenious idea in the controversy came from a reader who wrote in suggesting that the composers get busy and blend a few bars of all the Allied anthems into one potpourri, the medley to begin, he proposed hopefully, with "O say, can you see."

August 10

The classic English topic of conversation, the weather, has vanished for the duration and now would be good for animated chat only in the event of a brisk Biblical shower—of oranges, cheese, cornflakes, and prunes instead of manna. Everyone talks about food. An astonishing amount of people's time is occupied by discussing ways and means of making rations go further, thinking up ingenious substitutes for unprocurable commodities, and trying to scrounge a little extra of whatever luxury one particularly yearns for. Nearly everybody now and then finds himself thinking of some kind of food to which in peacetime he never gave a second thought. Strong men, for instance, who normally wouldn't touch a piece of candy from one end of the year to the other now brood over the idea of milk chocolate with morbid passion. No matter how comparatively well one eats, deficiencies in diet lead to occasional empty moments which the individual mentally fills in to his own liking with filet mignon, plumcake, or a dish of ham and eggs.

Quite a lot of Americans in London, who earlier in the war irritably curbed a tendency of anxious families at home to shower them with things like tinned butter, are wishing they hadn't been so hasty. Since Americans here are not allowed to write home and ask for what they want, all they can do is pen effusive thanks for the delicious ham or whatever (which actually was never sent) and trust to their dear ones' sagacity to put two and two together. The official attitude toward food parcels is divided between reluctance to check these friendly impulses and a wish that precious shipping space could be left clear for bulk consignments, which would benefit the many instead of the few.

On the whole, the food situation, although it's far from good, is a long way from being desperate. The average number of calories which each member of the population consumed during the first year of the war was only one per cent lower than it was in peacetime and it is expected that it will be no lower this year. Those feelings of emptiness are more the result of turning rather suddenly to a thinner diet; obviously, a nation which once consumed a lot of meat and fats can't switch abruptly to vegetables and cereals without experiencing discomfort under the waistband. The urban poor come off the worst, owing to their distaste for such substitutes (the unshakable aversion of cockney evacuees to green-stuffs is the bane of many a communal feeding centre) and to their habitual partiality for delicacies like tinned salmon, condensed milk, and endless cups of tea, all of which are difficult or impossible to procure. The rural poor do a good deal better because they grow a lot of vegetables, generally keep a few chickens, and poach a rabbit or two when they're lucky. The more moneyed classes are able to buy trimmings to furbish up the dull, basic necessities, but anything substantial beyond those necessities is becoming increasingly hard to come by, money or no.

The shelves of, say, Fortnum & Mason are dazzling at first sight, but closer inspection reveals that the bulk of the displays consists of sauces, chutneys, and other condiments, which don't go far toward assuaging the appetite unless accompanied by a good slab of fish, flesh, or fowl. At the moment, fowls have practically disappeared from legal markets because poultry farmers prefer to sell at black-market prices rather than at the government-controlled figure. Fish is expensive, and the meat ration is such that a small family probably gets no more than a modest joint once a week. Horse-flesh is on sale, ostensibly for dogs, but possibly it appears incognito in many of the cooked foods which shops offer for human consumption. Eggs are rationed at the rate of one a week to a person and often turn up stamped with a cryptic blue hieroglyph which pessimists say is a Chinese character indicative of age. Vegetables are plentiful; Londoners dug for victory so manfully this spring that scarlet runners in every back yard seem to be trying to strangle the house, and for the time being there is a greater danger of being hit by a marrow falling off the roof of an air-raid shelter than of being struck by a bomb. Among unrationed foods, the following are likely to elicit a regretful no from one's shopkeeper: breakfast cereals, tinned and dried fruits, olive oil, tinned fish and soups, jellies, biscuits, lemons, lime juice, honey, chocolate, and macaroni and every other variety of pasta.

Now that marketing has become one long dialogue of queries and negative answers, the job of feeding a family is one which requires ingenuity, stamina, and endless time. The time factor has been sympathetically studied by the authorities in their drive to get women into line in the war industries. Some of the factories solve the problem by letting married women off for a couple of hours during the morning so that they can do their household shopping. In certain towns, food shops are trying out a scheme of reserving a proportion of their goods for war workers who can only get in late and would otherwise find everything sold out. The housekeeping difficulties of families in which both husband and wife go to work every day are simplified to some extent by the government-run chain of British Restaurants, of which there are now six hundred operating—two hundred and fifty of them in the London area—and about four hundred more under way. These restaurants, which were originally planned for bombed-out people and workingmen who didn't have the use of a works canteen, serve a good meal of meat, dessert, and a cup of tea for a shilling. The amount of meat served to customers at a British Restaurant or at a West End place like the Savoy is the same one-penny-worth a head, though the Savoy may add a few champignons.

Lately, there has been an acute shortage of beer, which is a big hardship to the workingman. Except in bars, hard liquor is equally difficult to buy. Often chagrined customers, after pointing wrathfully to displays of Scotch and rye in a shop window, discover that the bottles are dummies. The resulting skepticism about the nature of things sometimes has unfortunate results, as when a housewife stared coldly at a mound of lemons in her greengrocer's shop under the gloomy impression that they were hollow papier-mâché mockeries. She discovered later, after they were all gone, that they were part of a crate of the genuine article which had just come in that morning.

August 17

[*August, Churchill and Roosevelt meet "somewhere in the Atlantic."*]

The meeting of the week was also, as was to be expected, the big topic of the week for everyone. For quite a number of

Londoners, it had been the private, though not particularly confidential, topic of the preceding week, too, since the rumor that Churchill had gone to confer with Roosevelt had been leaking out around the town for some time. An alternative version of the story was that Churchill had flown to the Russian front to see for himself how things were going there. Even those who were skeptical about either possibility had to admit that there hadn't been a picture of a cigar in the press for days. The papers confined themselves to announcing, with a good deal of overemphasis, the fairly trivial social news that Mrs. Churchill had gone on a holiday, leaving no forwarding address, and followed this up, in an agonized attempt to lead their readers along the right path without giving anything away, by highlighting the President's fishing trip and hinting at some possible appointment he might have with somebody on the Atlantic.

In spite of all this, Mr. Attlee's broadcast came as a dramatic surprise to most people, who had spent the fateful time up to three o'clock that afternoon wondering uneasily what new sacrifice for themselves and their families the important announcement was going to demand. The news effectually jerked them out of their reveries, but many Britons seemed to feel that their Premier had gone the dickens of a long way merely to reiterate a stand which, in their simplicity, they thought everyone knew they had been prepared to die for, probably unpleasantly. This was the view publicly expressed, alone among the chorus of press enthusiasm, by the still, small voice of the respectable family picture paper, the *Daily Sketch*. Editorially, on the day after Mr. Attlee's announcement, it took the line that "this façade and eloquence" must conceal "some grave, practical, and highly important decision and act of warfare calculated to further our mutual cause and the very aims [with which] the document is so concerned." If this was not the case, it flatly stated, the risking of so many indispensable lives would go on record as "the most astounding piece of unjustified recklessness ever recorded in history."

It's true enough that the most solid satisfaction here was

not so much over the matter contained in the eight-point declaration, which certainly was nothing new, as over the fact that it seemed to be a significant step for both countries toward that communal design-for-living which most people see as their only hope of working out a braver new world. Apart from the universal pleasure in the surface circumstances of the meeting, about which the whole country seemed to feel as chucklingly benevolent as if two ideally suited people had at last got together, there was a strong conviction that its underlying implications carried even greater promise than its expressed results for the future of humanity.

The news which anxious Britons are waiting to hear right now is that Mr. Churchill has returned safely to Downing Street. The delay in its coming has started people wondering whether he hasn't gone on to continue the conference at the Soviet end—a gesture which would certainly do a great deal to obliterate from Moscow's excellent memory the Chamberlain government's unfortunate choice of a comparatively minor emissary to Moscow at the time of the abortive Anglo-Soviet negotiations of a couple of years ago. All the same, there will be a good many sighs of relief when it is announced that the Prime Minister is home again, especially as the second big transatlantic air crash in five days has made the public a bit jumpy. The deaths of Mr. Arthur Purvis, head of the British Supply Council, in Thursday's crash and of so many important technicians in the two disasters are a sobering shock in the middle of the excitement over the Churchill-Roosevelt meeting. Millions who didn't know a great deal about Mr. Purvis felt much as they did at the time of Lord Lothian's death and realized that the country had lost a man whose life work had made the spirit of such a meeting possible.

The Russian news at the moment is being treated with a good deal of caution, because it is difficult to form any sort of accurate estimate of what is happening from the contradictory communiqués issued by both sides. Ordinary people who figure out what's what from the things they read in the papers have come to the conclusion that the German communiqués stick to the truth when things are going well and lie when they're not. One hears considerable gloom expressed on all sides over the failure of British forces to produce any sort of land diversion to relieve the pressure on the Russian front. There is hopeful talk all the time that something of the sort is brewing, but the official view is said to be that unless made in sufficient strength any such expedition would be useless, that the necessary strength has to be deployed elsewhere, and that another evacuation from the Continent would be plain disastrous. The unofficial and uninformed view, especially of Dominion troops who have been kicking their heels in this country for the past year, is all in favor of trying out a bigger and better Lofoten as soon as may be.

Meanwhile, the newspapers are full of little Soviet items which would have read pretty funnily a short time back. Civilians have been told to study the success of the Russian scorched-earth policy, with a view to repeating in Sussex villages what has been found to work so admirably in the Ukraine grainfields; the *British Medical Journal* has pointed out the excellence of Russia's health spas, to which retired colonels could loyally take themselves after the war instead of to Pau or Vichy; the Archbishop of Canterbury has called the nation to prayer, with special intercessions for Russia, on September 7th, the anniversary of the first big raid on London; a wordy Communist drama, which discusses the visit of a Red general to a remote station on the Trans-Siberian Railway, was produced here by the highbrow Unity Theatre last Sunday; and, more accessible to the lowbrow public, there's a documentary film called "One Day in Soviet Russia," which recently arrived as the work of ninety-seven cameramen and got politely regretful notices from the critics.

Incidentally, record business has been done by the R.A.F. film "Target for Tonight," which should soon be on American screens. Although for transatlantic consumption there may be slightly too much Oxford accent and insistence on the casual British habit of underplaying tense moments, it is certainly the best propaganda film to come out of the war to date. Crowds queuing up for it stop the sidewalk traffic in Leicester Square every evening.

August 23

Mr. Churchill's broadcast tomorrow may effectually remove the slight flavor of disappointment which remains after his meeting with President Roosevelt. Certainly no one is better than he is at creating an illusion of producing good, satisfying bread out of stones. Although this may sound like a jejune metaphor in connection with the eight-point declaration, it would appear that the majority of people did feel when the meeting was over that they had been promised a fine loaf for the future but were still left with an empty sensation for the present. The truth is that there is a sharp disparity between what the press and the radio have been telling people they ought to think about the meeting's significance and what ordinary men and women have been thinking and saying about it. After Londoners had welcomed their Premier home, heaved a sigh of relief, and gone back to their dwellings, the kind of discussion in which they engaged was by no means an echo of the official eulogy of the declaration. Boiled down, the gist of plain, sensible British opinion seemed to be that it had been good talk but the public would have been even better pleased to be let in on the secret of some corresponding action, which for millions would speak louder than any amount of historically important words.

At the moment, the average Englishman is not entirely convinced that everything is being done which could be done to help Russia. Inasmuch as quite a lot of the English feel that there's no time like the present for a full-dress military diversion to turn the Nazis from the Eastern Front, there was a notable lack of excitement when some of the papers came out with streamers across their front pages announcing the glad news that Britain had jotted down 1943 in her engagement book as a suitable date for a rendezvous with Germany on the Continent. In multitudes of English homes there is the sombre certainty that if Soviet Russia is allowed to go down, the enemy will not be likely to wait obligingly until 1943 for a major settlement. There may be Tory strongholds in which the dangers of Communistic infiltrations are still gloomily pondered, but for the most part the Colonel's Lady and Judy O'Grady have become sisters under their skins with surprising celerity since it has been made clear that those skins are being fought for along the Dnieper as surely as they may yet be over the Kent orchards and Sussex marshes.

In a way, the ominous darkening of the Russian horizon hasn't had an unhealthy effect on morale here; until recently, the long letup in the blitz and the freedom from any immediate threat of invasion were creating a dangerous illusion of security. One of the most alarming signs of this has been the return of thousands of children to London, brought back, despite official disapproval, by parents apparently convinced that German planes will continue to fly east, not west.

It is realized that at best the coming winter is likely to feature among its attractions more intensive bombing, new food shortages, and cold. The last will probably be not at all funny, owing to the critical coal shortage—a scandal which has burst like a bomb and for which the reluctance of miners engaged in other industries to go back to the pits is said to be partly responsible. The response to a broadcast appeal for the return of fifty thousand ex-miners was described in a government White Paper as "most disappointing." Critics of the government's handling of this serious problem say that an increase in miners' rations would have a decided effect in getting the men back to the job, since the hewer has always been accustomed to nourishing food, including a good deal of meat, and doesn't feel able or willing to put forth the great physical exertion the task requires on anything less. Rationing of coal to the tune of a ton a month for each household is going to result, it is feared, in a wholesale re-turn of shivering people to the towns which may be more dangerous but will be considerably better heated than houses in isolated country districts where gas and electricity don't exist.

The threatened winter milk cut has stirred up a lot of crit-icism, too; overzealous ploughing-up of pasture land seems to have put dairy farmers in a bad way, something which has come as a complete surprise to the public. On the proposed extremely skimpy rations, children up to six will get a pint a day, those over six half a pint, and adults probably none at all if the shortage is really bad. As the nutrition experts have spent their time pointing out the importance of keeping up the supplies of this essential protective food, it looks as though the Ministries of Food and Agriculture between them are responsible for a situation to which the winter death rate may add its own grim footnote.

Just underneath Wednesday's *Court Circular* announce-ment that the Premier, on his arrival in London, had been received in audience by the King was a solitary paragraph to the effect that Miss Dorothy Thompson had left. This re-spectful treatment was in keeping with the general reception accorded to the lady, whose enthusiastic comments were wel-comed with gratitude here as the genuine voice of America. Unfortunately, this impression is encouraged by the newspa-pers, which naturally quote a fairly one-sided section of American opinion, and by the broadcasts of Miss Thomp-son, Quentin Reynolds, Harry Hopkins, and other favorably inclined observers. The resulting rosy picture of the United States as one big mass of interventionists, with just a few harmless little isolationists milling around in the back-ground, is one which leads to a good deal of extremely dan-gerous confusion in British minds. Many people consider that a broadcast or two by Lindbergh or by one of the fiercer isolationist senators would have a bracing effect, similar to that of the Soviet reverses. Of all the American observers who have spoken in England this summer, Herbert Agar has impressed everyone most by a series of remarkable speeches combining sincerity, hardheaded facts, and no compliments. "The war," he said in one of them, "will not be won by 'other men.' It will only be won by the blood and toil of all of us who believe in Western civilization." Words, those, to sink deeply into the consciousness of anyone who was beginning to believe that it might be won by the blood and toil of a few million Russians.

September 6

At the moment, any letter from London must be indirectly about Moscow, because the Russian news is effectually coloring most of the local happenings. As an aftermath to the general optimism about the magnificent Russian resistance, there seems to be a movement afoot to frighten the public into realizing that it's not frightened enough. In an effort to stop anyone's thinking that Russia is doing well enough for two, almost every orator of note this week has made warning use of that key word of a year ago, "complacency." Mr. Brendan Bracken, the new Minister of Information, spoke of it as Public Enemy No. 2 at a luncheon of the Foreign Press Association. Mr. Attlee and Sir Walter Citrine both deplored any tendencies toward it in speeches at the Trades Union Congress, which has been meeting in Edinburgh.

Both of the T.U.C. speeches were in support of a resolution, unanimously carried by the Congress, affirming the "unalterable resolve" of the British working classes to destroy the Nazi-Fascist regime, their pleasure at the prospect of Anglo-American unity, and the determination of the trades unions to give all possible assistance to the Soviet. Sir Walter also administered a sharp rap to the British Communist Party, which he described as "a totally unreliable agent for carrying out any policy." During the ensuing debate, he had to take the floor again in an attempt to answer Mr. Jack Tanner, the president of the Amalgamated Engineering Union, who accused the Minister of Aircraft Production,

Colonel Moore-Brabazon, of expressing the hope that the German and Soviet armies would write each other off and leave Britain as the dominant power in Europe. Mr. Tanner declared that he could and would substantiate his statement that this was the sabotaging point of view of certain people "in high places." Lots of people in middling and low places feel that they'd like to hear more about this, because it might help to clear up an uneasy current of suspicion that the impediments in the way of swift maximum aid to Russia aren't entirely geographical. Considering the note of urgency in the statement on Russia drawn up at the Atlantic conference, it is felt, perhaps not unreasonably, that practical action is being disappointingly slow in getting under way.

Besides dealing out warnings against excessive optimism over the Russian campaign, the papers seem to have taken alarm over the generally rosy view of those Anglo-American relations which the T.U.C. officially welcomed. From assuring the public of a stupendous flow of American arms to this country, the press has abruptly switched to a more cautious line, apparently in an attempt to convince the British that neither United States industry nor Russian bodies are going to win their war without a corresponding straining of every muscle here. A Mr. Philip Hewett Myring wrote a letter on this subject to the *Times,* which printed it under the subtitle "Fool's Paradise" and followed up with an article educating innocent Britons in some of the facts of life regarding the workings of Congress and the powers of the President. This sudden change of tone is probably the direct result of the recent broadcast by Mr. Churchill, who really did administer a much needed jolt to the large section of the population which felt that if America hadn't yet actually waded into the war, she had certainly taken a shoe off. It was a shock, possibly an astringent one, to find that the Prime Minister still thought it necessary to utter the same plain warnings that he used to give this country in the queer nightmare period between Munich and Prague.

In the lighter intervals between being prepared for hard times ahead, Londoners have been packing into a couple of highly topical exhibitions. One is an exhibit of Soviet life which has drawn crowds to the small Suffolk Galleries every day since its opening by Mme. Maisky. Its principal feature is the intelligent use of remarkably beautiful photographs of happy workers, contented cows, Old Testament patriarchs, New Utopia babies sunbathing in G-strings, and grandiloquent architecture. Russian war posters on display are brilliant, savage, and sometimes almost funny in their brief messages, which are not, as in England, polite injunctions to the civilian population to stay put or to avoid careless talk, but simple commands to kill as many Germans as speedily as possible. It would be instructive to know what British matrons up from the country for a day's shopping and colonels dropping in from their Pall Mall clubs think as they peer cautiously at the photographs of collective farms, high-cheek-boned Soviet airmen, and "The Pickwick Papers" as presented by the Affiliated Moscow Art Theatre in a setting less reminiscent of Dickens than of "Chauve-Souris." A gramophone at the gallery ceaselessly grinds out the popular melodies of the U.S.S.R., and records and sheet music of the songs are on sale there, so British homes may soon be ringing with "Soviet Fatherland," "Salute to Life," and "Song of the Collectives."

The second exhibition shows art by and of London firemen, and is being held in the sacred purlieus of the Royal Academy. The canvases cover every aspect of the job, from a terrifying impression of a red-hot wall heeling over on two firemen to a still life called "And So to Bed," a poignant little arrangement of a dirty uniform, sodden socks, a waterlogged pack of cigarettes, and the impedimenta of helmet, axe, and respirator thrown down on a chair by some tired man. The sensation of the show is a blank space left by a river scene which was withdrawn by the censors, who presumably didn't object to the fact that it was reproduced in the catalogue. The firemen themselves, artistic and otherwise, have been turning up in force, inspecting the pictures from a realistic point of view, and chuckling happily as they identify "some of the fellows at my station" or ask each other

"Brings back that night in Queen Victoria Street, don't it, Bill?" The collection has brought back several nights so vividly that the notes and silver dropped by the public into firemen's helmets at the door should benefit the firefighters' benevolent fund quite handsomely.

October 1

Clothes-rationing has been going on in England since the first of last June and most people have now recovered from their early panic, in which it seemed to them that there were only a paltry sixty-six coupons between them and loincloths. In the scheme's test period, if the last four months may be considered that, all sorts of complications and weaknesses have been detected and some of them satisfactorily fixed. Minor rackets have budded and flowered in profusion. On the whole, however, the British seem to be executing one of those wonderful grumbling jobs, at which they excel, of making the best of things. Some people see their jobs disappearing, and are understandably bitter. Others don't expect the new measures to make much difference. Almost universally, there has so far been an inability to realize that what happened on June 1st wasn't just a temporary nuisance but a revolution, an important upheaval in the clothing habits of a nation.

The Board of Trade, which is in charge of the rationing system, explains to anyone interested that the fundamental plan of apportioning clothes on a basis of sixty-six coupons a year for each individual was decided upon some time ago by a huddle of economic experts, working in closest secrecy. They geared their calculations to the needs of the average three-pounds-a-week wage-earner, who is said to refurbish his wardrobe at a rate which will leave him with one or two coupons still on hand at the end of the year. Obviously, the well-to-do, accustomed to spending much more on clothes, have had to adjust themselves drastically in order to get along on such a skimpy scale of buying. These people, however, are presumed to have well-stocked wardrobes, which their sixty-six coupons can supplement more or less adequately. The Board of Trade either has never heard or pretends to ignore the famous and impassioned prayer of the lady who cried, "Oh God, to be naked with a checkbook!" In the eyes of the Board, no Britons, with or without a checkbook, are naked except those who are unlucky enough to lose their clothes as the result of bombing, in which case they receive an additional grant of coupons; the Board assumes that everyone else possesses a nucleus of garments, to which a shirt can be grafted here and a pair of shoes there as the old things fall to tatters.

Even newly born infants are treated with an impartiality which seems to assume that they have brought their own reserve of diapers with them. On the whole, death is regarded more sympathetically than birth, since shrouds are an item on the list of coupon-exempt goods. By a recent amendment to the rules, however, expectant mothers may draw a double allowance of baby clothes if they can produce a certificate from a doctor or midwife that twins are to be expected. If the diagnosis turns out to have been overexuberant, the Board of Trade jovially writes the mistake off to good will. One of its officials, Mr. Nicholas Davenport, goes on the air now and then in a dialogue with a young lady announcer of the B.B.C., in which he makes a point of such admonitions as "Cut your cloth according to your coupons" and "Never coupon today what you can put off till tomorrow." The young lady always acts as a stooge who has done all the wrong things, frittering her precious coupons away on nonessentials like bathing suits and annoying overworked officials by leaving her old ration book at home when it comes time to apply for a new one. It is Mr. Davenport's rôle to show her, in a jolly, avuncular way, how naughty she has been.

The Board of Trade professes to know nothing of the black market in silk stockings, which operates in a rather murky atmosphere. Bootleg hosiery of a quality legally retailing at about four shillings and sixpence a pair can be bought without coupons at around seven shillings and six-pence from seedy little men at bars in some parts of town. Plenty of other rackets, more or less legal, have evolved from the new order, too. During the first weeks of the scheme, when it was announced that exemption would be given to custom-made clothes ordered before rationing began, many persons were startled but gratified to receive a polite note from their tailor asking when they were going to come around and fit that tweed suit they had ordered quite a while back. Showing up at the shop in a slight daze, they were received with a courteous wink and shown the order book, in which everything was written down in black and white, plain as you like.

In some shops business is good, in others it's terrible. Tai-lors are mostly doing well, because customers consider that a good, classic tweed salted away now will be comforting in the lean days ahead, when honest woollen fabrics probably will have disappeared from the market. The Savile Row tai-loring establishments received a great fillip from the visit of the Russian military mission, whose members behaved like the delegates in "Ninotchka," heading straight for double-breasted English suitings when they stepped off the plane. Dyeing-and-cleaning shops are also booming; it's a question of weeks, not days, before you get a garment back.

On the whole, most of the more expensive shops were sur-prised by the briskness of their trade after the rationing of clothes started. They had expected a lull during the first few days while the startled public sat at home and brooded over its coupons, but instead there was an immediate rush of shoppers, who were apparently going on the principle that they might as well buy the stuff while it was there to buy and before the government had time to think up any more restrictions. This artificial buoyancy didn't last long and the rate of purchasing soon fell off, though not too noticeably. Although the scheme hasn't been operating long enough for its full effects to be felt, it's obvious that the big stores are in a better position to stand the drought than the small shops are. If you take a walk down any London shopping street, you are likely to see shutters over the windows of dozens of modest businesses which struggled through the blitz but couldn't survive clothes-rationing.

October 19

Although Mr. Churchill refused—rightly, most people think —to arrange for a debate in the Commons on the Russian situation, this didn't stop the debate's taking place privately in British homes up and down the country. The protagonists have seemed to be divided roughly between those who feel that Britain hasn't sent enough help to Russia and those who argue that she couldn't possibly have sent more and that what precious stuff she has spared may be enough to delay the expected British push in the Middle East. It's a fact that not since Crete have there been such discussions and such general uneasiness.

Except for the Prime Minister himself, Lord Beaverbrook is the man who probably has the most solid backing of public confidence (barring the extreme Conservative element, which still regards him suspiciously as a terrible fellow), and his personal success in Moscow was heartening. All the same, to the average uninformed individual trying to make head or tail of the various communiqués and to figure out whether yesterday's denial was likely to become tomorrow's admission, the need seemed terrifyingly urgent and the help promised at the Kremlin conferences terrifyingly distant. Several newspapers, including the *Daily Telegraph,* took the line that it wasn't the public's rôle to reason why and that armchair strategists who were talking so blithely about the desirability of an invasion in the West were doing so irresponsibly and possibly harmfully. This provoked an acid retort from Beaverbrook's *Evening Standard,* which has been clamoring consistently for active help to Russia and which pointed out that the *Telegraph's* military expert had dropped a bad brick out of his own armchair on June 16th when he observed, "I cannot believe that even Stalin has any confidence in his armed forces." The *Times* was more moderate and conceded that "there is no need to despise these ideas" of how to aid Russia, adding that "some of them are held by very intelligent men and supported with cogent arguments." It decided, though, that the ideas were useless and confusing without knowledge of what was really going on.

Because this is just what nobody knows, not even those who might be expected to, the resulting frustration is acute and the public is carrying on like an angry prizefighter who wants to get up and slug somebody somewhere but can't because his manager is sitting on his head. The deduction that Whitehall had decided not to slug anyone anywhere at present was drawn unwillingly from Lord Halifax's surprising statement that Britain was not yet ready to invade the Continent, which turned out to be one of the biggest bricks dropped in or out of anyone's armchair.

Not without reason, the principal criticism of most thinking people is that the emotions of the moment are not being used as intelligently as they might be to get the public into a state of mind for fresh stringent sacrifices at home rather than for more immediately satisfying adventures abroad. The timid reluctance of those in authority to demand such sacrifices is felt to be uninspiring in a situation which could have all the invaluable emotional impetus of another Dunkirk. The same newspaper posters which recently announced new Russian losses soothed Londoners with the news that they were going to be allowed to draw bigger food rations, when a national poll would probably have shown that people would willingly eat less butter if it meant giving up more shipping space to guns. Even Mr. Churchill was disappointedly felt to have sounded a note which was less of a clarion call than a dinner bell in his recent promise that Britons would sit down to a better-stocked table this Christmas. To people occupied in wondering what sort of Christmas Moscow families would be celebrating, such talk seemed hardly the bleak request for further blood, sweat, and tears which most of them would have welcomed.

It's also a current criticism that although the conscription of women is being pushed along so fast that the thirty-one-year-olds will be registered by December and those up to fifty by spring, there are still too many young women notice-able behind the counters of big stores and in other unessen-tial positions. In an effort to get them into the factories, it has been announced that in the future only key shopgirls are to be exempt and that the whole schedule of reserved occu-pations for women is going to be drastically overhauled. Slow as the authorities seem to be in following through with call-up papers after registration, the new sweep is having the effect of making plenty of girls leap before they're pushed, so that they can have their own choice as to what particular form of national work they enter. The domestic-servant class, for one, has been noticeably affected. At the moment, house-wives who are lucky enough to have any kind of help are in the envied minority, their complacency slightly tempered by fear that some unscrupulous friend will come along and lure the cook to a rival kitchen with the promise of higher wages.

While everyone's thoughts were on the Battle for Moscow last week, a bloodless but spirited battle was being fought right here by the book trade. Several eminent publishers and printers sharpened their pens and charged into a rumpus over the new government restrictions on paper and binding materials. These shortages, combined with a dearth of skilled labor, are leading to a terrible situation in the pub-lishing business. People are reading as they have never read before (Hatchards, the bookseller in Piccadilly, says that it has had its best season in years), but few new books are com-ing out now and thousands of old books were destroyed in the air raids. There is an increasing demand for technical works to meet the needs of training machine workers, R.A.F. apprentices, and others, and it appears that the tighter ra-tioning of publishers' materials will mean a future shortage of texts of this kind as well as of the unessential novel.

When the new restrictions were announced, Mr. J. H. Blackwood, of the old publishing firm of Blackwood & Sons, snorted that although the legitimate book-making trade was being strangled, there was still apparently plenty of paper for the Civil Service to maintain its "overwhelming flood of government forms of all descriptions." Another plaint came from one of the masters at Marlborough College, who drew attention to the severe shortage of schoolbooks. "When the booksellers inform us, as they have done, that they cannot supply a French grammar or even (incredible as it sounds) an Oxford 'Milton,'" he said mournfully, "matters are come to a pretty pass."

November 2

These long, strangely quiet nights are giving everybody plenty of time for talking. If they were less quiet, the talk which is going around at the moment might well be less noisy. If London were still being blitzed, the ordinary individual might at least be cheered to know that he was taking a share of the punishment and not just gloomily reading how the Russians were taking it. Meanwhile, the general dislike of a situation which is of nobody's choosing, however much it's Whitehall's dismal necessity, is causing high words in public and private among all sections of the population. More practically, it has caused the rich to dig down into their pocketbooks for the Red Cross Aid to Russia Fund, which is sponsored by Mrs. Churchill and has a list of subscribers headed by the King and Queen and Queen Mary. Those in more modest circumstances have had to content themselves with digging into their storerooms for old magazines and love letters in response to Lord Beaverbrook's appeal for a hundred thousand tons of wastepaper to convert into shell casings for Russia.

Apparently, the increasing number of letters to the newspapers, which mostly begin in the vein of "Sir, it would be folly to ignore the fact that there is a growing sense of uneasiness, etc.," finally convinced the authorities that the public needed to be made to feel it was contributing personally to Russia's aid. When the clarion call at last came, however, it was found to be an invitation to a paper chase instead of an order to get in line for a munition-factory job. Various embittered people living outside the urban areas pointed out that they had collected their wastepaper months back, when there was a similar drive for salvage, and that it was still sitting right at home waiting to be collected. There was also a wail from scholars who had visions of priceless records being destroyed in the holocaust and urged that professional spotters be employed to snatch a possible contemporary Pepys or Fanny Burney from the salvage bins. Probably the funniest reaction came from certain government departments, which complained with dignity that the fuss about over-verbose official forms was unnecessary, since it was the invariable practice to turn these back into pulp after they had served their purpose, thus implying that it is patriotic to waste as much paper as possible in order to make more wastepaper for Lord Beaverbrook.

November 11

Although there's still plenty of private and public discussion about the efficiency of Britain's current assistance to Russia and the timidity of the government's policy at home, the shouting for a military diversion in the West seems to have died down. At a recent North Country workers' conference in Manchester, where delegates met to listen to Lord Beaverbrook and discuss the problem of production with him afterward, it was noted that no one raised the subject of a second front, although this was an audience to which the question of achieving the maximum Anglo-Soviet collaboration must have been an especially vital one. At the moment, the last shred of hope that England will try an invasion in the West would appear to have vanished, probably because it is sensibly realized that while actions may speak louder than words, production figures speak louder than either.

Instead, public expectancy is turning in another direction. Stalin's recent broadcast reference to the imminent creation of a second front was thought to have great importance here, and it doesn't require the forecasts of currently popular astrologers—whose daily newspaper columns of predictions about the war are eagerly read by the public and periodically denounced with fury by their more seriously minded colleagues—to convince the layman that Britain's belligerent star is due to rise shortly in the Middle East. Because of the fresh focussing of attention toward that part of the world, General Wavell's candid admissions about his miscalculation in the Cyrenaica campaign in Libya were naturally read with much interest. Unlike the Gort dispatches, which sketched the portrait of a commander who felt that his rôle wasn't to reason why but to do or die with whatever the War Office saw fit to send him, the Libyan revelations showed Wavell reasoning why, all right, but reasoning a month too late. Britons hope to goodness that whenever and wherever the new showdown comes, this dismal sort of postmortem on the part of the High Command won't again be necessary.

Among thoughtful people of all sections of the population and all shades of political coloring, anxiety continues over Britain's use of the four months which have gone by since Russia was invaded. Lately, however, the general feeling has seemed to be more cheerful, for a variety of reasons. The Stalin speech, coinciding with Goebbels' gloomy article in *Das Reich,* contributed a note of encouragement, which was backed up by Mr. Churchill's speech at the Mansion House on the occasion of the annual change of Lord Mayors. Although the Prime Minister has been speaking recently to workers in Sheffield, the Tyneside, and Hull, this was his first major utterance in public for some time, and Londoners found it heartening. The humble millions who couldn't actually sit down with the bigwigs at the Lord Mayor's lunch table that day were able to enjoy, without any cards of admission, the traditional pageant, which they weren't treated to last year and which it's in their bones to love. They got a fine show of marching men and women, of the skirling pipes and blaring brasses of seven military bands, of the King taking the salute at Buckingham Palace, and of both the new and the old Lord Mayors in their cocked hats and furred robes taking it outside St. Paul's. The outgoing Mayor, Sir George Wilkinson, was described by one journalist as "a wistful figure," because he didn't get his rightful show last year at the start of his term of office, London at that time having been more preoccupied with digging its citizens out of debris than with squeezing them to death in cheering crowds on the sidewalks.

The fact that the City was still there for anyone to march through this year is undoubtedly due to the members of the Civil Defense contingents in the procession, who must have had their own grimly reminiscent thoughts as they passed along Cheapside, Queen Victoria Street, and the strange, silent deserts which the excavators have scooped out around St. Paul's Churchyard. Those who agree with Mr. J. B. Priestley that the dullness of ordinary wartime existence is one of the chief problems which those in authority have yet to tackle imaginatively probably felt that, for a starter, it wouldn't be a bad idea to treat Londoners more often to this kind of combination of thumping good martial music and a view of marching men.

Lord Beaverbrook's paper chase continues in its effort to collect wastepaper for munitions and, as one journal mournfully observed, for all the "other infernal uses to which man can now put the material which enabled Shakespeare and Milton to express their thoughts." Recent restrictions have forbidden the use of more than ten posters to advertise any one entertainment, as well as the manufacture of cleansing tissues, of paper handkerchiefs, and of permanent-wave sachets made of wood pulp. In view of the Board of Trade's refusal of an appeal to make handkerchiefs ration-coupon-free as a safeguard to public health during the common-cold season, it would seem that the nation will have to wipe its nose on its sleeve this winter. Another order which has just come into force rules out the use by shops of wrapping paper for any purchase except food, so string bags will soon be as common in the grander shopping streets as they have always been among the public which spends its money at coster stalls. Christmas cards are among the types of stationery which the new restrictions affect. This Christmas, if Britons have the amiable impulse to wish each other the compliments of such a particularly murderous season of peace on earth and mercy mild, they will have to do it with pictures of robins and frosted Yule logs that are already in stock, for from now on not a single Yule log will come off the presses.

November 30

The first public reaction to the news of the joining of the Libya battle seemed to be one of unqualified relief. Finally, after all the uneasy months of discussion and speculation, a British army was facing a German army—not, to be sure, on a European battlefield, which Stalin would have found more useful, but at least apparently not at a disadvantage. It was this last point which seemed to go slap to people's heads. There was such welcome novelty in the absence of the usual apologetic newspaper editorials, which have so often pointed out that, although greatly outnumbered in men and material, the British forces could be relied upon to give a good account of themselves. This time, the papers exultantly went to the other extreme and more or less implied that since the R.A.F. had control of the air, the Eighth Army of the ground, and the Navy of the sea, the battle would be in the bag within a week at the latest. Unfortunately, this impression was backed up by the statements from the Cairo General Headquarters and by the Prime Minister's comparison of the struggle with a sea battle in which "all may be settled one way or the other in the course of perhaps two hours."

When it became obvious that this one was not going to be

settled for a great many hours and when the papers suddenly started talking about a tough struggle still ahead, the sense of letdown was inevitable and painful. Britons somewhat justifiably grumbled that a little less official flag-waving at the start might have been a better idea. Before long, most people were suffering from the depressed hangover which follows early elation. Although the news of the recapture of Rostov raised their spirits, there was grave anxiety over the general Russian situation, which is obviously far more critical than the Libyan campaign. Even if the decisive desert battle, when it comes, does end in a success, it won't greatly ease things for the Soviet, observers here seem to feel, unless the British are able to keep going and not stop until they're in southern Italy.

Mr. Churchill recently gave his blessing to a remarkable French-language periodical called *La France Libre,* which celebrated its first anniversary to the accompaniment of a shower of good wishes and of generous praise from its fellow-reviews, like the *Nation* and *Nineteenth Century.* Its editor, André Labarthe, used to be a well-known journalist in France and also taught science at the Sorbonne. He started up here, with little official encouragement, on credit given him by a friendly printer. Now his review has the largest circulation of any periodical of its kind in Great Britain. Although it's in French, not more than ten per cent of its twenty-two thousand subscribers are French, according to Labarthe, who has just completed an arrangement whereby he will send copy to the States by air mail and have an American edition printed in New York. The current anniversary number contains contributions from Dr. Beneš, General de Gaulle, and General Sikorski, besides a letter from the Prime Minister which contains at least one unmistakable bit of Churchillian phrasing. "On the soil of England," Mr. Churchill writes, *"La France Libre* keeps the bright flame alive for that sure coming day when all good Frenchmen will once again be free to think and write the truth as they see it."

December 14

Events of the past week have been so closely packed and the emotional pressure has been so intense that items of news which at most times would have made headlines for days, such as General Cunningham's retirement from the Libyan command, were received with practically no comment. On Monday, December 8th, London felt as it did at the beginning of the war. Newsdealers stood on the corners handing out papers as steadily and automatically as if they were husking corn; people bought copies on the way out to lunch and again on the way back, just in case a late edition might have sneaked up on them with some fresher news. Suddenly and soberly, this little island was remembering its vast and sprawling possessions of Empire. It seemed as though every person one met had a son in Singapore or a daughter in Rangoon; every post office was jammed with anxious crowds finding out about cable rates to Hong Kong, Kuala Lumpur, or Penang.

The initial shock and anger resulting from the Sunday-evening radio announcement of the Japanese attack on the United States were terrific, but comfort was taken in the assumption that these early blows would be returned with interest at the earliest opportunity. When nothing happened except new and harder hitting from the Japanese, there was gloom which culminated in the stunned silence that met Wednesday's news of the loss of the *Prince of Wales* and the *Repulse*. For sheer mass misery, this was probably England's blackest day since the collapse of France. The satisfaction over the arrival at Singapore of the Prince of Wales with her consorts was still so recent that her loss seemed at first almost incredible. It was as if some enormously powerful and valuable watchdog which had been going to keep burglars away from the house had been shot while exercising in the front yard. The big battleship's disappearance made the landscape look so menacing that British spirits, which always react better to disaster than to triumph, promptly rose to a new high pitch of belligerence. This found immediate outlet in angry questions as to how the *Prince of Wales* disaster had been allowed to happen in the first place. Mr. Churchill's preliminary statement to the House of Commons didn't stop people from asking why capital ships had been given inadequate air support or from concluding bitterly that liaison between the services is something which democracies learn slowly and at hideous cost as they go along, while the Axis strategists cut their teeth on it.

Because most people's store of excitement had been used up on the entrance of Japan into the war and the events surrounding it, the United States' declaration of war on Germany and Italy was received quietly. There was little outward jubilation over an event which every intelligent Briton has been quite frankly praying for ever since it became evident that, for all the fine phrases, something more than the tools was going to be necessary before there could be a possibility of finishing the job.

At the Savoy on Monday night, the American correspondents had everybody worked up to slapping backs and singing "O say, can you see . . ." On Thursday night, there was little emotion and no singing. Instead, there was a feeling that the war was going to be tougher from now on, that it would certainly be longer than people had expected, and that this country and America may easily have to take some knocks which will make the loss of a couple of capital ships seem like chicken feed. As a start to the expected toughness, the blitzes are expected to open up here again at any moment, following the return of German bombers from the winter-clogged Russian front. While waiting for this to happen, Londoners have found homely reading in what sparse news there has been of the first American blackouts and false air-raid alarms.

In spite of the sickening wallops which the democracies have taken at the beginning of this latest phase of the war, the general mood is confident.

December 21

For feelings, it was a mixed week in London. Counter-bal-
ancing gloom over the Pacific situation, the really good news
from Libya at last seemed to justify the premature and
much-criticized chirpiness of the famous Cairo spokesman,
whom Mr. Churchill recently defended with a characteristic
impetuosity reported to have drawn "indulgent smiles" from
his listeners in the House. Above all, the news from the Russian front continued to be of such incredible goodness that
someone suggested inserting the word "from" in the middle
of the "Aid Russia" slogan on the flags which appeared in
English buttonholes a few days ago. The realization that this
and not the Middle and Far East is the front upon which the
Germans could lose the war seemed to have sunk well into
the public consciousness. All sorts of rumors were going
around London of an Allied grand alliance of strategy which
would shortly and dramatically be brought out of the bag.
The necessity for something of the sort was among the subjects scheduled for secret debate in the Commons.

Also down to be discussed in the same manner was the loss
of the *Prince of Wales* and the *Repulse*. Though it's unlikely that any statement will be issued to the public about
this tragic setback, which has already altered the British sea-
scape in the East to an extent that has prompted observers to
recall France's temporary naval domination in 1781, there's
no doubt how people in millions of British homes have interpreted the sinkings for themselves. The anger over the
loss of those two ships has had a furious, personal quality.
The ordinary Briton's criticism of the action leading to the
disaster has not been softened, either, by the attempt to justify Admiral Phillips' judgment in deciding that he didn't
need an aerial escort because the weather was overcast, an
explanation which has led cynics to hope the High Command isn't banking on the chance that the Germans will

pick a rainy day for an invasion of this island. Those who think precious capital ships should be assured of a slightly more lethal umbrella than a cumulus were also noticeably unassuaged by the speech of the First Lord of the Admiralty, who remarked that lack of air support had not prevented the Fleet from taking men out of Greece, Crete, and Dunkirk, "although at great loss." It had been hoped that those three occasions might have provided the experiences which would make large sacrifices a less inevitable part of future actions, and the discovery that this was not so has been a profoundly shaking experience for a people to whom faith in the Navy is part of their faith in life.

The wholesale reshuffle of American commands in the Pacific brought but slight comfort to the British, who, occupied as they have been with their own naval tragedy, could only feel that the neighbors were having their upsets, too. Echoes of American criticism of unpreparedness at Pearl Harbor at least had a mitigating effect upon the susceptibilities of Englishmen, who were good and tired of hearing that, whatever happened, it was always the British who weren't ready for it. To find that others were just as fallible was not altogether unsoothing, human nature being what it is, though people wish glumly that the demonstration hadn't come off at quite such a dangerous moment.

There was nothing mixed, unhappily, about feelings in regard to the Far East news; all were of deep anxiety. The fall of Penang had been expected but nevertheless came as a nasty shock, and there seems to be no great optimism that Hong Kong will turn out to be a second Tobruk. The uneasiness was increased by the now open and grave references in the press to the approaching danger to Singapore, a place which relatively few Englishmen have ever seen, although so many of their hopes and fears are centred on it. Relatively few Englishmen had ever seen the *Prince of Wales,* for that matter, and the public now feels that Singapore is a sort of geographical *Prince of Wales*—something impregnable, by all the rules, though these rules may turn out to be unreliable in the end. No one felt particularly cheered by the unfortunate remark of Sir Shenton Thomas, Governor of British Malaya, that "things hadn't gone as well as they had hoped" there because of Thailand's throwing in the towel. All that sensible people could think was that Malayan defenses must be in a pretty queer state if a force of thirty-six thousand inadequately equipped Thailand troops strung out along a vast frontier had been really reckoned as an effective barrier to the Japanese advance. Air Chief Marshal Brooke-Popham was hardly the most popular Englishman, either, having said of the Far East in October, "We are in a position to handle any situation that may arise." His handling of the situation which has arisen in December has made an anxious public at home wish to goodness that those in high places would stop issuing cock-a-hoop predictions without first crossing their fingers and looking twice at the defenses of their air fields. The scandal over the lack of foresight in this respect is expected to leave as many casualties as the Pearl Harbor explosions did in the American command.

With so much to worry about, it doesn't feel much like Christmas to the adult population of this island. In the last day or two, however, the familiar fever has got under way, and the shopping streets have been crowded with people who, however much Singapore is graven on their hearts, carry on their brows the unmistakable lines of anguished worrying over what to give Aunt Ethel. They have been lucky if all they have had to carry were lines on their foreheads, since the shops require customers to take away their purchases, and this, coupled with a lack of wrapping paper, has made most shoppers look like harassed and cruelly overloaded camels. Enterprising gift hunters have been toting suitcases around with them, and the resulting casualties among the young in crowded stores prompted a *Times* reporter to remark, "Many people have discovered how large a proportion of small children are in height just about suitcase level."

Any children who survive the perils of these expeditions are going to have to do with fewer toys this year, since they are scarce and expensive. So are adult gifts, such as handbags, for which no coupons are needed. The gift which every Briton would like best would be news of a resounding Allied slapback at the enemy in the Pacific. Seasonably enough, their anxious attention is turned to the East, where they still hope that their country has wise men to direct their affairs and good shepherds to watch by night and by day over their great heritage.

December 28

Because of the well-known Axis predilection for staging coups on days devoted normally to Christian peace and quiet, most people here approached the Christmas holiday with the feeling that it might very likely be ticked off in red on the Hitlerian calendar. Having filled the children's stockings, parents retired to bed, leaving their flashlights and warm clothing extra handy in case something noiser than a herald angel should drop in, and families gathered around their radios on Christmas morning expecting to hear a new tale of aggression mixed in with the carols.

Hitler's taking over of the German High Command was looked upon here as a tipoff that the mystical prow of the *Herrenvolk's* destiny was going to be turned in a new direction. Just what that direction may be is the problem which press and public are busy trying to solve at the moment, and it is devoutly hoped that the Allied intelligence services have their own information, which will enable them to dispense with the usual chorus of astonishment over yet another caddish surprise offensive. Half the papers seem to think that the Eastern Mediterranean will see Hitler's début as an active Napoleon. The other half has been prudently guarding against any possible holiday relaxation of vigilance by prophesying that an immediate invasion of this country was the nut which Hitler's generals had jibed at cracking.

Whatever their individual fancies, people were not inclined to repeat the old error of viewing the latest Nazi reshuffle as a desperate last move which would turn out well for the British. The idea of Hitler as a crazy, Chaplinesque commander who would quickly blunder toward disaster isn't so popular as it was before some of those supposedly crazy notions of his proved pretty sound after all. The cautious general feeling has seemed to be that the last-minute new casting looked like an admission of embarrassment on the part of the management, but it would be a mistake to pass judgment on the show before the curtain went up. Since Hitler was never a slow worker, most Britons expect to hear the warning bell even before they've taken down the Christmas decorations.

There was nothing cautious, however, about the feeling that the news of the Prime Minister's arrival in Washington was good news, word of which came as a surprise to the majority of Londoners. The secret had been better kept than the story of his journey to the Atlantic rendezvous, which was leaking around the town long before it broke in the papers. Those in modest working-class homes seemed particularly pleased by the latest development. They were disappointed by the Atlantic Charter, which they regarded as a lot of incomprehensible words their Premier had had to go a dickens of a way to formulate; now that the second series of discussions is being conducted on dry land, they hope for some correspondingly more solid outcome, which they will be able really to get their teeth into. Mr. Churchill's speech to Congress and his warm reception were heard by millions of Britons, who sat beaming by their radios, feeling that old Winnie was doing them proud.

Last week, unhappily, nobody found anything to beam about in the Far Eastern war news, which was bad and was openly expected to become worse. Mr. Churchill's promise that Singapore would be held brought only moderate comfort to an anxious public, whose Christmas had been saddened by the loss of Hong Kong. There was relief, however, over the removal of Air Marshal Sir Robert Brooke-Popham as Commander-in-Chief of the British forces in the Far East. Of his successor, Sir Henry Pownall, little is generally known, but plenty of truly perturbed Britons can only pray that the incoming Commander-in-Chief may prove a little slower on the verbal trigger and a little faster everywhere else than the disastrously chatty outgoing one was. It wasn't exactly cheering to people who for months have been handed a complacent line of talk about Singapore's impregnable defenses to learn that those defenses had serious gaps or to read the wails of the Malayan authorities that their nice plans for a scorched-earth policy had been spoiled by the suddenness of the unsporting Japanese attack.

To date, the most graphic account of the Malayan fighting has been sent back by a *Times* correspondent, whose dispatch read something like a "Jungle Book" account of a conflict between puzzled elephants and tribes of agile, inventive monkeys. "If they [the Japanese] come up against heavy opposition," the correspondent wrote indignantly, "they make no attempt to launch a frontal assault but creep round and attack from a flank. Similarly, when our troops advance, the enemy disappears into the jungle on either side."

Many on this island had personal anxieties to pile on top of last week's grave public ones. There were individual uncertainties concerning the fate of friends and relatives in Malaya and Hong Kong; moreover, the fate of incomes derived from rubber and tin-mining industries in the East were distinctly tottering in the balance. The chairman of the Ayer Hitam Tin Dredging Company expressed the latter situation with admirable moderation when he observed at the annual general meeting of shareholders in the firm, "It is hardly necessary to add that recent events must adversely affect production at the mine." Recent events are also going to affect adversely the production of corsets, fly swatters, tobacco pouches, garden hose, rubber bones for dogs, and golf tees, the manufacture of which will be prohibited by an order of the Ministry of Supply, effective next Monday. Motor tires, already at a premium, will be more difficult than ever to obtain because of what is happening in Malaya. Those who were fortunate or foresighted enough to salt away a couple of spares are looking a good deal happier than motorists who are running on faith and old retreads.

1942

January 4

LONDON felt that its nicest New Year present had been popped into its pocket by the Commandos. The news of the two successful Norwegian raids was better than a case of Mumm to the spirits of those multitudes who have believed, with Admiral Sir Roger Keyes, that a series of brisk, small-scale operations would be well within the scope of accomplishment and excellent in effect. The death of the Admiral's son, Colonel Keyes, in the Commando action in Libya added a tragic footnote to the success story for which the public had been waiting so long. The raids themselves seemed like a timely footnote to Mr. Churchill's Ottawa speech, with its promise of a roughhouse for anyone who wanted it. Before delighted Londoners had finished chuckling their appreciation of this attitude, invasion barges scraping on Norwegian beaches supplied proof of its earnestness.

Although the enthusiasm over the steadily good news from the Russian and Libyan fronts remained high, the principal feeling last week was one of anxiety over the steadily bad news from the Pacific. General Wavell's new appointment raised spirits over the weekend, because the majority of civilians look upon him as a talisman and believe things will go better now that he is taking charge. However, his colleague, General Hutton, the new Commander-in-Chief in Burma, raised gooseflesh by reputedly saying on his arrival there that he was confident that with the forces at his command he could defeat any aggression. This sounded so like one of the remarks which the ex-Commander-in-Chief in Malaya was in the habit of throwing off that sensitive Britons crossed their fingers and shuddered.

At the moment, there seems to be a definite attempt by the press to switch the public from thinking about Singapore to thinking about Rangoon, possibly because it's certain that the Burma Road will have to be held and it's not nearly so certain that Singapore, even if held, will not be rendered more or less ineffectual as a key defense point. This is an idea which will deal a crushing blow to proud British notions of prestige and sentiment, but the fall of Hong Kong has already made people wonder whether prestige and sentiment are not expensive luxuries in such a crisis. Naturally, there was emotion over the courage and fortitude of Hong Kong's defenders against hopeless odds, but the fact that those odds were plainly hopeless long before the fighting began has given rise to the reflection that if the forces and equipment locked up there had been employed elsewhere, Penang and the vital airfields of Kota Bharu and Victoria Point might still be in British hands. With so many scattered and precious eggs to keep an eye on, lots of anxious people were feeling last week that it might be best to go against the proverb and pick out one basket to put the lot into. That basket, informed opinion seemed to hold, may be in Burma rather than Malaya.

Meanwhile, the immediate lesson, which to the ordinary individual sticks out a mile as a result of the fighting in Malaya, is the life-or-death importance of effective airfield defense. Public concern on this count has swelled so enormously that there's no longer even an attempt at polite acceptance of the usual official assurances that the defense plans for Great Britain are going ahead nicely. The same assurances unfortunately were part of the all-too-recent official handouts in Malaya, where things are now seen to be going ahead nicely for nobody but the Japs. Those who think that the plans of the new German Commander-in-Chief certainly include an attempt at an invasion of Britain sometime in the next few months would like rather more positive evidence than this sort of talk that Penang and Kota Bharu won't be repeated disastrously one day in Lincolnshire and Sussex.

January 11

The Houses of Lords and Commons in their Thursday debate on the war situation sounded pretty much like most British homes at the moment—anxious, highly critical, and just plain wrathful. Londoners were pleased to hear that a noble Lord had upped and called Air Chief Marshal Brooke-Popham a nincompoop, a polite version of what they have been calling him in private. They were not so pleased, however, by the dexterity with which Mr. Attlee, standing in for the Prime Minister, avoided committing himself or anybody else in a statement which, as the *Times* dryly commented next morning, "could scarcely have been more economical of information." The questions which everybody is asking were put back on ice, presumably to be dealt with by Mr. Churchill on his return. It's hoped that they will then be answered as fully as possible within the limits of national safety; if they're not, many people expect a major blowup of public and Parliamentary indignation. Canberra is not the only worried capital in the Empire by a long chalk. Londoners react superbly to disaster, but they, no less than the Australians, would like to know whether the current disasters couldn't have been avoided and to be reassured that they won't happen again. At the moment, the British feel that neither information nor assurance is forthcoming.

About the outcome of the war, there are no doubts; about the immediate present, there are unfortunately plenty. Enthusiasm over the President's stupendous armament program and the Russian successes couldn't quite make the public forget that its own troops were falling back day by day in Malaya and that a monkey wrench, officially described as bad weather, had been slipped somewhere into the Libyan works. To the thousands of retired eastern administrators who in Cheltenham or Tunbridge Wells now lord it over half an acre of garden and a detached villa called Darjeeling or The Peak, the loss of ground in the East is not so tragic as is the loss of prestige. Ground can be recovered, but those same former servants of the Empire fear that the prestige of the British Raj, which they and their fathers have tended in years of lonely exile, is taking a sickening wallop. There is now open apprehension that there will be more and harder wallops to follow before Wavell is likely to be able to pull anybody's chestnuts out of the fire. Those who know Singapore have been looking grave over the possibility of blood perhaps proving thicker but less precious than water in the community's defense. It was thirst that ended the resistance of Hong Kong, and old-timers from Malaya fear that Singapore, most of whose water is piped over from Johore, may find itself in no better shape to withstand a long siege.

Mr. Attlee made the public a present of one bit of good news on Thursday, which was the information that something was at last being done about training a special branch of the R.A.F. for the defense of airfields. The general relief at this was tempered by the exasperated wish that experience had filtered the lesson into official skulls a trifle earlier. Quite ordinary people grumble that they have been alive to the danger ever since Crete. Meanwhile, they hope that Hitler won't mind holding off the invasion until the new airfield force is ready to cope with it. The name of the director general in charge of the force, Major General Liardet, was unknown to the majority of the public. His home village remembers him as a cheerful, energetic man and a great hand at producing local amateur theatricals. Behind the scenes, he was once responsible for a good deal of the success of the yearly military spectacle, the Aldershot Tattoo. Maybe this is a happy omen, as it suggests exactly that dramatic instinct and flair for handling large masses of men and material in which British military organizers have so often and so disconcertingly seemed to be deficient.

January 25

The English public, already sufficiently confused by the spectacle of the Japanese rising sun sending ever more trenchant beams over that empire on which a benign British sun was supposed never to set, has been further fogged during the past week by the contradictory antics of the press. Some of the papers declared with apparent authority that the Prime Minister, as soon as he had finished hanging up his hat, was going to celebrate his return by a big reshuffle of the Cabinet and would probably replace Lord Halifax at Washington with Sir Archibald Sinclair, the Secretary of State for Air. Readers of other journals got for their pennyworth the statement, from what purported to be equally authoritative souces, that nothing of the kind was contemplated. At the moment, the glum general feeling seems to be that the second prophecy is the authentic one. Mr. Churchill's attitude of hostility to criticism has perplexed and chilled the millions of his devoted followers who still think back to the days when he was the noblest and hardest-hitting critic of them all. Distaste for naming individual scapegoats, the excuse put out in some quarters for making no changes in the present administration, has had a bad public—and a worse private—reception. The mistakes of the past, people say, can take care of themselves; what the public is interested in is grounds for confidence that Mr. Churchill's team is going to be better equipped to take care of the future. At the moment, that confidence simply doesn't exist, and the valuable impetus which a fresh start would give hangs fire, wasting time, money, and hope.

Behind the worried gentlemen in Parliament, who will be able to air their uneasiness in a three-day war debate, are the worried ordinary people, whose concern must remain unvocal. These people are accustomed to weigh the news by simple, everyday standards of success and failure. By all the

rules for running a home, a business, or an empire, readjustment would seem to be necessary. By all the signs, it won't
be forthcoming without a struggle. This is adding anger to
the profound disturbance with which the public is watching
the growing threat to Mr. Kipling's Empire, an empire
which, now that the "dominion over palm and pine" seems
to be so palpably wobbling, has suddenly become a reality to
lots of Englishmen who hitherto had hardly credited it with
existence outside of the Wembley Exhibition. Most Londoners seem to accept without resignation the bitter probability
that Singapore will be rendered useless strategically, even if
it doesn't actually fall. What with the weekend accumulation
of bad news from Australia, Malaya, Burma, and Libya, even
the magnificent Russian successes couldn't lift the prevailing
gloom.

Maybe Mr. Churchill's eloquence, when it comes, will succeed as it has succeeded before. This time, however, there
appears to be a real and urgent demand that, in addition
to the golden words of which he is master, he give valuable
new blood its golden opportunity. It would be nice to think
that the Prime Minister was going to concede the need for
this as gracefully as he did the rejection of a proposal that he
broadcast his speeches direct from the House. The inexplicable system of having him repeat on the air an obviously
weary version of his big addresses to the House has never
been satisfactory to himself or to his audiences, and the decision to continue it may have pleased M.P.'s but certainly
didn't please the nation. The objection that right honourable gentlemen's objections might obtrude on the air and that
regular broadcasts from Parliament might cause members to
address their radio public rather than the Speaker didn't
make up for the general disappointment. With the invigorating impact of the Washington and Ottawa speeches fresh in
their minds, people felt that if they couldn't have first-run
Churchill, they'd rather just read the thing in the evening
paper.

One of the minor local repercussions of the monotonous
British retreat in Malaya is the sudden difficulty of buying

anything made of rubber. Recent arctic weather, which bogged railway travel in the north, burst pipes in houses left empty by evacuated families, and turned remote country-sides into beautiful but hopelessly marooned fairylands, set prudent people to thinking about buying a new hot-water bottle and giving the old one to the salvage-rubber department of the Ministry of Supply. This proved to be such a universal notion that harassed drugstores were soon hanging out signs reading, "No more hot-water bottles." Before long, other things, such as shoes with crêpe-rubber soles, are going to be collectors' pieces, and motorcars may well be on the same list if something isn't done soon about rubber reclamation and the manufacture of the synthetic article. Tea is another small trimming of civilian life which, it is mournfully expected, the bad news from the East will finally affect.

January 31

Now that the tumult and the shouting of the war debate has died, people are beginning, metaphorically speaking, to take their own temperatures and ask themselves if they are feeling any better. On the whole, it does seem as though those three days of hearing their anxieties aired have done the British good, though not all the good they hoped. On Tuesday, as office crowds went to get some lunch, they heard newsdealers shouting that the Prime Minister's statement was out. "Cheerful Charlie, ain't 'e?" was the comment of one particularly hoarse cockney to his companion as he jerked his thumb toward a poster on which a newsie had chalked up "Churchill says bad news and worse to come." The cockney didn't sound displeased, however. Most Britons enjoy a fight and a good fighter, and the Prime Minister had turned in a display of pugilistics that was practically faultless. Seemingly, the House, though dazzled, wasn't knocked completely groggy, judging by the hard hitting that went on in the ensuing debate. One of the speeches, which impressed moderate people because it summed up excellently what they are feeling and fearing, came from Sir John Wardlaw-Milne, a Conservative member of high standing, who didn't mince his words in what he had to say about military strategy abroad and production efforts at home. A strange feature of the proceedings was the apparent reluctance, in the course of all the talk about unsatisfactory Ministers, to name them. The landslide vote of confidence was expected; nine out of ten ordinary Englishmen would have voted the same way if they could have squeezed into the lobby with the critics.

This isn't to say that Parliamentary or public uneasiness has subsided. Totting up what has been gained by the debate, worried citizens note that they have been given a Minister of Production, which is a somewhat vague answer to the clamor for an Imperial War Cabinet, and a promise that the House's criticisms will be considered with an open mind. In spite of the Prime Minister's admission that he felt the burden of office weighing heavily upon him, the desired shifting of some of the load onto other shoulders was not mentioned. As for getting rid of those deadweight colleagues, whom loyalty apparently prevents him from dumping, someone suggested in a letter to the *Times* that those colleagues, since they must realize that nobody's confidence dwells with them, should do the gentlemanly thing and dump themselves. On the whole, the only clear point which has come out of the debate is that nobody can envisage being led to victory by anyone except Mr. Churchill, who will lead them, he has made it equally clear, only at his own pace and by the route he considers best. With that, at the moment, it would appear the public must be content.

There's very little else in the news, unfortunately, that is contributing to local contentment. One of the few bright spots was the arrival of the American troops in Ulster, which cheered people here enormously, not least the Canadian troops, who were hopeful that the new garrison would eventually release some of them for action. The news of the Japanese naval losses in the Strait of Macassar was also heartening, and there's mounting admiration for the Dutch, who

wasted no breath telling the world that they were ready for
anything but realistically set about proving it. Except for
these items and the new Russian successes, the British public
has had nothing but gloomy reading. There is no getting
away from the fact that the Libyan setback has been a bitter
blow. This hasn't been softened by the newspaper reporting
of the campaign, which started off by having Rommel tied
up and pretty well annihilated every other day; then spoke
indignantly of bad weather, as though the elements had un-
sportingly put an obstacle exclusively in the way of the British; and finally trotted out the old one about "superior
forces of the enemy," which bewildered Britons had supposed was for once a boot on the other foot. The sad general
conclusion to be drawn from all this seems to be that history
is again repeating itself, with Auchinleck standing in for
Wavell in this year's revival.

An immediate local effect of the serious events in the East
has been a tightening up along the food front, including rationing of cereals and dried fruits. Those who have the difficult job of shopping for a family find that the pinch of shortages has both more and less acute moments, of which this
would seem to be one of the more acute ones. Milk rationing, under which adults are allowed only two pints a week,
has probably been the biggest hardship to date, and there
was considerable glumness over the recent announcement
that it would be continued, with but a slight increase in the
quota, through the summer. The Food Ministry has been
flooded with letters, including one supposedly from a kitten,
who plaintively announced that he caught mice for the government and hoped Lord Woolton would see his way clear
to allowing him his little saucerful. In the country, the milk
shortage has brought about a boom in goats, which appeal to
people who haven't got the space or the nerve necessary to
tackle a cow but who trustingly imagine that a goat is a
handy sort of animal which keeps the lawn neat and practically milks itself. Country folk, who before the war were accustomed to paying perhaps thirty shillings for a nice nanny,
are scandalized by the way rusticating Londoners, intent on

insuring milk puddings for the children, are now scrambling to acquire the same creatures at around twelve pounds.

There is unfortunately no clearing up of the unhappiness over the news from the Pacific, where General MacArthur's magnificent stand has provided the only note of cheer. It is generally accepted by raging retired sahibs, who know what the fall of Singapore would mean to British prestige in the East, as well as by Englishmen who have never got nearer to the place than seeing its name on a can of pineapple, that the naval base has been lost and that the continued Japanese assault there is only a matter of stealing the belatedly locked stable in addition to the horse. Having conceded this severe loss, the public is turning its concern to the possibility of holding Burma and Java, and is debating once again what new unpleasantness spring will offer. Plenty of people now think that an invasion of this island is unlikely, while others feel that, however badly the war may be going for Germany, Hitler will risk everything to bring off such a desperate last move. Those who anticipate an invasion weren't particularly encouraged by the peer who recently recommended that pikes be issued to the Home Guard. They were handy things, he said, though he didn't specify how handy they'd be against a tommy gun.

February 14

This is one of the bad moments in English history. It may also be a bad moment in the political history of the man who has more power here than any individual has wielded since Cromwell. As always in a crisis, the English have had a sudden spurt of un-English chattiness. When London was being bombed, total strangers loosened up and plunged into conversation with a sense of relief. Now that there's again the feeling of acute national danger, there is an unprecedented amount of discussion going on among people who seem ready to air their anger and anxiety to anyone who will listen. Maybe discussion isn't the word, since all the talking arrives at approximately the same conclusion. From what is being said in every bus and train and on every street corner, from the conversations of bewildered yokels in country pubs and of equally bewildered ex-Empire administrators in London clubs, it is obvious that millions who a short time back wouldn't have dreamed of criticizing Mr. Churchill are now openly criticizing him.

This reluctant change has been brought about by what is happening to English power and prestige abroad, by what isn't happening in the directing of the war at home, and by Mr. Churchill's supporters' sad suspicion that he has set the tone for military leaders who are in the habit of issuing optimistic statements which subsequent events don't justify. His promises that Singapore would be held and that Rommel's forces would be destroyed haven't helped the public to view with equanimity the ignominious British retreats in Malaya and Libya. You hear people say that they have always trusted him in the past because they knew that he would let them have the truth, however unpalatable; now there's an uneasy suspicion that fine oratory may sometimes carry away the orator as well as his audience. You also hear people say that anyway they've had enough of fine oratory; what they would like is action and a sign from Mr. Churchill that he understands the profoundly worried temper of the country.

Up to now, no such sign has been forthcoming. The perfect fusion of spirit between leader and led which won the Battle of Britain has been allowed to lapse, leaving Britons feeling like naughty children being scolded by an irate headmaster for daring to criticize his staff. From all the bitter comment and hasty judgments, all the shock and alarm of England's blackest week since Dunkirk, one fact stands out, however: there are few people either in Westminster or the country at large who would like to see Mr. Churchill fall, partly because it is obvious that there is no alternative to hoist in his stead and partly because of the unshaken conviction that he has all the great English qualities which the British want in a leader, as well as the few great English fail-ings which they don't. What the general feeling seems to boil down to is that Britons don't intend to lose Mr. Churchill, but they don't intend to lose the war either. From the grave plain speaking of press and public it is evident that nothing but a fresh start will convince the English that they're on the right road to win it. That fresh start should certainly include a change of ministers and the setting up of the less hampered and unwieldy War Cabinet for which there has long been agitation.

[*February* 11–12, *the German battleships Scharnhorst and Gneisenau and other ships left Brest and escaped to Kiel.*]

Coming on top of the tragic news from Singapore, the bad news from Libya and Burma, and the good news from nowhere, the incredible happenings in the Strait of Dover were the straw that finally broke the public's capacity for bearing disaster. The waters of the Channel closed over unlimited British pride as well as over forty-two British planes on Thursday, when dwellers in Kent heard the guns and wondered if the invasion had come at last. "If we had got the *Scharnhorst*," was the gloomy general comment, "it would have been something." What the people did get proved to be almost as much of a moral knockout as the loss of the *Prince of Wales* and the *Repulse*. The Air Ministry's explanations didn't do much to soothe the galling realization that the Germans had strolled right past Britain's front yard in broad daylight and cocked a snook in at the open window. Most people felt that wormwood had been added to gall by the discovery that the strollers, despite the R.A.F.'s repeated expenditures of bombs, machines, and lives over Brest, were still in good enough shape for such a promenade.

The whole episode has started up old questions, which this time, it is felt, someone will have to answer satisfactorily. There's increasing doubt as to the wisdom of relying largely, as the High Command is known to rely, on the heavy bomber as a weapon for winning the war, but above all the Channel failure is making people ask more in anger than in sorrow why there should be sporadic boasting about an increasing liaison between the Army, Navy, and Air Force when it's pitifully evident that liaison, as the Germans know it, hasn't even begun.

Among the uncertainties of the last dark days, the only voice that has seemed to make sense to the harassed public has been that of Sir Stafford Cripps, whose radio talk the other evening inspired one cartoonist to depict him as Disney's Jiminy Cricket. Certainly Sir Stafford only said what all thinking Britons' consciences have long been telling them when he commented on the dangers of taking the attitude that it's all right to settle back into a spectator's seat and let Russia get on with the war. This was the kind of straight talking which people have long and in vain hoped to hear from the Prime Minister. What Sir Stafford said confirmed the growing feeling that the Russian news, which has been London's one solid comfort in the daily accumulation of disappointments, may soon make more anxious reading. Because it's obvious that in such an event the help which British factories can send Russia will be vital, Mr. Churchill's recent outline of the duties of the new Minister of Production was received with a chilly lack of enthusiasm both inside and outside of Parliament. It seemed to most observers that the new lineup was only a rehash which was no better and might even be slightly worse than the old one, since it depends for smooth working on the complete coöperation of Lord Beaverbrook, controlling material, and Mr. Bevin, controlling labor. The hopes of a fruitful outcome from this marriage of minds don't at the moment appear to be particularly rosy. As one commentator dubiously put it, "We can only trust that grace will be bestowed on both of them."

February 20

Although it had been regarded as inevitable, the fall of Singapore sounded to Britons something like an earth-shaking rehearsal for Judgment Day. Maybe it really was a sort of judgment day on the lack of prevision, the absence of dynamic planning, and the sahib mentality which made the supposedly impregnable fortress a pushover for the first determined nation that came along. While millions of words were being spilled on paper to explain the defeat, simple and pious Englishmen who took their troubles to church that morning may have felt that the Psalm for the day summed up the situation adequately with the nine words "The proud are robbed, they have slept their sleep." Everything one has heard since then, both in public and in private, seems to show a grim national determination to end that sleep before the rest of the world mistakes it for *rigor mortis.* Because the British character does best when stimulated by anger, the current feeling over the loss of possessions, prestige, and trained manpower is probably a good thing. Anger saved the day when France fell and, later, when the bombs fell.

By postponing the debate on the conduct of the war until next week, the Prime Minister indicated that he thought Parliamentary discontent might cool off by then. However, it is likely that the Members at Westminster, and certain that the worried men and women they represent, will still be in a mood to ask searching questions, not so much about what wasn't done in the past as about what's going to be done in the future. The Battle of Singapore is over. The Battles of Burma, of Java, and of Australia are to come. What has been going on right here and what has resulted in the hoped-for reconstructed and strengthened War Cabinet is the Battle of Winston Churchill. In a single session of the House of Commons the Premier was twice called a Führer, once by Conservative Lord Winterton and once by Communist Mr. Gallacher, without a peep of protest being raised by the newspapers next morning. Actually, what seemed to emerge from the recent government crisis was a picture of the difficulties encountered by Mr. Churchill in trying to be at once a Führer and not a Führer and to turn a democracy

into an efficient totalitarian state while retaining the democratic rights of free speech and free press.

What intelligent people of all classes wanted to be rid of
was the suspicion that party considerations and personal loyalties might be hanging a millstone around the neck of the
war effort. The hope of the worried little man everywhere
—the patient, good-humored citizen in a bowler hat who
pays his taxes, builds his air-raid shelter, grumbles, suffers,
and is the best willing-horse material in the world—is that
the big man at the top has given the all-out signal to go
which won an earlier battle when informed opinion in many
quarters said that it was lost. The loss of Malaya has already
had disastrous effects on thousands of British lives. Not only
large fortunes have crashed with it but smaller incomes de-
riving from life savings put back into the East by elderly
former planters and businessmen out there. Many a villa at
Cheltenham or any of the other English spas of the comfortably retired now finds itself facing ruin.

Difficulties of communication have naturally sharpened
anxiety. Most of the big London firms which once operated
in Malaya have been without word from their planters or of
their estates. The Colonial Office and the department of the
Red Cross which handles inquiries about missing people
have been jammed by anxious relatives hopeful for news.
There has been none to give them, and judging by the scarcity of information so far received from Hong Kong, it is
likely to be many heartbreaking weeks before any gets
through. On the Monday after Singapore fell, it seemed that
every Londoner one talked to either had a friend or relative
on the island or knew someone who had. It also seemed that
there was a general realistic acceptance of a longer, harder
war, which, even if it doesn't make its full bloody horror felt
here (and many people think that the expected spring offensive may be switched to England), will certainly make Britons look back upon the last two years as a dream of luxury
and easy living. The cut in the basic petrol ration was just a
start, it is believed, of further stringent civilian disciplining

to come. Because of the grave turn of events, no one would be surprised and many would be pleased to see that basic ration cut to nothing for all except those with some very good reason for motoring.

Whether or not radio listeners were unusually sensitive this week, the B.B.C. got into hot water again over its reporting of the unhappy *Scharnhorst-Gneisenau* episode. People have been complaining that the way in which this news was presented made the whole thing sound more like a triumphant R.A.F. exploit than what it undoubtedly was—a shocking British disappointment. The sensible public isn't taken in for a minute by any soft-pedalling of bad tidings. What it is in the mood to hear, because this is what it believes to be true at the moment, is that things are bad, that it will likely be a long time before they'll get any better, and that nothing but the undivided effort of every man and woman in this country will decide whether the proud are to go on sleeping or wake up and beat hell out of the robber.

March 1

Disasters sometimes accomplish quickly what the slow will of the people, bent on the same results, can't achieve in months. It took a Singapore to bring about the remodeling of the War Cabinet and the shifting of unpopular ministers for which the country had been hoping for so long. Maybe Mr. Churchill bowed to the public's opinion; more probably he had changed his own somewhere in the stormy passage of the last black days in Malaya. On the whole, people seem inclined to feel truly thankful for what they have received in the recent shakeup, though there's a sensible reservation of enthusiasm over the shift of men until it can be seen whether the new ones mean shifts of policy and administration too. The profoundly concerned and critically disposed public doesn't suppose that, just because the old roof has been patched up at the top, all the supporting structure has necessarily been made sound, but the general mood is certainly more hopeful than it was.

Some of the names in the new administration were practically unknown to the average citizen until last week. For instance, to most Britons the appointment of Sir James Grigg to head the War Office was totally unexpected, and they weren't displeased by a vigorous press campaign which assured them of his toughness, bluffness, and lack of compunction about kicking brasshat inefficiency all over the lot whenever he encountered it. Since these are also the much-publicized qualities attributed to Lord Beaverbrook, maybe the Grigg buildup was intended to console people for the dropping of the short-lived Ministry of Production, which surprised everybody. The appointment of Lord Cranborne to the Colonial Office was popular. One of the younger statesmen of the Eden school, he has a reputation for integrity and courage, characteristics that he demonstrated in his first speech as Minister to the House of Lords, in which he frankly admitted that the quick collapse of Singapore was as staggering a shock to the government as it was to the man in the street. Nowhere, it is ruefully conceded, are such ventilating powers more needed than in the dusty depths of the Colonial Office, which the recent disastrous events have brought into critical daylight.

While the present dreary post-mortem over Malaya is in progress, there is fresh hope that the problem of India is at last going to be tackled with imagination, and before it's too late. Few intelligent Britons think that postwar Asia will settle down into the cozy old pattern of Empire, with mad dogs and Englishmen in sole enjoyment of the midday sun. How realistically Britain intends to coöperate in the new pattern may be indicated by the declaration of Indian policy which Mr. Churchill is expected to make this coming week.

Because of the concessions which the Prime Minister made to the general uproar of dissatisfaction, there was little noise over his decision to go on doubling in the rôle of Minister of Defense.

In all the talk in every kind of circle, and especially

among the fighting services themselves, there seems to be the same desire for even a token showing of the spirit of initiative which is envied as well as admired in the Russian achievements. Friday's parachute raid on France may have been only a small straw in the wind, but it was the best-looking straw that vastly cheered Britons had seen for some time. People are eager, too, as those at the top until recently have apparently failed or been too timid to realize, for a more toughly waged war on the home front as well as elsewhere. The readiness to be told unpalatable facts was pointed up by the tremendous enthusiasm over the elevation to the Cabinet of Sir Stafford Cripps, who doesn't hesitate to deal them out without any polite shilly-shallying and whose appointment raised cheers even from sections of the press and public which previously might have been expected to fight shy of the former stormy petrel of the Labour Party.

The hold that Sir Stafford has obtained over the popular imagination, largely on the strength of two successful years in Moscow and two first-rate speeches since his return, is an extraordinary one. Here, people seem to feel, is a man who is capable of asking them for blood, sweat, and tears, not impersonally at some unspecified date but as a personal contribution to be delivered immediately. His austere opening speech as leader of the Commons, in which he insisted that all extravagances and popular amusements, such as dog racing and boxing matches, should be drastically curtailed, sounded just the note the public needed. His remarks about boxing matches were a result of the rumpus over a recent bout at the Albert Hall which forty-five hundred people took time out from the war to attend. Plenty of critics would like to see horse racing put on ice for the remainder of the war, too, since race meetings mean a large gathering of cars and cars eat petrol; it's also felt that the seven hundred and twenty-seven horses in training in England today eat up fodder which could be more usefully diverted to increasing the milk supply. Other measures which have been suggested lately are a severe rationing of tobacco and alcohol, further reduction of the sale of cosmetics, and the prohibition of the serving of any meal costing more than five shillings.

Britain seems to suspect that until she has been geared to a more Spartan way of living her outsides won't look right to the Russians and, what's more, that her insides won't feel right to the British. That Spartan living, like it or not, is plainly indicated for the future was the unmistakable message which emerged from the Prime Minister's alarming announcement of the jump in shipping losses—the gloomiest item in a week of gloomy news. The Director of Mining Supplies has prophesied that food for pit ponies is going to run short and urges feeding them straw-pulp silage. The public has been asked to overcome its prejudice against eating eels, which are to be more extensively caught and marketed, and to try washing clothes in the peasant French manner, with wood ash and water instead of soap. A priest has suggested that, to save precious metal, brass name plates might be left off coffins. Even the dead, it appears, will be asked to go short in the long, hard siege which the living now know is just ahead of them.

March 8

The government crisis is over, but the public uneasiness which brought it to a head hasn't abated noticeably. Last week's final tidying up of loose Ministerial ends was greeted with cheers by no one and even with a few sniffs from the press, which pointed out that a government that had introduced only ten new faces in the course of seventeen changes —and those mostly belonging to relatively unimportant undersecretaries—couldn't be said to have reconstructed itself along particularly dynamic lines.

Anyway, the public was in no mood for cheering, what with the news from the East going rapidly from worse to plain awful. It had been hoped that Java had been selected as the last ditch where the Japanese tour of aggrandizement might be checked—that tour which, like the itinerary of a prewar pleasure cruise, has already stopped over in Malaya for the picturesque rubber plantations and tin mines, and in Sumatra for the oil fields, and which is expected to look in shortly at Trincomalee and Port Darwin for the fine view that can be got from the harbors. By this weekend, hopes of delaying the tourists in Java longer than the Tokio timetable allowed hadn't quite gone but they weren't exactly rosy. Universal admiration for the Dutch has been accompanied by bitter regrets that more couldn't have been done to help them.

The abrupt announcement of complete Japanese air supremacy over Java only heightened the extremely critical frame of mind in which the public had followed Wednesday's debate on the R.A.F. in an equally critically disposed House of Commons. Recent events have badly shaken the ordinary individual's confidence, not in the personnel or tactical efficiency of the Air Force but in the directing of general air strategy and supply. Naturally, all the questions couldn't be answered in public, but it is felt that the lengthy statement by the Air Secretary, Sir Archibald Sinclair, didn't completely settle the urgent one of the moment. Angry Britons can't figure out why, with an immense air force here to draw on, British troops should again and again have been forced to fall back in the East for lack of air support. It has been suggested that the success of General MacArthur's surprise attack on enemy shipping shows what brave men can do with only limited material resources, provided they're led by someone who fights with his head, and not a thick head, either. People think that if the Malayan campaign had thrown up only a few proofs of an equally resourceful spirit, its nature might have been entirely altered. It is certain that they would be feeling a good deal less sensitive about the whole sad business than they are at the moment. As a footnote to the current anxiety, a correspondence has been going on in the *Times* between scholastic gentlemen who have been arguing whether the upper-class public-school education and its insistence on character rather than intelligence haven't been responsible for the thuds of empire builders going down for the count instead of building, and whether, if Waterloo was won on the playing fields of Eton, Singapore wasn't lost in its classrooms.

Plenty of people consider that a lot of education in self-denial is certainly going to be necessary for everyone before it can be said that the war is being won in the parlors and kitchens of Britain. Among the intelligent of all classes, who feel that something is wrong, though they can't tell what, there's a real and almost pathetic desire for a drastic tightening up in the daily war effort. The recent order that service uniforms and civilian utility clothing are to be cut with new economical skimpiness was a step in the right direction. However, Englishmen of limited means, who are going to be the chief consumers of these utility garments, would probably be even better pleased with the regulated single-breasted, pleatless suitings they're to get if they didn't know that the wealthier spenders can still order clothes regulated by nothing but the depth of their pocketbooks. Similarly, there was no grumbling about the hints of new rationing restrictions, which are regarded as a necessary outcome of the recent bad news, but the bulk of the population, always ready to pull in its belt without complaint, is reasonably resentful of the continued ability of the few to order an expensive meal in a restaurant that probably maintains the standard of its menu by means of back-door dickerings with the black market.

To date, the courts have been disappointingly lenient toward black-market racketeers, though the exasperated mood of the country as a whole is probably nearer to that of the irascible Labour M.P. who at intervals during the Parliamentary debate on the subject spluttered that his way of dealing with such gentry would be to put them up against a wall. The *Daily Express* has turned itself into an unofficial OGPU to expose the black market and, promising strict secrecy, has invited its readers to write in and tip it off about neighbors who may have bootleg hams in the attic and tins of petrol buried in the herbaceous border. One of the suggestions put forward during the food debate in Parliament was that a maximum price be fixed for all restaurant meals and that all luxury hotels be taken over and turned into clubs for the armed forces. If adopted, this is likely to add to the difficulty of finding accommodations in London, which is already fierce. Hotels and clubs are packed; flats which during the blitz period stood like gaunt and deserted cliff dwellings now have waiting lists of would-be tenants. So many of the big blocks of flats have been taken over by government departments that war workers in search of a small furnished apartment either can't find one or, if they can, are confronted with rents so steep that some sort of control seems indicated in the future.

March 15

Nothing which has happened so far to British power and possessions has produced quite the emotional rage and shock that were sensed when it was learned what had happened to British subjects in Hong Kong. Many people think it was late in the day to be shocked, considering the awful lessons which Nanking offered and which the Western democracies viewed with cynical indifference. For their indifference those democracies are certainly doing penance during this Lenten season of loss and discipline. Hong Kong destroyed with one brutal blow the complacent British notion that a Japanese soldier might conceivably rape and murder a Chinese woman but would be bound to behave toward an English lady with the circumspection of a *Bushido* Galahad. Maybe the distress of the discovery, coupled with the new torture of wondering what was happening to friends and relatives in Singapore and Java, will be all to the good if it succeeds in injecting a stiff shot of hatred into the sluggish national bloodstream. Many of the papers seem to feel there's a danger that in remembering Hong Kong people may forget Poland and get the idea that in contrast to the Japanese the

Germans are nice and humane. The public has been urged to drive into its head the difficult notion that smoking Polish villages could one day be duplicated, complete down to the last dangling yokel, in Kent and Sussex hamlets.

What with all this news in addition to concern over Australia and Ceylon and the final announcement of the heavy naval losses in the battle off Java, it's been a black week. Because of the public mood, it was probably a good week in which to introduce the expected new disciplinary measures affecting civilian life, such as the curtailment of horse and dog racing, the denial of gasoline to pleasure drivers after June, and the introduction of the wheat-meal loaf, which must take the place of white bread on April 6th. Lots of Britons felt that they'd gladly keep their bets in their pockets, walk their shoes through, and eat black bread if doing so would help to wipe some of the Hong Kong debt off the slate. The only grumbling seemed to be that, after two and a half years of war, these first timid attempts to put the nation on a proper war footing were a bit late. The restriction of greyhound racing to Saturday only will mean that Londoners will have a choice of eighteen meetings on the same afternoon; however, it's expected that when double summer time comes in, some of the tracks may switch to evening racing. Horse racing is restricted to five courses—Newmarket, Windsor, Salisbury, Stockton, and Pontefract.

The disappearance of gasoline will certainly put a crimp in the currently prosperous second-hand-car market, which has been doing a fine business in low-horsepower cars that are economical to run. The gasoline order has already cast a chill on people who live in remote country districts, who rely entirely on the family Morris for such necessary chores as taking the children to school and fetching home household supplies which tradespeople haven't got enough gas to deliver, and who hope to goodness that the government will give their plight the sympathetic consideration they've been promised.

The same isolated country dwellers heaved the loudest sighs of relief when a new interpretation of the hoarding

order was issued the other day in answer to agitated inquiries from housewives who weren't sure whether the state of
their supply cupboards rated official congratulation or a jail
sentence. The Ministry of Food's previous reluctance to
come right out and say what constituted the week's supply of
food it permits and the recent whacking fines imposed in
test cases had been worrying many. Those who live far from
shops and had obediently stocked up during the various invasion crises, so that they would be self-sufficient whatever
happened, have been gazing nervously at their tins and wondering how such reserves would strike a food inspector. The
answer, just made public, is that a reasonable accumulation
is all right provided it's "legally acquired." "The prudent
and honest housewife," the paternal official dictum reads,
"has nothing to worry about"—which sounds pretty nice in
times like these.

March 22

Without reservation, the British seemed to feel that the best
news of the week and of several weeks past was the appointment of General MacArthur and his arrival in Australia.
The universal chorus of enthusiasm, both public and private, was a nice reply to the propaganda the Germans have
been putting on the air for some time in the hope of chilling
British homes with the notion that Downing Street is now
answerable to the White House and that Britain is coming
more and more under the domination of the United States.
Millions of British homes remained comfortably unchilled
by Australia's eager welcome to the new commander and by
Mr. Curtin's request that the Pacific War Council be located
in Washington rather than in London. The thought is realistically accepted here that, regardless of the sentiment
involved—if, indeed, any sentiment has managed to survive
the recent gruelling tests of bitterness and criticism—
common sense must inevitably swing Australia toward the

young rather than the old country for support at this stage of the war.

What lots of anxious people in the old country can only regard as highly unfortunate is the current triangle situation which has developed because of Mr. Churchill's decision, so irksome to Mr. Curtin, that Mr. Casey would be more useful in the Middle East than as Australian Minister to the United States. This has created a setup similar to the old one of the daughter who resents what looks like maternal interference and accuses the old girl of having stolen her best beau. It's feared that, with family relations on the strained side anyhow, the latest crop of misunderstandings, however honestly arrived at, won't exactly have conciliatory effects.

The MacArthur appointment so cheered London that an alarmed press had to rush and point out that it was too early to be talking of tides turning and that the job the General now had on his hands was roughly comparable to defending the British Isles with a force only big enough to make an impressive showing on the little Isle of Wight. The public, which has the notion fondly implanted in its mind that the General can't spell the word "defend," didn't seem to share this concern; it is inclined to think that MacArthur and not Foch was responsible for the saying "My right has been rolled up, my left has been driven back, my centre has been smashed. I have ordered an advance from all directions." That, to people fed up with parrying blows instead of giving them, sounds pretty much like what they want to hear.

The press itself has made news in various ways this past week. The shortage of newsprint resulted in fewer papers on the stands and readers have been urged to go back to the Victorian custom of sharing their copies with neighbors. Those with a partiality for the *Daily Mirror* were faced with the possibility that they might soon find themselves without a copy to lend to anyone when the Home Secretary came out with a plain warning in the House of Commons that the paper would join the *Daily Worker* in the outer darkness of suppression if it didn't mend its caustic manners fairly quickly. The parentage of the *Mirror* is an old mystery which the House proceedings failed to clear up, although a Socialist member asked, bang-out, who owned it and a Conservative member twice suggested, without getting an answering bite, that Hearst was at least a parent.

Orphan though the *Mirror* may be, it didn't lack powerful champions to jump in and declare that while its way of presenting the news might depress half the public and enrage the other half, the country would suffer a defeat indeed if the cherished freedom of the press to speak its mind were imperilled. The *Mirror's* colleagues in Fleet Street have rallied round and accused the Home Secretary of threatening to use an emergency regulation which was framed only for use in an invasion. Every degree of journalistic opinion has been heard in the ensuing rumpus, from a dignified reproof in the *Times* to the dictum of Beaverbrook's *Express* that "the purpose of this war is to enable every man to be able to speak his mind and pray to his god" and the *Mirror's* own breathless editorial sentence: "If we are called defeatist, unpatriotic, irresponsible, and dangerous, it is manifestly useless to defend outselves against those who have succeeded in convincing themselves that we have the monopoly of a sort of criminality in criticism."

The big local news of the week, however, was not concerned so much with paper as with coal, which is finally to be rationed, together with gas and electricity. Coal is a very grave problem indeed, which the coming summer will have to settle; otherwise, vital industries are going to be pinched and a vast number of Britons are going to have the problem settled for them by an epidemic of pneumonia next winter. The chief reasons given for the paradoxical shortage of what Britain so abundantly possesses are difficulties of transport and the drafting into other industries and the Army of some seventy thousand of the youngest and huskiest coal hewers. It is being urged that the miners who are now in the forces should be released to meet the emergency, but a House of Commons debate on the subject seemed to show that the trouble goes deeper than the draft. There is the old bitter conflict between the miners and the owners, in which the minors are now alleging that they are being exposed to additional fatigue and danger and, what's more, that the public is getting inferior coal palmed off on it by the practice some owners have of working only the poorest seams and so keeping the more fertile seams for the days of unlimited profits they expect after the war. Leftists insist that such ugly evils can be knocked on the head only by a complete nationalization of the industry, which they believe would result in stepping up the morale of the mine workers. Lots of people besides Leftists honestly believe that it is about time some use was made of the powers to conscript private property which were voted way back in the bad days of 1940.

April 5

Over Easter, the big subject of discussion was naturally the chances of success of the Cripps mission to India. Though informed opinion has been dubious from the beginning, uninformed opinion has continued to cling to its belief that Sir Stafford is a miracle worker who will somehow pull an acceptable solution out of the bag. At the moment, the attitude of the press, which started out hopeful and then became despondent, is back to hopeful again on the strength of Wavell's visit to New Delhi. There's a good deal of sympathy toward the Indian desire to have a leading say in defense matters, but no one seems to feel that this particular horse can change riders in midstream at such a dangerous moment without giving the parties who are watching from the bank a chance to nip in and take advantage. Britons can merely pray that the Indian leaders will realize that with the Japanese sitting in the Andamans, Chandra Bose in Germany, and the situation in Burma not so good, this is no moment for arguing whether there are to be two men on the horse or only one.

[*March 28, naval installation at St. Nazaire, France, raided by British Commandos.*]

The invasion season is officially due to open on April 15th, after which date people wishing to take a trip to the East or the South Coast must consult the police before setting out, but lots of Britons are wondering hopefully whether offensive action isn't going to originate on this side of the Channel instead of the other. The St. Nazaire action raised spirits wonderfully because it was considered possibly a sample of the shape of things to come, but not until after a nasty period of suspense during which the papers were unadroitly allowed to publish the German communiqué alleging complete failure without any accompanying British statement of success.

Last Sunday was militantly observed by a crowd of some thirty thousand people, who packed around Nelson's Column to hear speakers of every shade of political coloring declare that England expected a second front to be opened up this year. An orator in a Home Guard uniform got the biggest response of the proceedings when he inquired whether it was reasonable for the uninformed public, however much it wanted a second front, to try and tell the government and the High Command what they ought or ought not to do. The rousing answering shouts of "Yes!," though not quite the effect intended, must have carried nicely to nearby Whitehall and, it's hoped, reassuringly to far-off Moscow. The setup on that particular speaker's platform was a good illustration of a strong nationwide movement away from the traditional old party groupings of Tory, Liberal, and Labour —a movement which is becoming more and more evident in British political life. As the great formula of Empire is rearranging itself or being ruthlessly rearranged in new patterns every day, what is happening to domestic formulas is also of profound importance to the world of tomorrow.

April 19

The breakdown of the Cripps negotiations has resulted in some sad post-mortems this past week. Even though most people now say they felt all along that the case was an inoperable one, general disappointment over the outcome has been acute. The only cheering features, the public seems to feel, are that the sincerity of England's desire for a workable settlement of the India question is now established without a doubt and that she retires from the whole involved business with a great deal more kudos than she had when she went in. As for Sir Stafford, if he isn't exactly coming back as a conquering hero, he is nevertheless looked upon as a conquered hero who did nobly. What has been said of him in private has only echoed the praise which the Prime Minister expressed in the House of Commons on the day when he also had the less pleasant job of answering questions about the loss of the aircraft carrier *Hermes,* the cruisers *Dorsetshire* and *Cornwall,* and the Malayan peninsula. These funereal items received no floral tributes, unless one so classes Mr. Churchill's defense of the admiral responsible for the dispositions leading to the naval disasters, which all too vividly reminded the M.P.'s of the earlier and bigger losses off the Malayan coast. Because ordinary British people hope to goodness that nothing of this sort is ever again going to remind them of the loss of Singapore, there is considerable public uneasiness over the Prime Minister's flat refusal to hold a full inquiry into that catastrophe and untangle some of its unhappy lessons from the mass of accusations and counter-accusations and the evidence of heart-breaking, heroic muddle which must now be available.

The one lesson which, to the little man outside Westminster as well as to his representatives inside, seems to stick out a mile is the need for a united strategy and for creation of a great General Staff on the German model, headed by a commander-in-chief in supreme control over the land, sea, and air forces. Though this question had often been in the offing, it's now plumb in the foreground, placed there by an admirable article written by Sir Edward Grigg, former Undersecretary for War, and by powerful editorial support in the *Times,* which nowadays frequently supplies not only thunder but, surprisingly often, thunder on the left. Since the appointment of such a commander-in-chief would lessen Mr. Churchill's importance as Minister of Defense, it's likely that before long England will see a return performance of the recent set-to between Prime Minister, Parliament, and country, with a reorganized High Command as the prize this time instead of a reorganized War Cabinet.

April 26

In the spring a young or old Englishman's fancy lightly turns to thoughts of invasion, judging by the kind of talk which is going around at the moment. What makes the talk different from the invasion chat which circulated last spring is that this time it mostly concerns an English invasion of the Continent, although the press has hastened to point out that von Rundstedt's new troop dispositions may just as easily have an offensive significance as a defensive one and that it's quite in the cards that the Germans may be hustled into trying something here before anything drastic is tried out on them there. The general public, however, continues to be convinced that the strong daylight sweeps over France, the Commando reconnaissance trips, and the recent presence of General Marshall in London are all hopeful straws in a wind which may at any moment touch off a spark along one of the occupied coastlines.

This new optimistic feeling that something is up at last has sent spirits up too, after the doldrums of the long, disastrous winter. Because most of the English full-dress heavyweight expeditions of this war have turned out to be things about which the British prefer not to think, all hopes are now centred on the exciting new discovery of the old national talent for the brilliant impromptu, the type of piratical, sea-borne foray which has often studded and sometimes made English history. Millions of English, hardly less ardently than millions of French, Norwegians, and Dutch, are waiting for the day when the shock troops will drop in and won't drop out again—that day, in fact, which the civilians of St. Nazaire obviously thought had come. Right now there's a feeling that the day may be just around the corner.

May 9

News of the swift, smoothly running occupation of Madagascar, coupled with reports of United States naval successes, raised spirits here enormously. It was a heartening corrective to the universal regret over the fall of Corregidor and gloom over the situation in Burma, where the inevitable end now seems to be in sight. Worried Britons, who have felt that the Burmese failure was another example of the British strategists' disinclination to make up their minds which was going to be the most important basket to plump all their eggs into, were relieved to learn that there was nothing undecided about the operations in Madagascar. In its enthusiasm, the press slightly lost its head and gave hastily scratched together descriptions of what it variously referred to as the third, fourth, and fifth largest island in the world. "Whatever we do, something seems to go wrong with it," one Londoner remarked sardonically to his neighbor after reading that Madagascar had shrunk yet again.

The public's satisfaction was only slightly clouded by fears that, with Allied strength being more and more widely dispersed, a second front on the Continent might not be established in the near future, where popular hopes had placed it. The second front, with all its hows, wheres, and whens, is now the burning topic of conversation in every discussion of the war. What makes ordinary people feel that perhaps it isn't so far away is the increasing strength of the R.A.F. raids and the comparative feebleness of the German reprisals. Instead of the two hundred planes a night the Nazis used to send, twenty now appear, and it's a new and encouraging experience for country dwellers to hear bombers roaring over nightly and to know that in all probability they're heading for enemy territory, not for British cities. Naturally, there was sadness over the loss of life and of historic architecture in Bath and the cathedral cities, but the papers were fairly moderate in their indictment of the outrage, since they had only just finished candidly admitting that British bombs had made a considerable mess of the beautiful ancient buildings in Lübeck. The general feeling seemed to be that much as one might lament the disintegration of a gem of eighteenth-century English architecture, it was more sensible to reflect that Nash's elegant inspirations had served a good purpose as bait to draw more German bombers away from the Russian front. It is doubtful, however, whether the refugees from Bath whom one saw arriving in London last week, mostly frail and elderly people who had lost everything, were yet in the mood to appreciate such bracing arguments.

Since the Germans have announced their new cultural policy of visiting Britain with an open Baedeker propped above their bomb sights, residents of historic spots which haven't been picked on so far are feeling understandably apprehensive. A house next door to Anne Hathaway's cottage is today an uncomfortable liability, it seems, not a picturesque asset.

The clamor for a second front was mentioned a few days ago by Hugh Dalton, president of the Board of Trade, in a House of Commons debate on fuel rationing, which is still the principal local controversy. In defending the government's fuel-by-coupon scheme, he pointed out that people who are asking for an invasion of the Continent this year aren't thinking logically when they use their next breath to demand that thirty-five thousand miners, some of the huskiest fighting men in the British Army, be released from the forces and sent back into the pits. Arguments over the rationing plan have been intense. Ordinary householders naturally feel resentful that the government didn't do something about the problem long ago. The *Daily Express* has launched a campaign urging its readers to save heat and light voluntarily and so stun the government with the results that official action won't be necessary. A lady wrote to the *Times* to complain that, owing to Westminster Abbey's frugal use of its chandeliers, the twilight in Poets' Corner was so thick she couldn't tell whose distinguished dust she was treading underfoot.

When all the smoke attending this particular combustion has cleared away, it's likely that the rationing plan will be put into effect, firmly and swiftly, since the rate of coal production and the needs of expanding war industry are running a race which makes some form of drastic control a necessity. The fresh batch of coupons which this rationing will entail will certainly be a strain on the sanity of the housewife who has just learned that a ration book for candy would soon be part and parcel of the few pounds of assorted bits of paper which she now has to tote around with her on shopping expeditions. This was good news, however, to sugar-starved war workers, who haven't the time to queue up at candy counters with the more leisured customers. It has always been a strange and startling sight to see middle-aged Kensington matrons in fur coats standing grimly in line waiting for sixpennyworth of gumdrops, as though it were Biblical manna.

The past week has produced two speeches which sounded the same note: one by the Archbishop of Canterbury and the other by Sir Stafford Cripps. Both spoke of the better social order that would follow the war, with special stress on housing, nutrition, employment, and education. Such talk has often been heard before, but cynical Britons, who have quite a vivid memory of how the Utopian aftermath of the last war shaped up, haven't paid much attention. This time, the personalities of the speakers have made the ideas sound different. When the Primate of England and the man whom most people expect to see one day as Prime Minister both speak the same language of Christian Socialism, it sounds like a genuine happy augury for the millions on this island who would like to be clearer in their minds than they are as to what sort of world the boys are going to come marching home to.

May 24

While Parliament was gravely debating war strategy last week, most Britons, whether inside Westminster or out, were preoccupied with what was happening on the Russian battle fronts. All other news seemed pale before the crucial importance of this. The mood of the moment here is something like the impatience of a pugnacious fellow who feels that he's destined to hang around holding coats while the greatest fight in history is going on under his nose. The way the ordinary man is talking seems to indicate that politicians and editorial writers might as well save their breath to cool their porridge for all the good it's doing in cooling public opinion. It's apparently useless for them to point out that the R.A.F. is regularly battering Germany's production bases, that the steady stream of British war material to Russia continues at considerable sacrifice to this country, and that Britain is already fighting on three fronts—the Pacific, the Middle East, and the Atlantic. From the tone of private conversations and public utterances at mass meetings, it appears that the British people can't or won't recognize the existence of any substitute for a genuine, slap-up opening of a land offensive on the Continent. Although stern things have been said in the House of Commons about uninformed, emotional *vox populi* clamor, the same kind of clamor has demonstrated its power before now in this war by throwing Chamberlain out and bringing Churchill and Cripps in.

The prudent can only share the hope expressed by Hore-

Belisha, among others, that the new spirit of activism which is sweeping the country won't stampede the government into moving a man or a muscle before it is good and ready to do so. The government has certainly showed an extreme reluctance to be stampeded into a change of the war-planning machinery, and the recent two-day debate on the matter had a disappointingly flat flavor, possibly because a good deal of it boiled down to criticisms of the Prime Minister, who, by being absent on both days, gave the proceedings the pointless appearance of King Charles without his head. Members found themselves standing with their slingshots ready but no target in sight. What hitting there was turned out, generally speaking, to be of a pretty polite order, most of the attackers wrapping up their missiles so delicately that a more forthright naval gentleman rapped out with quarterdeck directness that he hoped to goodness they wouldn't have to see the Empire go down in a blaze of discretion.

Across the way, the Lords were mincing words a good deal less finely in what they had to say about the urgent necessity of investigating the authorities in London responsible for the Singapore disaster. The continuing resistance of the government to this demand has caused real uneasiness, since the public not unreasonably would like to feel assured that what has been wrong with the top layer of strategical planners is being corrected, so that it will be ready for a future test, which, it's felt, may not be so far away. Loyal old Savoyards who remember their "Mikado" can't very well be blamed for deducing, even though they're loyal old Churchillians as well, that there's a possible excess of Gilbert and Sullivan in a system which calls on the Minister of Defense to criticize plans which, as Chairman of the Chiefs of Staff Committee, he has helped to draw up.

The vital importance of the aid which Britain will be sending in one form or another to Russia this summer gives particular interest to a remarkable review of British war production just issued by Mass Observation, an organization which reports man-in-the-street reactions to social changes. The report, based on reactions collected between October and March, is a weighty affair covering every human aspect of war industry, from boss to worker, in about eighty firms in seven sample areas disguised by such names as Tanktown, Planetown, and War Village. The investigators found that roughly eight out of ten managing directors in big concerns were satisfied with war production and that about half the workers felt the efficiency level was pretty much all right. Things which may tip the scales one way or the other in the output of a factory were found to include the idiosyncrasies of the boss, the temper of the works manager, good or bad cooking in the canteen, the local bus service, and even the proportion of women workers married to soldiers. Women workers were bothered by the problem of shopping for their families, because they had found that most of the food was gone by the time they could get out of their overalls and reach for the market basket. (This situation has since been straightened out in some districts by the Women's Voluntary Services' scheme of collecting shopping lists and money from factory workers in the mornings and bringing back the required goods in the evenings.) People were reported to be getting less sleep than they did before the war, and over-sleeping was often given as a reason for absenteeism, which was discovered to be higher among women than among men. The report found that there was a general feeling of uneasiness among workers as to what shape the postwar economic world would take. The incentive of high wages is, it seems, surprisingly unimportant. "What the average worker wants more than a lot of money is a little security," the report sums up, and maybe that sums up nicely for the rest of us too.

Meanwhile, various large and small changes affecting ordinary English lives are either in the offing or have come into force during the past week. The prohibition on the manufacture of lace curtains, those primly drawn veils over a million suburban lives, will put a temporary crimp in the Nottingham lace industry. The battle for coal rationing has trailed off into an uneasy truce, in which there's still talk of nationalization of the industry. Milk rationing is to be called off altogether for the next few weeks, thanks to a spate of good grass-growing weather. Reports from the country say that crops are doing fine, too. English farmers, encouraged by Göring's recent gloomy estimate of the German harvest, think that even English soil is going to turn in something special in this critical summer of 1942.

June 20

This has been a bad week. Londoners getting off their buses and pouring into the tube at the evening rush hour every day seemed afraid to glance at the headlines, for developments in Libya had a way of getting graver with every edition. For the time being, public concern has naturally shifted from the critical Russian front to the Eighth Army's struggle. The current bad news from Libya hasn't actually caused as much of a shock as its predecessors, since by now everyone is pretty well primed to expect the tide of battle in those parts to be a dingdong affair, but even so, the seriousness of Rommel's new push toward Egypt has made a gloomy impression here.

It's possible, though, that the setback will prove a beneficial corrective to the alarming optimism which was in the air only a few weeks back, when everybody was talking as though a thousand planes were going to drop in on Germany every other night and a Continental invasion was as easy a jaunt as a prewar cheap-day trip to Dieppe. Though there seems to be less irresponsible shouting for a second front than there was, it is still generally hoped that this is the principal subject being discussed by Mr. Churchill during his visit to President Roosevelt. Londoners took the news of the Prime Minister's arrival in the United States more calmly than they did that of the Atlantic meeting and the first Washington hop. Those occasions seemed in themselves to make history; on this one, the British are engrossed in wondering what sort of history is going to be made by the decisions their Premier and his host arrive at.

Although the press and the people's minds were largely
taken up with what's happening in Libya, most of the newspapers this week assigned reporters to make the rounds of
eating places and learn the effect of the first few days of the
five-shilling-maximum meal order. The general opinion
seems to be that the order hasn't made much difference either to the state of a diner's stomach or to the total of his
bill, since the one feels and the other looks much the same,
thanks to the extra "overhead house charges" which most
good restaurants are permitted to make. Some establishments, which for one reason or another haven't been allowed
to make house charges, have stated quite frankly that they
intend to take the difference out of their customers on
wines, as the prices of these aren't under control. Anyone
who kicks will probably find that all the tables are reserved
when he makes a return visit. Even with such dodges, it is
likely that many small places which had kept up their standards and prices by a little black-market funny business will
be forced to close now that they've had to lower their tariffs.

The Food Minister's new discipline is generally approved,
however, as a step in the right direction in the gradual levelling process that is taking place day by day, not only in
Englishmen's pockets but in their minds. Another sign of
changes which will affect the old privileged orders was in the
news during the last week. In the House of Commons, the
president of the Board of Education mentioned the possibility that after the war the zealously guarded traditions of the
great public schools may be broken down to allow any
bright boy to enter, whether his father happens to be a peer
or a plumber, and that in such an event some measure of
state control will have to be introduced to compensate the
schools for what they lose on fees from parents. With taxes
strangling the rich so efficiently that they're having to dig
down into capital to keep even half a wing of the family seat
open, a lot of peers probably feel ruefully that their sons are
going to need state assistance to put them through Eton
every bit as much as the plumbers' sons will.

Londoners are beginning to get accustomed to the uniforms of American troops, who are now seen in ever-increasing numbers on the streets. Middle West and Southern accents are heard in the crowds as frequently as the French, Czech, Polish, and Norwegian which make a blackout saunter down Piccadilly a nostalgic Cook's tour.

July 5

The mood of the moment here can, alas, best be summed up in the disgruntled British wartime phrase "browned off." The most thorough browning off of Londoners since the fall of Singapore hasn't been reflected in any spectacular way. No anxious crowds have collected in Downing Street, and there have been few impassioned words except in Westminster. People go about their work and their amusements, queue up in the food shops, and buy their evening pennyworth of bad news from Egypt, all with complete surface calm. The average man, patiently and courageously getting on with the job while hoping to goodness that his leaders know theirs, has simply been conscious for the past grave week of a feeling of discomfort, like a sort of perpetual mental indigestion. Unfortunately, the remedy for this particular malady, which would be a socking British counterattack, doesn't yet seem to be at hand; on the contrary, the public, though hoping, naturally, to see Rommel's weekend troubles increase, shrewdly suspects that the press, by its series of brisk pronouncements that the fall of Alexandria would be serious but not disastrous, is trying to prepare people for fresh pangs right ahead.

Bewilderment has been the outstanding national emotion ever since Tobruk, which had come to stand for the unbreakable tenacity of man's spirit in the minds of all Britons, was taken with the seeming ease of shattering a child's toy fort. Astounded Britons, who couldn't believe their ears, realized with anger that they had only too readily believed their eyes, which had assured them, thanks to the newspapers, that everything was going well, that the British forces in Libya were superior in equipment to the enemy's, and that the R.A.F. had complete control of the air. If such was the case, reasons the average uninformed citizen, it is difficult to understand what suddenly overcame the fighting men, in whom the public still believes. The no-confidence debate in Parliament didn't throw light on what had or had not been done by individuals or committees here to make sure that the English troops had up-to-date sinews of steel as well as old-fashioned hearts of oak. As a means of assuring the rest of the world, and particularly the United States, that this family, though it couldn't be called happy at the moment, is at any rate sternly united, the overwhelming vote in Mr. Churchill's favor was certainly eloquent. Here at home it was possibly unnecessary, as the English are perfectly familiar with their own misleading habit of grousing about their leaders in the corner pub while remaining fully determined to fight behind those leaders to the last ditch.

Though the corner pubs have had their full quota of grousers, and though the question of whether the Premiership was in danger of passing to Cripps or Eden may have been raised at a few dinner tables, the threat of a major political shakeup no doubt looked more imminent from a distance than it really was. The bulk of the population, particularly in the loyal rural areas, which haven't time or patience for the loose political chatter of city folk, hoped that the Prime Minister would somehow be able to explain away the inexplicable. The speech of his leading critic, Sir John Wardlaw-Milne, lost in effectiveness because of its surprising suggestion that a present-day royal duke might, as did the Duke of York of the old nursery rhyme, march up a hill with ten thousand men rather than follow them at a discreet distance in a staff car full of brass hats. Judging by the reception of the House and the comments of the public, a nursery rhyme is just now the most likely place for such martial royal excursions.

What did emerge from the debate was the Prime Minister's insistence on retaining his office as Defense Minister. Although he suggested that the whole rumpus over this had

been artificially stimulated by the press, there's no doubt
that plenty of disturbed Britons feel, without any guidance,
that something is very wrong with the present setup. Now
that the current reverse has followed the already sadly familiar pattern laid down for all democratic reverses—military
disappointment, angry debate, sweeping vote of confidence
—the ordinary people can only trust that this one will differ
by being more profitable than earlier bitter educational experiences seem to have been.

The most heartening thing to the observer here during
the recent black days, which have also been saddened by the
fall of Sevastopol and made tense by waiting for the next
Egyptian communiqué, has been the behavior of the ordinary people themselves. What they have been through in the
last six months has been less noisy, perhaps, but no less wearing to the spirit and nerves than were the bad times of 1940,
when the bombs were falling. In the present ordeal, civilians
have had to listen to the monotonous falling of British arms
and strongholds abroad while being harassed at home by rising prices, dwindling business, increasing curtailment of lib-
erty and comfort, and anxiety about their menfolk overseas.
It's good, and to the Axis it should be profoundly discourag-
ing, that the public has refused to become defeatist even
under the impact of defeats that in a more excitable country
might have resulted in governments and heads being broken. On the morning after the news arrived that Tobruk was
lost, a seedy Londoner in a bus summed up the general
point of view nicely by saying to a crony, "I can't rightly see
at the moment exactly how we're going to win, but if anyone
told me we wasn't, I'd bust out larfing." This quiet and
dogged confidence in themselves which the people of England can feel at such a time is worth a good deal more than
all the votes counted at Westminster.

In these grave days, Londoners have been glad to be able
to find something to crack a smile, however grim, about. It
seems that some earnest fact-finding agency, keeping its
finger on the national pulse, saw fit to circulate a little
house-to-house questionnaire to find out the public's reac-

tions to the Army, which at best has never enjoyed the great
popular kudos bestowed upon the Air Force and the Navy.
One of the questions asked was whom the householders fancied as the outstanding general. Naturally, the agency meant
a British general, but a horribly large and candid proportion
of Britons picked up their pens and regretfully, though with
their countrymen's typical admiration for a first-class per-
former in any game, wrote "Rommel."

July 19

Londoners who have recently been dropping in at the Soviet
Exhibition in Piccadilly to see the handsome saddle bought
for Marshal Timoshenko with British subscriptions were
hoping last week that the sympathy of this country with the
Marshal's present struggle would soon be expressed in a
more acceptable form of leatherwork—the planting of British and American boots on occupied soil. Now that the
Egyptian news looks a little better and the Russian news a
lot worse, the Second Front is back once more as the primary
topic of private and public speculation. Whatever Whitehall
thinks and knows about the possibility of an Allied landing
in force during this critical summer, there's no mistaking
how the bulk of the population feels. Maybe this is one of
the times when the powerful uninformed instinct of a nation
is as valid as the informed caution of its military leaders.
     What instinct seems to be telling Englishmen right now,
to judge by what they're saying over the nice cup of tea in
the canteen and the half of bitter in the pub, is that next
year would certainly be better but it would almost certainly
also be too late. For at the bottom of English teacups last
week even people with no particular clairvoyant gift for
reading the leaves but with just ordinary ability to read a
map could make out the shape of ominous things to come if
the German thrust to the Volga should succeed in eliminat-
ing Russia as a striking force. Though the difficulties of getting a foothold across the water are apparent even to civil-

ians who would have trouble in getting a platoon across a road, it is also plain that the undertaking looks healthier now in many ways, however it might appear in a sober staff report, than it would after the release of the crack panzer divisions currently tied up near the Don.

Perhaps it's bluff and perhaps it isn't, but the press continues to drop hopeful hints that something is brewing. Since papers and politicians have been throwing out similar remarks for months and nothing has happened, the British public continues to fret, but this time there is a general belief that the situation is so urgent that the chiefs of staff may well be forced to improvise an entrance several pages ahead of their cue as they originally wrote the script. There's no disposition here to minimize what doing so would mean in fresh blood, tears, and sweat for the British people. Yet millions are hoping, as the summer days peel off the calendar, that the one will dawn before long when the guns will again be heard on the coast, telling England that danger has once more moved right into her front yard.

With the question of shipping so much in the news at the moment, the shipping debate was naturally Parliament's most important piece of business last week. The public was left in the dark about Parliament's findings, for a resolution to hold the debate in private session was adhered to in spite of Labour objections. Even in the absence of official figures to back up unofficial suspicions, shipping conditions are known to be so bad that there has been widespread approval of Mr. Churchill's appeal to American generosity to cut down on Bundles for Britain, so that precious space can be set aside for potential bundles from Britain—lethal ones this time. Although it is realized that detailed publication of shipping losses would give away information valuable to the enemy, lots of people think that the gravity of the situation could be hammered home a bit more forcefully to the public by placing more restrictions on food. There are said to be qualms in the government about the effect on civilian morale of any further cuts in the present perfectly adequate, if not bountiful, standard of living. The thing which members of the government are maybe too busy governing to find out is that the great, patient, courageous mass of British people who make up Britain's real strength will gladly pull in their belts till it hurts if by doing so they can bring a successful western offensive one second nearer.

So far they haven't been asked to do so. Lord Woolton is the only Minister about whom one rarely hears a grumble; some conscientious Britons feel that he does his job as purveyor to the national stomach perhaps a shade too well. Up to date, the only warning he has given of new austerities ahead is the threatened poultry-rationing plan, under which, because of the shortage of feed, the average household would be allowed to keep only one hen. (Another hen or so would be permitted in cases where a deal can be made with a poultryless family next door to trade eggs for table scraps, though ministerial advisers have not yet indicated how they expect to handle the appalling neighborly feuds that are certain to arise when the eggs don't divide up evenly.) Since Englishmen have so far been officially encouraged to become egg producers and have been doing so in large numbers, to the expensive tune of acquiring laying pullets at twenty-five shillings apiece, there is understandable consternation over the new order, which is scheduled to take effect in October. Country people will naturally be the chief sufferers, though henhouses frequently blossom in surprising places, such as London barrage-balloon sites and at least one rooftop in Grosvenor Square. No matter where, chicken owners say that they hope Lord Woolton will see his way clear to leaving them their birds and suggest that he save shipping space instead by a liberal rationing of bread, which is as yet unrationed and consequently, they claim, often wasted by the thoughtless.

August 16

In recent years, for some occult reason, Augusts have been months of more-than-usual suspense in England. This year is no exception. Once again, many people are looking anxiously toward the coming weeks and what they may bring, although the principal anxiety seems to be that they may not bring anything at all except a gradual deepening of the gravity of Russia's already desperate situation. So far, however, the counsel of the cautious, who consider that a second front at this point is impossible, appears to be heavily outweighing the opinion of those who believe that impossibilities must sometimes be attempted. There's no mistaking Labour's feelings on this score, and these may simmer into explosive discontent if summer slips into autumn and nothing is done.

To the general atmosphere of watchful waiting has been added the impatience of the American troops now in London, most of whom talk as though they were somewhat doubtful of being able to give the town a quick once-over before leaving to keep a date with von Rundstedt, which they seem to imagine will be around Thursday week at the latest. Any Canadians who happen to be present when this little jaunt is outlined usually smile with the weary irony of men who thought much the same thing two years and several hundred pints of English-village beer ago. Rumors are naturally as prevalent as they were when the invasion boot was on the other foot. Now, as then, people confidentially mention dates that may prove interesting or tell you about somebody's nursemaid who came back from her holiday announcing that tanks were rumbling past her window all night and that it's an open secret at home, no matter what the word may be from Whitehall, that the men are expecting the word to go at any minute. The truth is, of course, that everybody knows precisely nothing.

To offset a heavy dose of sombre news, the papers have dutifully been giving their readers stories about the American troops who arrived the other day and have caused an unprecedented scarcity of taxis throughout the metropolis. Fleet Street solemnly reported that all the boys, when asked what they were going to do first in London, said they couldn't wait to rush off to Westminster Abbey. The press was equally dead pan in reporting an interview with a private from Texas who, when asked what he had liked best so far in England, replied, "The climate."

Lists of "do's" and "do not's" have been issued for the benefit of hospitable Britons who want to ask the boys home. Prospective hosts are cautioned to steer clear of such tactless subjects as the tardiness of the United States to enter the war, since it has been found that the guests are likely to crack right back with something equally disconcerting to Englishmen. Motherly ladies, who might want to get out the best tea service for their uniformed visitors, are warned that most Americans do not look upon tea as a customary afternoon rite. At the same time, British householders are told that they had better not produce their precious monthly ration of whisky, as the guests are liable to knock it off blithely at one sitting, without realizing that it's hard to come by in England nowadays. For all the "do's" and "don't's," Anglo-American relations still seem fine.

August 30

[*August 19, Allied forces stage a nine-hour attack on Dieppe, on the French channel coast.*]

To a nation hungry for decisive action, half a loaf is certainly better than none, even if it has to be made to last a long time. The Dieppe raid is still being chewed over by press and public, both of which earnestly hope that it was merely an appetizer before the real *plat du jour*. On the whole, informed opinion here seems to hold that the operation was worth its considerable costliness if only because it forced the Luftwaffe to part with some of its fighter strength, which usually remains prudently grounded when the R.A.F. goes over in daylight sweeps. The effect on public morale was immediate throughout England. According to reports from various pits and factories in the industrial Midlands, output for the day when the news first broke was stepped up to a new and enthusiastic high by workers who believed, in spite of the B.B.C.'s careful early-morning warnings to the contrary, that the expedition was the genuine article after all. It's not recorded how much production slumped when it was disappointedly realized that the boys were home again as advertised.

Now the public seems to have returned to its pre-Dieppe condition of watchful waiting while trying to decide how bad the Russian news is and how good the Solomon Islands news may be when complete information, so far lacking, turns up on the subject. There's also anxious discussion over British teacups and beer mugs of the surprising calm in India, of the lull in the Middle East, and of what the real results of Mr. Churchill's visit to Moscow may have been. Although few people, incidentally, seem to connect Dieppe with the Kremlin conversations, there's a strong local tendency to look upon the official lifting of the ban upon the *Daily Worker* as a sort of graceful bread-and-butter letter to Stalin.

This being the time of year when the English summer usually begins to make its excuses, Britons' thoughts are turning gloomily toward a possibly chilly autumn and a downright shivering winter. The fuel problem remains a grave one, which so far hasn't been drastically tackled. Plans for coal rationing seem at the moment to have been replaced by a sort of honor system whereby householders are asked to fix their own fuel "target" and appoint a member of the family to keep an eye on the gas meter and the boiler gauge. Maybe this public-school sort of appeal will do the trick, but it is most people's cynical guess that it won't.

If reports of bumper harvests in the country are reliable, Britons may be cold this winter but they shouldn't be hungry. At the same time, it's more than likely that they'll be increasingly shabby, since the president of the Board of Trade has just announced that the next issue of clothing coupons must be made to last nearly six months instead of five. "Anybody who retains his natural hair," the president added with apparent inconsequence, "ought to go without a hat," thereby setting rumors afoot that headgear would shortly be placed on the list of rationed articles.

London at the moment is a boom town, owing mostly to the money of the American troops on leave. Restaurants, bars, and theatres are packed, and so is every means of transport and every square inch of living space. Strangers crowd together in shared taxis and amiably double up in the matter of hotel bathrooms. Whatever gaiety there is, however, is principally manufactured by the boys to whom war is still a novelty. To British men and women entering their fourth year of it next week and wondering if Stalingrad will have fallen by then, life is largely grim rather than gay these critical but by no means despondent days.

September 13

The struggle for Stalingrad has naturally been uppermost in everyone's thoughts during the past week. Mr. Churchill's cryptic remark in the House on the Russian situation— "This is September eighth"—was taken by the pessimistic to mean that the Russians must rely on bad weather as a substitute for a second front and by the optimistic as a reminder that there was still plenty of time ahead in which to put decisive plans into action. The average Briton, who tries to steer a middle course, can't help feeling that the deadline for effective aid to Russia is drawing dangerously near. The mood of the moment here is naturally one of acute anxiety, though the talk is less noisy than it has been at other perilous points. Maybe people feel as the M.P.'s presumably felt after Mr. Churchill's war statement last Tuesday: that there's nothing further to be said and that all that remains is to wait and see what's going to be done. There was astonishment, however, when what was to have been a two-day debate fizzled out in an hour and a half, since the last debate on the war went on for a full two days and ended at three o'clock in the morning of the third, with members still queuing up to speak.

On the whole, it's felt that the Prime Minister's balance sheet of results achieved was an impressive one, though from it Britons doped out for themselves that the Moscow visit probably wasn't quite the roaring success it had earlier been made to seem. What Mr. Churchill had to say about the changes in the Middle East Command didn't clear up the mystification of the uninformed over the retirement of General Auchinleck, but the Prime Minister's reading of the desert sands for the near future confirmed the prevailing cautious feeling that the Egyptian situation was looking a good deal healthier. The British have had so much good news go sour on them overnight, before the ink was even dry on the adjectives, that the tidings of Rommel's recent setback were received with considerable reserve. Though some of the correspondents had been taking the line that his retreat was a British victory, their dispatches were read skeptically by the folks at home, who seemed determined not to be caught again in the act of cheering a premature victory. "The news from Egypt doesn't look so bad today," was the usual way Britons had of saying they hoped it was really looking downright good.

October 4

Most Britons, their attention fixed first of all on the continued miracle of Stalingrad and secondly on the locally vital question of fuel, haven't had much concern left over to bestow on the exasperated remarks from the Berlin Sportpalast. Hitler's oratory—including the reference to coming air reprisals, which was presumably intended to make British flesh creep—provoked only absent-minded comment from a press and public which have been holding their collective breath over the outcome of the entire Russian struggle.

The problem of keeping the home fires and blast furnaces

burning was discussed during the past week by Parliament and, less formally but no less earnestly, by the occupants of mansions, cottages, and every in-between-grade dwelling up and down the country. Few Englishmen, sitting beside fire-places in which they patriotically won't have any fires until November, seemed much encouraged by Major Lloyd George's account of how things were going or by his hopes that the formidable eleven-million-ton gap between produc-tion and consumption would somehow be bridged this win-ter by voluntary economies. The Tories, who killed fuel-ra-tioning when it was first proposed a while back, were sufficiently alarmed this time to back up Labour's Mr. Gren-fell who held that twenty thousand miners should be re-leased from the services and factories to improve a situation which may otherwise have disastrous effects.

The government knows it is facing the nasty fix of not being able to guarantee supplies of coal, however meagre. Deliveries may easily be bogged down by transportation snarls or renewed blitzes, and, since a householder with a ra-tion card would not unnaturally expect to get his full ration, prudent officials probably think it is safer to urge people to use a minimum of coal rather than to promise them one. Meanwhile, some of the coldest places in London are govern-ment offices, where Civil Servants sit shuffling buff paper forms through blue fingers and counting the minutes until it's time to go and get a breath of nice stale air in the can-teen. (The warmest place, according to a reporter who toted a thermometer around town with him, is the comfortably frowzy top of a bus at the rush hour.) Many Britons suspect that the Queen, by coming down with bronchitis last week, set a fashion which will be more loyally copied this winter than ever were the Alexandra hair-dos or the Mary toques.

Since a resumption of big raids on England may be ex-pected at any moment after the end of favorable bombing weather on the Russian front, the existing compulsory call-up of women in certain groups to serve as fire-watchers has been coming in for a good deal of attention. Various civic authorities, in a sudden burst of old-fashioned chivalry, have been digging their toes in against the idea of women fire-watchers, principally because of the dangers involved but also on what are darkly referred to as "moral grounds." Sensible Englishwomen are naturally mad as snakes about this. Specially privileged femininity, they argue, has no place in total war, as the women of Stalingrad would certainly testify, and the notion that there might be carryings-on on the roof-tops has only added to their indignation. Those who think women physically unsuited for what may be a tough and dangerous job were put right by the chairman of the Westminster Emergency Committee, who pointed out that in a recent fire-watchers' competition the fourth place was won by a team of determined matrons, with an average age of thirty-five, who scuttled over tricky old roofs like lady Tarzans.

October 18

The public had a right to look thoughtful this weekend, what with every public speaker, from the Prime Minister down, telling it that the war was about to enter a new and sombre stage and the headlines announcing that the Stalingrad struggle was already in one. Most Britons feel that it isn't much good trying to read between the lines of official utterances, particularly since the eighty-day period which the Minister of Production had darkly predicted would be the crowning test ended recently, leaving everyone much as they were before and irritably wanting to know what the dickens the Minister had meant anyway. The Minister explained that he had simply picked on eighty days as a handy sort of time interval, in which, after all, plenty of things were bound to happen.

Millions of Englishmen had hoped that a second front was one of those things. Now that summer is gone and the tweeds of last year but one are being tenderly lifted out of the mothballs, there's less talk about the opening of a major

Continental offensive in 1942, although Fleet Street continues to plug for or against it, depending on editorial policy.
The *Times,* the Leftish *News Chronicle* and *Daily Herald,*
and the Beaverbrook papers have all, with varying degrees of
caution, consistently advocated early military action. The
Telegraph thinks that bigger and better bombers over Germany is the best method of aiding Russia at the moment, the
Daily Mail roots for keeping the northern supply lines open
at any cost, and the *Manchester Guardian* wistfully asks its
readers to consider the attractions of a diversion on the Italian coast. The papers skirted uneasily around the Stalin letter, like well-bred guests trying to ignore the fact that a dinner companion has shaken dynamite out of his dinner
napkin.

A movie that is drawing crowds is the magnificent "In
Which We Serve," which is the life story of a destroyer, written, directed, produced, musically scored, and starred in by
Noel Coward. The real star, however, is the Navy. Lots of
Englishmen, who were made a trifle warm under the collar
by "Mrs. Miniver," are glad that America is at last going to
have an authentic picture of how the British acted under
bombings, came back from Dunkirk, and generally conducted themselves in time of acute stress and strain. None of
the anxious wives and mothers in this picture is a Greer Gar-
son, but you should like it nevertheless.

November 1

The vaguely bullish feeling here that things are looking better culminated in the news that the curtain had gone up at
last on the big British offensive in Egypt.* This gave a great
boost to the spirits of the stay-at-home public, already considerably encouraged by the success of the R.A.F. and American raids over Europe and by the enemy's seeming reluc-

* In October the British Eighth Army began the final successful offensive
against the German and Italian forces in Africa.

tance or inability to sock back in kind. No civilian will ever be able to complain that he was led into premature optimism this time, though. Official taciturnity has been so profound that newspaper accounts of the fighting have had to fill in with cautious theorizing and handy chunks of Clausewitz. Among ordinary Londoners there's been no soft-pedalling of elation over the Allied air successes. The British were cordially enthusiastic about the Flying Fortresses' great day at Lille but even more so when the R.A.F. boys hedge-hopped over France and beat hell out of the Schneider-Creusot plant. The papers, demurely mentioning that the Lancasters had no fighter escort, were like the crowd at a rural cricket match which courteously claps the visiting team but lets out a roar when the village policeman smacks a boundary into the churchyard.

With the exception of Saturday night's raid on Canterbury, the German retaliations up to date have been so feeble that Londoners are puzzled, and there now seems to be a school of thought which doesn't expect that "they" will come over in big numbers this winter, just as "they" surprisingly didn't last year. All the same, it's noticeable that the steel bunks on tube-station platforms are better patronized these nights than they have been for some time. Those who frequent them maybe feel that with good, long bombing nights back again there's no use getting caught out if anything does happen.

One of the strangest popular reasons given for the temporary immunity from blitzes is that it's due to Mrs. Roosevelt. "The President must know that there won't be no raids," one stout matron comfortably remarked to her neighbor in a food queue the other day, "or else 'e wouldn't never 'ave let 'er come." Canterbury presumably shook this faith a bit, but though Mrs. Roosevelt's potency as a mascot may have waned, her popularity hasn't. The crowds, which would mistrust too much elegance, love her because she looks homey and, as they approvingly remark, "motherly." The press has devoted so much space to her doings that it's occasionally difficult to keep track of the war, what with her own "My

Day" column and the adjoining ones filled up by other writers who describe her day all over again, just in case she forgot something. Her indefatigable lopings have apparently
left the journalists so limp that there was more than a hint
of relief in the *Mirror's* midweek observation, as it panted at
the Roosevelt heels, that she was beginning to look tired.

The relaxing of the restrictions on the use of central heating was greeted with cheers by the majority and jeers by the
Spartan minority, which pointed out that the government
had made a poor beginning in its fuel-economy campaign by
being tenderhearted over the public's chilly toes in comparatively mild weather. The real reason for the official action
probably was the havoc that an epidemic of colds was causing in the unheated government offices. There had also been
solicitude about the health of the American troops, who, it
was pointed out, were used to warm houses.

Reports are now coming in from the country, incidentally,
as to how the boys are settling down with the natives. In one
village the elderly and autocratic lady of the manor over-
heard herself described by her guests as "a swell old guy."
She was as delighted as if the President had sent her a decoration. In such small and simple ways do many of the minor
punctures in the reservoir become, thank God, self-sealing.

November 15

It has been exhilarating to live through the last ten days in
England. There has been the biggest wave of national emotion since Dunkirk, when, in every town and village, one felt
the quiet but stubborn resolve immortalized by Low in the
famous cartoon that showed a solitary Briton facing the
Channel and bore the caption "Very well then—alone." Last
week, with Stalingrad holding and Morocco falling, Britons
had good cause to realize thankfully that they were not alone
and that the beginning of the unified grand strategy for
which the critics had long been clamoring was right there on

the mat with the morning paper. The excitement over the American landings in the west of Africa and the British advances in the east was terrific, and this time not particularly quiet, either. On the morning when British families switched on their radios and heard the news that the Nazi forces were in full retreat, London was a city of smiling people who walked as though they were stepping out to the music of a Guards' band. Neither the girls behind shop counters, nor the taxi-drivers, nor the humorous bus conductor who tinkled his bell and shouted, "Next stop, Bengasi!" needed any encouragement to demand of the customers, "Well, it looks all right, doesn't it?" For once, these Britons were not referring to the weather. At the circus, which has just arrived in town, one of the clowns, wearing a pith helmet and mounted on a camel, had only to ask, "Which way has he gone?" for the smallest tot in the audience to understand gleefully whom he was talking about.

The present universal *Te Deum* is naturally all the louder because throughout the past year there has been precious little to sing about. Although the press during the past week hasn't omitted an occasional warning that the Germans may still have a trick or two up their sleeves, and although the public doesn't need any warnings to remember far too well that Libya has often been the stage for a grim sort of dance in which first one side and then the other went through the figure of advance and retreat, there is a general conviction that this time the victory is going to be decisive. People seem to feel that the current success is a far more solid one than any previous gain in that area has been. The event which gave perhaps the deepest satisfaction here was the retaking of Tobruk, the battered citadel which has come to stand for so much in British minds. The news that the Eighth Army was back there again was a profound psychological relief to the public.

Maybe psychology has had a good deal to do with the events of the past fortnight. The British success effectually knocked on the head the dangerous notion that German arms and leadership are infallible and left the pessimists who had been talking gloomily of what would happen when the second front did come off right out on a limb. Though General Montgomery, the leader immediately responsible for smashing the German lines, is naturally the man of the moment, the Prime Minister has also had his share of the kudos. In the past months, Mr. Churchill has often had to justify events to a critical audience when things were going badly. Last week, his cheering listeners in the House seemed to feel that events justified themselves and that his defense of the British plan was convincing. The section of the press which had been noisiest about tackling the job of prodding the government for a second front has in the last few days been indulging in an orgy of eating its own words. Though Africa is not the second front that many had been thinking of, it's a preliminary on such a brilliant scale that even the most truculent prodders now seem convinced that it was better to postpone the attack on the Continent until spring and concede handsomely that maybe Mr. Churchill knew best, after all.

It was a typical Churchillian inspiration, and one that helped the public let off steam in its desire to do something suitably festive about the great tidings, to order that the church bells should be rung today from the long-silent belfries all over England, which weren't to have given tongue until the invasion of this island. Although some of the more cautious felt that this was tempting Providence rather prematurely, and shuddered at the thought of what Monday bad news might follow Sunday's jubilation, there was general pleasure over the idea. Some of the ruined City churches necessarily remained silent; in other famous steeples bells were being tried out for the first time since they were damaged in the raids. In the country, lots of little churches which wanted to join the celebration found that their ablebodied bell-pullers were all away in the armed forces and had to dig old gaffers out of retirement to totter around and do their best to produce a joyful clashing.

At the moment all local concerns and all kinds of conversation are dominated by what is happening in North Africa.

The nationwide wave of emotion is not the only thing that makes this moment something like those moments in the summer of 1940. There's a big difference, however. Those were grim days in 1940. Today, though sensible Britons think there's certain to be plenty of grimness ahead, for the first time they believe that sober reasons for hope are at last in sight.

November 29

[*November, Russians under Marshall S. K. Timoshenko begin counteroffensive at Stalingrad.*]

Things are moving so fast and dramatically that the morning papers can be, and often are, hopelessly dated by noon and the radio is listened to eagerly by thousands who are as anxious as in the old days of a victorious Hitler not to miss a single footfall of destiny. These new days are fateful ones, too, all right. Even hyper-cautious Britons, used to apparently good news that comes back like a boomerang, are inclined to interpret the events in North Africa, Russia, and Toulon in a manner which, a short time back, would have seemed like wishful thinking.

The Russian news, coming on top of the excitement over the Eighth Army's success, set spines tingling. It is extraordinary to see the excitement which the mere mention of Stalingrad creates in the average Londoner. On the day the newspaper sellers were jubilantly chalking "Old Timo Again" on their boards, their papers were being grabbed up so fast by people who stood reading them in the street that late-comers had to content themselves with matily looking over the shoulders of the more fortunate customers. The military relief of a city which has been in everyone's thoughts for so long was as big a mental relief as was the recapture of Tobruk, that other symbol of the resistance of men of good will. This time, Britons felt that, besides throwing their hats in the air over the Russian successes, they could look Moscow in the eye, in view of the announcement that considerable units of the Luftwaffe had been milked from the Russian front to bolster up the North African one.

The public reaction to the news of the scuttling of the French fleet was the one that might have been expected from a nation which loves ships deep down in its bones. Though it would have been reasonable for Britons to cheer because a danger which has long threatened them had been removed forever, their first impulse apparently was to groan. Maybe the tragic explosions at Toulon will help to blast some daylight into a situation which people here have found perplexingly murky; namely, the real position of France, of Pétain, and of Darlan. Local feeling over the complicated political goings on in North Africa is demonstrated by the strong sympathy for General de Gaulle. Though Britons glumly concede that it may be profitable at this stage of the game to sit in with undesirable partners, it doesn't follow that they enjoy doing so. The views of the Fighting French in London are also the views of millions of Londoners who are convinced that appeasement of a man of Vichy or a man of Munich smells just about the same, no matter what fancy name you want to call it.

December 13

The most important news of the last fortnight here has not been concerned with the war but with the peace. The Beveridge Report, which had been "heard of" for so long that people were beginning to wonder whether a limp wet blanket hadn't been pressed over its mouth, finally came out, to the accompaniment of many cheers and surprisingly few howls. For the first time, ordinary Englishmen, who had felt that the Atlantic Charter was only a lot of big words for a lot of difficult abstract things, thought that, in Sir William Beveridge's proposals for postwar social security, they saw a practical design for living. Londoners queued up to buy this heavy two-shilling slab of involved economics as though it were unrationed manna dropped from some heaven where the old bogey of financial want didn't exist. Those who couldn't get hold of a copy were able to take the report in easier doses from the press, which favored it over the war in all the editorials that day, and from the B.B.C., which added enthusiastically off its own bat (and was subsequently reproved in Parliament for doing so) that the cost of putting the scheme into effect would tot up only to the amount needed to keep the war running for a few days.

Since the plan would in effect do away with the various voluntary insurance companies and benefit societies which make such a big drain on the English workingman's pay envelope, these powerful interests are naturally expected to kick the hardest, supported by such Tory elements as dare to rally to their defense. Opposition so far has mostly and shakily been on the ground that if you guarantee a nation won't starve you thereby remove its spirit of adventure and initiative, the critics having apparently and queerly figured out that hungry men make the best potential Drakes and Livingstones. Meanwhile, the plain British people, whose lives it will remodel, seem to feel that it is the most encouraging glimpse to date of a Britain that is worth fighting for and (more important still, in view of the groggy state of the birth rate) into which it need not be so much of a hazard to be born.

German radio reports of a new Eighth Army offensive have ended a period of comparative calm, in which the headlines and the public temperature had got back to normal after a long spell of excited shouting. There has recently been a general tendency to caution regarding the situation in Tunisia, which was too glibly taken to be as fine as everything else until Mr. Eden abruptly described it in the House as "critical." Considerable consternation is expressed both in private conversation and published comment over the recent maneuvers of Admiral Darlan, which the British fear look like the digging in of a man who has come to stay. Since

British propaganda to Occupied France has busily plugged Darlan as Traitor No. 1 for the past couple of years, it's suspected that the underground movement in France may find his sudden siding with the Allies a little hard to understand. Bewilderment here is right out in the open. Lots of Britons, though perfectly willing to agree that necessity makes strange bedfellows, seem to feel that Darlan is the crumb in the bed which keeps you awake until it's removed.

Talk about this and other phases of how the war is going hasn't diverted people's attention from the inescapable fact that Christmas is coming. Though the stern official view is that presents should be given to nobody but children, shops of all sorts have been seasonably crowded all week with customers who maybe were there for their health. Even the children won't come off so handsomely this Christmas, for toys are scarce, poorly made, and appallingly expensive. Judging by the comments of harassed parents, gloomily pricing toys that are ugly and costly enough to give the tots nightmares and their elders apoplexy, plenty of young Britons are going to find books in their Christmas packages. The personal column of the *Times* carries frenzied appeals daily for second-hand tricycles, doll prams, and constructional toys, none of which can be bought new any more.

The Christmas dinner isn't going to be so particularly festive, either, from all accounts. Turkeys are difficult to find, though it's rumored that tinned ones will be available—a bleak prospect for those who can't work up any suitably seasonable emotions at the thought of getting out the yuletide can-opener. The outlook for the dessert course isn't much rosier, since dried fruit for the traditional puddings and pies is scarce and requires a forbiddingly high number of food points when finally discovered. Even the self-sacrificing who had planned to wrap up a little of their tea or sugar ration and pop it into some friend's Christmas stocking received a setback from the Food Ministry, which unhelpfully announced that it was illegal to give away rations.

Not only the shops are currently crowded. London's hotels, restaurants, theatres, cinemas, snack bars, and taxis are doing record business. The theatres, which still begin at early-evening blitz hours though there's no blitz, have been packing them to see Shakespeare's "Henry IV," Shaw's "The Doctor's Dilemma," Wilde's "The Importance of Being Earnest," and Congreve's "The Way of the World," besides the usual girl shows. There are waiting lists at many big blocks of flats, where in 1940 the few remaining tenants jumped at the sound of their own voices in the elevators. Undeterred by the thought of the return of raids, owners of damaged houses who two years ago moved out into the country are having their collapsed ceilings put back as fast as the over-worked builders can manage, taking their furniture out of the dust covers, and moving in again. If you compare this confident mood with the deep anxiety and uneasiness last Christmas, there's reason to feel encouraged.

December 27

[*December 23, Admiral Darlan assassinated by a French anti-Fascist.*]

What with the superbly good Russian news and the continued retreat of Rommel, most grownup Britons felt that their Christmas stockings had been generously filled, even though the children's were on the meagre side this year. If, in the occupied countries, there was anything like the surge of grim satisfaction with which Darlan's removal was received here, this shouldn't prove a happy New Year to Quislings anywhere. With the best will in the world toward the known American opinion, few Britons had apparently been able to look at the Darlan deal from a purely military angle. Darlan's record was too much hated a part of the black sheet of European events for that. The feeling of the man in the street was recently summed up by Low's cartoon in the *Evening Standard* showing Mr. Eden as a dapper conjurer plucking the Admiral out of the hat and being heckled from the audience by Wendell Willkie with a shout of "Now make him disappear." Though it's not supposed that Darlan's departure has completely cleared the French political horizon of the threat of future squalls, it has undoubtedly brought to London a general sense of relief.

It's now reasonable to suppose that this fourth Christmas of the war may be remembered as the one which brought the phrase "after the war" back into active circulation. Certainly one hears it being used far more frequently and confidently now than for some time past. People talk about the end of the war as though it were a perfectly matter-of-fact objective on the horizon and not just a nice pipe dream.

The recent holiday season, besides being the brightest as far as outlook goes which this country has had since the horrors started in Europe, is also likely to linger in the public's memory less cheerfully as one of the most expensive which ever bore down upon the pocketbook. The cost of all traditional garnishings which weren't price controlled, from mistletoe to food and drink, soared alarmingly during the last few days before Christmas. The toy racket tardily drew stern official attention, rather too late to do much good for parents who had already in desperation shelled out high prices for shoddy rubbish.

One of the gayer manifestations of the festive spirit has been the bower of tents and greenery which suddenly blossomed in the sombre, gutted shell of John Lewis's bombed Oxford Street store. This was a Potato Christmas Fair, sponsored by Potato Pete, a creation of the Ministry of Food's propaganda department to make starch-stodged Britons eat even more home-grown tubers and go slow on the imported wheat loaf. The show was visited on its opening day by Lord Woolton, by a baby elephant called Comet, who proved too heavy (perhaps from too much patriotic spud-eating) to be able to negotiate the wooden gangway down into the wrecked basement, and by hordes of the public who dutifully received hot baked potatoes from Father Christmas and signed a visitors' book beneath the vow "I promise as my Christmas gift to the sailors who have to bring our bread that I will do all I can to eat home-grown potatoes instead."

Those who remembered that particular Oxford Street site as a scene of blackened, smoking desolation may well have felt that its lively new lease of life was just another sign of the optimistic spirit in which 1942 is ending. Maybe it's thought at the top that too much optimism is as bad as none at all, for several official utterances lately have warned the people that the ramparts they watch are still the white cliffs of Dover and that an attempt upon them is quite in the cards at some moment when Hitler may believe that popular attention has been diverted elsewhere.

Should this moment arrive with the spring, Englishwomen may be fighting, if not side by side with their menfolk, at any rate just behind them, for it was announced last week that the War Office was about to break down and admit women into the Home Guard for noncombatant duty. The noncombatant clause is likely to disappoint the more militantly minded, who, led by Dr. Edith Summerskill, M.P., have been gunning for some time for the formation of a corps of housewife snipers on the Russian model. It is certain, anyway, that during the coming year, whether or not women will be shouldering guns, an increasing number will be drafted into making them, inasmuch as Mr. Bevin's plans for a further call-up of employees in the retail trades are sweeping. Luxury shops, on which the Minister has naturally come down hardest, won't have a salesgirl under forty-five when the new regulations become effective, and competition for the services of the rest will obviously be fierce. Perhaps the only Mayfair tradesmen who weren't gloomy about the prospects last week were the hairdressers, to whom Mr. Bevin thoughtfully accorded easier terms for keeping their key operators out of the factories, since a neat head is held to be an invaluable booster of feminine morale, as much for factory girls themselves as for that now rare species, the lady of leisure.

If the latter commodity is in short supply over here nowadays, so is old-fashioned pride, judging by the fascinating advertisements which appear daily in the columns of the

Times. Eighteen months of clothes rationing are presumably responsible for the increasing number of ads offering, with full name and address and no stuffy British reticence, to sell and buy second-hand furs, shoes, men's clothes, and even such intimate articles of apparel as pure-silk lingerie. For some time, parents have been passing on their children's old clothes to friends with younger offspring as a coupon-saving measure, and boys and girls have become accustomed to meeting last winter's coat walking down the street on someone else's back. Maybe this habit is now going to gain ground with the adults, too.

1943

RITONS FACED UP TO THE

January 10

B RITONS FACED UP TO THE opening days of 1943 in a state
of delayed and possibly healthful mental hangover. In
the excitement of the big emotional jag after November's
program of military triumphs there had been a dangerous
tendency to talk as if the rest of the war were going to be
equally swift, brilliant, and easy. It is possible, too, that the
immense interest which all sections of the community have
taken in the Beveridge Report helped to accent postwar reconstruction in the public's mind and to blur the inescapable fact that, if 1943 lives up to its commitments, thousands
of young men now alive will not be around to help that reconstruction along. Maybe the growing realization that Tunisia is proving tougher than was first expected and that over
in Tripolitania Rommel is likely to do a lot of other things
besides run, has jerked people back into a saner frame of
mind. The rosy early-winter honeymoon period is now over.

Though the Russian news is good enough to make jubilation still in order, Londoners are talking over their beer
mugs and teacups in a way which shows they know that the
worst in casualties and sacrifices are yet to come before Mr.
Churchill's "end of the beginning" can be said to look like
the beginning of the end. The new National Service Bill,
which went into effect last week, when the first batch of sev-
enteen-and-a-half-year-olds queued up to register for the
armed forces, has been a sobering pointer toward a future
when casualties may be almost on the Russian scale. This

[261

registration, incidentally, means that the already hard-pressed universities will practically have to shut up shop, except those prepared to give medical and technical courses and to teach women students.

January 24

Probably the happiest people in this town last Sunday night, when the Germans paid their return visit to revenge the bombing of Berlin, were the ack-ack boys, who had been moping beside their new guns for months like kids with a slingshot and no alley cats in sight. That Sunday, it was obvious that they were having the time of their lives. Lots of other less military Londoners merely had the fright of their lives, for the sound effects of the new barrage were something special, and even old-timers thought that a really big blitz was on until they realized that most of the bangs were from shells going up instead of from bombs coming down. That the former can be as lethal as the latter was proved by the high number of shrapnel casualties, presumably among people who hadn't been able to resist stargazing at the weird and wonderful constellations flowering in the heavens.

Next morning, Londoners were slipping back easily into the old 1941 vocabulary. Earnest conversations in buses and on street corners were filled with expressions like "So I says to our warden," and people carrying on these conversations appeared not uncheerful, as if they had just had a dreaded session with the dentist which had proved to be not so bad after all. Those who view the raid as a costly tit-for-tat affair which probably won't be attempted again are offset by those who think it was in the nature of a tryout for really heavy attacks in the future. The immediate minor reactions included a slight flurry of cancellations of reservations at hotels and clubs. There was also an increase the following evening in the number of people seeking shelter in the tubes, and soon after dark many prudent early arrivals, who didn't fancy being caught out in another stupendous barrage, were begin-

ning to settle their bedding and bundles on the steel bunks
underground.

Londoners have not been so preoccupied with this bit of
local shooting that they forgot to be jubilant over the relief
of Leningrad and the other magnificent Russian successes.
The Eighth Army's advance has also naturally been celebrated, though exuberance has been slightly checked by a
few warning dispatches pointing out that the toughest part
of the North African job is yet to come. On the whole, however, people seem to feel a lot happier about the military
outlook there than they do about the political setup. The
hoisting of yet another collaborationist into office has apparently made the London Fighting French fighting mad and
has certainly made plenty of Britons bewildered and disturbed. Those who had heaved a sigh of relief over Darlan's
exit not unnaturally feel that Marcel Peyrouton is a mighty
queer sort of cement to choose for the delicate business of
joining the dissenting French factions.

A considerable local to-do has been raging meanwhile over
the question of opening theatres on Sunday, which has apparently split the British theatrical profession from top to
bottom. There have been resignations from Equity, heated
words from ladies and gentlemen of the stage at an open
meeting which sometimes looked as if it were about to turn
into a free-for-all, and fuming letters to the *Times* signed by
an assortment of names which could easily make up the cast
of an all-star production. Those who want the ancient ruling
against Sunday shows revoked argue that servicemen and
women, often far from home and friends, are given the
choice of a Sunday-afternoon movie or a mooch around
strange streets while the other theatres' civilizing doors remain inhospitably closed. An equally passionate faction
clings to the thought that Sunday is the one day on which actors can shed the buskin and don the domestic carpet slipper.

Last Sunday night's raid by the Nazis coincided with an
ambitious effort by the theatre's younger competitor, the
radio, when the B.B.C. broadcast one of its eight hour-long

installments of "War and Peace," which it is gallantly attempting to present as a serialized drama. "What with the battle of Austerlitz inside the studio and the battle of Hyde Park outside, it was a lively evening," a harassed B.B.C. official observed later. The project, which was launched with the blessing of the Soviet Ambassador, seconded by an enthusiastic cable from the Union of Soviet Writers, is the climax of a tremendous Tolstoy boom here. A new thirty-thousand-copy edition of *War and Peace* has sold out in less than a month, and those who failed to get the book must now wait for the next printing, promised in May if the necessary paper is forthcoming, or else get along with the radio version, in which the fascinating voice of the woman narrator is supplied by the balletomanes' old favorite, Lydia Lopokova.

The keen interest in anything Russian has even penetrated the nurseries, it would seem, judging by an exhibition of children's war pictures now on view in London and destined for the States this spring. One of the most striking exhibits is called "The Defense of Stalingrad," the large and rather horrific joint effort of a class of London school kids. Children apparently don't favor pretty subjects for their brushwork nowadays. They paint bombs bursting, buildings collapsing, and men facing Nazi firing squads. A picture called "Daylight Attack," showing German raiders swooping out of a blue sky, might easily have been painted by one of the London youngsters who, in last Wednesday morning's raid, learned only too well, alas, that it's an ugly world right now for painting or just for living in.

January 31

[*January 14–24, Churchill and Roosevelt meet at Casablanca.*]

Sentiment in London about the Casablanca meeting seemed to be rather subdued. In general, the public acted like the cautious reader who thinks the blurb on the cover of a book promises well but wants to wait and see what's inside. Maybe there was a slight feeling of disappointment that this time there couldn't have been four leading characters instead of the conventional two. Maybe, too, the repetition of Mr. Churchill's sudden appearances in unexpected parts of the globe has blunted the popular excitement which resulted from his first Atlantic rendezvous. At any rate, the average Briton, whose own travelling is mostly restricted these days to following his nose to work and back again, appeared to accept the dramatic locale of the conference with as much calm as if it had come off in a board room in Liverpool. Every local discussion of the Casablanca meeting has centred not so much on the journeys which immediately preceded it as on the big-scale ones of men and materials which are presumed to have been decided upon at the conference.

How to provide the transport necessary for these 1943 excursions is the question which, though it wasn't mentioned in any of the vague Casablanca communiqués, is at last engaging the alarmed attention of press and public. Suddenly every Briton seems to have awakened from a comfortable night's slumbers and seen a periscope in his backyard. Past official statements on the U-boat problem, from the Prime Minister downward, have tended to lull people into feeling that it was bad but not so bad that it couldn't be licked. Right now, the sombre certainty is that the situation couldn't be worse. Lots of people are saying that this is one of the occasions when ignorance isn't bliss and that it would be less dangerous to relax the official secrecy about our shipping losses, even at the risk of informing the enemy, than to allow the present state of anxiety to continue, since it gives rise to fears that matters are even graver than they were in 1917. Now that the jubilation over Allied land successes is moderating, people are soberly remembering that the sea is the battlefield on which the outcome of the war really depends. If the impending Parliamentary U-boat debate is held in secret, as has been proposed, it won't do much to dispel the growing uneasiness of the public, which wants more assurance than it has had so far that the next twelvemonth won't see the boys all dressed up and plenty of places to go if only they could get there.

Possibly a peek at the figures on the number of ships being sunk would also help cajole people into going slow on the precious wheat loaf. In an effort to avoid rationing it, Lord Woolton recently called a meeting of delegates, from the immensely powerful Women's Institutes, who promised to help his campaign along and sped back to their village centres to urge some three hundred thousand members to push still more potatoes down their families' throats. Strictly vegetarian dishes are shortly to appear, marked with a persuasive "V," on restaurant menus, and at least one London railway station is doing a brisk trade with baked potatoes for a between-train snack instead of the now unpatriotic sandwich. Even if bread is not to be rationed, the general feeling is that the food situation, which right now is pretty good, soon won't be so good. The cheese ration, for instance, which has stood at a liberal eight ounces a week for some time, is about to be cut in half—a big hardship for the wives of workingmen, since they will have to find something equally filling but not "on points" to put in the daily lunchbox.

Wives of all sorts of men come within the scope of the new Bevin regulations, which are to take effect shortly. These, in addition to providing a close check on possibly slippery female labor by insisting that employers notify the Labour Exchange when a woman worker leaves them, will direct all childless married women under forty-five to take part-time jobs within a reasonable distance from their homes. Housewives have been, oddly enough, officially designated one of the "unoccupied classes," but it looks as though the days of many of them are not going to be so very leisured in the future, divided as they will be between household chores and office or factory. Tapping this last great reservoir of female labor is the follow-up of a recent drive to make it harder for women not only to get out of war service but to choose what form their service should take. Girls who are affected by the new call-up of nineteen-year-olds can no longer decide that they look better in Navy blue than in khaki and act accordingly, for they are being put willy-nilly into whatever service is shortest of recruits. It has also been ruled that once a girl joins a service, she cannot duck out after the fortnight probationary period because she finds the service life doesn't suit her. The effect of the demands Mr. Bevin has made on the personnel of retail business is already visible in some of the shops—notably in one on Regent Street where customers in the neckwear department were seen the other day timidly selecting purchases with the help of a commanding, white-haired dowager in a velvet train.

The daylight raids on Berlin were a fine tonic to Londoners. A relatively minor but no less cheering bracer was an announcement of certain small improvements in blackout regulations. For a long time, a faction of the press and public has been clamoring to have the blackout suspended altogether, which isn't a likely prospect. Still, everyone is grateful for the new ruling that lights in non-corridor railway cars will be left on while trains are standing in stations. Previously, everything but a solitary dim blue bulb in each compartment was turned off when a train entered a station and the unhappy traveller who proposed to alight was left to blunder his way to the door and possibly fall out onto the tracks instead of the platform. The new rule hasn't made a particularly dazzling difference in the prevailing murkiness after dark, but it is a spirits-raising token of brighter days ahead to a nation to which the command "Let there be light" sounds like just about the most beautiful sentence in the language.

February 14

The Prime Minister's statement in the House of Commons on how the war is going was enthusiastically received as the first square meal of sensible fare that the public has been able to get its teeth into since its appetite was sharpened by Casablanca. One ecstatic Labour member of the House, in a rush of scrambled but complimentary mythology, compared Mr. Churchill to Hercules holding up the canopy of civilization, to Venus drooping in on her native Cyprus, and to "the wise old Ulysses" returning from his wanderings to his faithful Penelope, the Deputy Prime Minister. However, it was obvious that the House, for all its approving and laudatory mood, was still uneasy about the North African political setup, although both in Parliament and out of it the reception of Eisenhower's new appointment * has been universally cordial.

There's no unduly optimistic tendency here to minimize the dangers ahead before history can deliver the events promised by Mr. Churchill during the next nine months. People are soberly certain that there are tough trials to come, starting off at any minute now with the struggle for Tunisia, but they're glad to know how they stand even though it entails guessing at when and where thousands of young Britons and Americans are going to fall. Meanwhile, the Premier's vigorous survey, together with Mr. Roosevelt's speech, provided a great boost to everyone's spirits. Stay-at-home Londoners, who don't know much about Ulysses but do know that they like to feel that Downing Street is itself again, summed their notions up affectionately over their morning papers with "The old man's done a good one this time."

Hints of spring are in the air. Though weather reports are forbidden, sleuths have been able to draw their own deductions from the *Times* correspondents, who have noted bumblebees bumbling and chaffinches warbling—phenomena which would presumably not be occurring during snowstorms. Spring blossoms are in the news for the government ruling that no flowers are to be sent by parcel post or rail—instituted to stop the public from paying the current exorbitant prices for such luxuries and to divert both land and

* As chief of Allied forces in North Africa.

labor to more urgent crops—has led to a beautiful racket among growers. Though boxes of flowers can't be shipped by rail, there's nothing to prevent anyone from stepping off the Cornish Express in London with a couple of valises stuffed full of bootleg jonquils. The authorities can't think up an answer to this, barring a customs inspection of suspect luggage, which would of course irritate innocent passengers the contents of whose baggage did not resemble a Riviera carnival.

Another seasonal sign, less welcome than jonquils, is the return of daylight bombings, for the Germans have been taking advantage of favorable weather to drop in again on rural southern districts. Once more, Londoners are hearing fewer sirens than their country cousins, who have had to relearn the old knack of taking bombs as part of the hazards of a market-day's shopping, and commuting City men are turning up at the office with tales of having been machine-gunned on the 8:20.

February 28

The Tunisian setback, while it lasted, provided a sharp and useful lesson in Anglo-American relations. The first news that things were not going so well as they might was received here with much the same reaction one noted back in the days of the bad blitzes, when the inhabitants of any frequently visited town, hearing that some previously unscathed neighborhood had caught a packet from the bombers, would shake their heads and say, "So poor old So-and-so got it badly last night. Now they know what it's all about, the poor devils. Well, well, they'll soon get onto it." Recently, this country, which has had its share of setbacks in the past, has been not unrelieved to find itself in the novel situation of being able to sit back and wag its head over the troubles of the folks across the way.

What has most impressed people is the tone of the American correspondents' dispatches from Tunisia, some of which have trickled into the London papers. These have been a fine corrective to any lurking suspicions that, while British military reverses get a bully ragging from the United States press, American dittos would be handled a good deal more tenderly. To find that this isn't the case has avoided what could have been a potent cause of Anglo-American unfriendliness and has made the relief with which the Allies' recovery was hailed a particularly friendly and delightful feeling. Indeed, the only danger now would seem to be that in the general lifting of spirits people may get the idea that all the troubles in North Africa have been permanently fixed, even though Englishmen have better reason than most to remember that cheering over good news from there may sometimes turn out to be slightly premature.

Meanwhile, national concern has been concentrated on Downing Street. The first admission in the bulletins on the Premier that pneumonia was his latest enemy only confirmed the worst fears of countless Englishmen, who remain perfectly calm when this valuable export goes skipping about the continents but have the fright of their lives when they learn that he's home in bed with a steam kettle. The *Times* has been publishing in adjoining columns daily bulletins on the health of those two highly dissimilar invalids, Mr. Churchill and Mr. Gandhi, about whose survival the Empire has equally good cause for feeling prayerful. Many Britons apparently don't consider the reasons for detaining the Mahatma * very sound, but on the whole opinion seems to be unhappily certain that the government of India was on a spot where it couldn't well have acted otherwise.

Though the Indian situation naturally continues to be one of the most popular weapons in the Goebbels propaganda armory, it looks as though the Nazis' old Bolshevist-menace blunderbuss, which was recently brought down from the top shelf and dusted off, is going to be a big disappointment; most of the British Government speakers at the Red

* From 1942 to 1944 Gandhi was interned because of his civil-disobedience program.

Army Day celebrations last Sunday referred to it wither-
ingly. The speeches were part of a vast program including an
Albert Hall pageant, called "Salute to the Red Army" and
composed by Louis MacNeice, with lots of symphony orchestras and Guards' bands to provide the sound effects. The Soviet flag flew gaily in the calm Sabbath air over a number of
cities, whose honest bourgeoisie were as pleased to tip their
hats to it as they would have been surprised to see it there
three years ago. There's no doubt at all about what the British think of the Russians, however difficult it may be to discover what the Russians think of the British. Londoners
have seemed particularly pleased about the sword of honor
which is to be presented to Stalingrad and which will almost
certainly be the work of the famous eighty-four-year-old
swordsmith Tom Beasley, who once made, among other notable blades, a flaming "Garden of Eden" sword for Emperor
Haile Selassie.

March 1

Now that the British have got around to revising their food
and clothing habits, it looks as though the nation's drinking
habits, already considerably affected, are in for further alter-
ation. Liquor is not officially rationed, but it often seems as
if it might as well be, since shops handling it won't sell more
than a bottle or so a month to a regular customer and won't
sell any at all to others. There are, of course, good reasons
for this. Distillation of grain for whisky-making was prohibited last September. Gin, which is manufactured from imported spirits, is in extremely short supply. Wines are scarce,
and anyhow are so appallingly expensive that they're way beyond the average pocket. The demand for beer has
accordingly grown, and a glass of it is often hard to come by
—especially in country districts whose population has been
swelled by evacuated townsfolk and the military. Those who
like to drink out usually still can do so, although at prices

which range from steep to suicidal. The problem is more difficult for the person who wants to have the makings of a nightcap around or a bottle of something handy to bring out when friends call. Hospitable gestures of this kind are not to be taken lightly these days, or so the harassed host feels as he counts heads and figures out that one round will mean that his monthly bottle of gin has gone bang. Even that one bottle a month is likely to look like a lot in retrospect six months from now. A big London store recently sent a regretful circular letter to its old customers telling them that from now on gin would be doled out at the rate of one bottle every four months.

All in all, the drink situation is bad and will probably become so much worse that most Britons will have to celebrate the armistice, when it arrives, with nothing more festive than beer, perhaps diluted even below its present strength, which is fifteen per cent less than what it was before the war. In spite of the agitations of the temperance groups, which frequently demand that Parliament explain why barley should be diverted from hungry hens to iniquitous breweries, the authorities have so far steadfastly refused either to cut the beer supply or to introduce the no-treating legislation which was put into effect during the First World War. This is because high prices and limited supplies are to a large extent achieving the results for which the dry elements are crusading. The official attitude seems to be that there's no good setting up regulations which might bring about high words in the corner pub and a sullen slacking-off in the workshops when the same end can be quietly attained without any drastic action by Westminster. Police records show that the country as a whole is becoming, maybe unwillingly but certainly steadily, more sober; the number of arrests in London for drunkenness, for instance, swooped down from the twenty-thousand mark in 1937 to an estimated nine thousand in 1942. Maybe this is because more and more Britons, obliged to drink nothing but weak beer, are finding intoxication a rather expensive and difficult state to achieve.

Consumers assuredly have their woes, but the liquor trade

has even worse ones. Distributors have to face a problem which only an alcoholic loaves-and-fishes miracle could satisfactorily solve. The fact that rationing is up to the liquor shops themselves is hard on people who move back to town after an enforced stay elsewhere and find no friendly wine merchant to whom to turn. Some of the big stores have an elaborate system of ration cards for their customers. The ruling against distilling grain for whisky doesn't seriously worry the trade, which expects that the considerable stocks in bond will last for the duration. It will have the effect, however, of putting younger and younger whiskies on the market. One firm which formerly prided itself on never having sold Scotch less than eight years old is now mournfully digging into supplies which had been earmarked for 1946.

Stocks are to be made to last as long as possible by frugal rationing, but blitzes on London and elsewhere have occasionally cut down supplies in a way that no rationing system could have prevented. There were sad faces in Scotland on the day that a lone raider came over and dropped a bomb, apparently by mistake, smack on top of seventy thousand gallons of whisky which had been stored in a hideout on a wild and lonely moor. Finding suitable billets for evacuated whisky stocks is a sizable headache, since the liquor must be kept at an even temperature. Owners of warehouses in vulnerable areas are not allowed to keep spirits on the top floors because of the inflammable nature of the stuff, and must take special precautions to prevent burning alcohol from flowing through the streets. All air-raid shelters uncomfortably close to whisky reserves have been closed.

March 28

Mr. Churchill's historic broadcast dominated the minds and the talk of the majority of Britons last week, at workshop benches or kitchen stoves, in Pall Mall clubs or the local Pig and Whistle. The general exhilaration produced by people's first and, some thought, overdue peek at the Churchillian shape of things to come was, however, overshadowed by the almost simultaneous setback in Tunisia. Public reaction to the news of the successful German counterattack was notably and sensibly calm. People really believe, like General Montgomery, that nothing can stop the Eighth Army. The principal anxiety, judging by the way Londoners discussed the reversal, was that any delays in the North African schedule might mean missing the connection with the first train to Europe.

The Churchill broadcast made history here for several reasons. In the first place, it neatly knocked on the head the widely held notion that the Prime Minister was less interested in the domestic issues of the peace than in the military problems of the war. Though on closer inspection a good deal of the proposed four-year plan didn't seem to amount to anything more revolutionary than a little Beveridge with Churchill trimmings, the way in which it was served up made it seem startlingly novel.

The public, which is used to being galvanized by "blood, sweat, and tears" oratory, was even more electrified at being cozily invited to draw up its chairs to the No. 10 fireside and discuss a practical postwar program which would include work for all, a more liberal educational policy that would rule out old-school-tie snobbery, television sets for happy agricultural workers, and milk for better and more babies. Some Churchill points were singled out for more discussion than others in different sections of the community. Possibly the most eagerly talked-over feature in the Pig and Whistle gatherings was the statement that, because of income-tax rebates, the end of the war would find several million people warming a neat little nest egg of two or three hundred pounds apiece. In political circles, the keenest interest was taken in Mr. Churchill's announcement that when peace arrives it is not his intention to utter a *nunc dimittis* and retire into political twilight, loaded with honors bestowed by a grateful nation. A large portion of his speech could hardly have been enjoyed by the more diehard elements in Mr.

Churchill's own party, and there is a fresh crop of speculations about the possibility of a new Centre Party, a notion
already much discussed, which Mr. Churchill might head
after the war. There was also, here and there, a certain feeling of disappointment over the thought that his outline of
social reforms must largely remain on paper until after the
cease-fire comes. Though the general reaction to what was
probably his most important domestic wartime utterance
was one of encouragement and stimulation, lots of his listeners hoped that the magic phrase "after the war" was really
going to turn out to be a trumpet call rather than a mighty
handy shelf.

Plenty of Londoners are less bothered at the moment
about what sort of postwar living conditions they're going to
have than about the question of where they're going to live
right now in this crowded city. The shortage of furnished
flats and the steep jump in rents are bringing furrows to the
brows of the local inhabitants and the floating American
population alike. Unfortunately, the old idea that every
American is a Rockefeller seems to have gained popularity
again, with the result that the managements of centrally located buildings are now demanding rents for one-room furnished flats that a short time back they were asking, and not
getting, for a sizable family affair. The situation is all the
more acute because many West End blocks have been taken
over as offices either by the British or the various Allied governments in London and most hotels and clubs now limit
the number of days that a guest may stay. Bona-fide war
workers, both English and American, wearily tramping
around looking for a place to lay their heads, not unnaturally feel rather jaundiced at the sight of the rows of deserted mansions in residential squares and crescents, emptied
by the big blitz and kept that way by crippling taxation and
lack of domestic help. Lots of citizens think that rents ought
to be controlled before any serious souring of Anglo-American amity occurs and that it would be a good idea to move
out some of the caretakers and their cats from the unoccupied houses and move in officials and their typists.

April 11

On the day Mr. Churchill announced the good news from Tunisia in the House, Londoners beamingly greeted each other with "So we've got 'em on the run again," as though even the puniest white-collar civilian had been right in on the attack by General Montgomery and the Eighth Army. The Russian and American successes have naturally come in for their share of the jubilation, but the cozy family feeling of being personally identified with what the boys are doing seems to have been centred on the veterans of El Alamein. If things continue the way they are going, even habitually cautious Britons will allow themselves to hope that the ribbon around this year's non-chocolate Easter egg will be the final cleanup of Tunisia.

However, the government has just firmly indicated, in an announcement of Easter holiday train schedules, which turn out to be rather stingier than the normal weekday ones, that the populace won't be allowed much of a breather in which to enjoy the triumph. Moreover, anyone planning to take a break later on in the year has been further and pointedly discouraged by new restrictions upon entering a large coastal area, which it was flatly stated may at any moment become the scene of invasion operations proceeding outward, not inward. The popular, though quite unofficial, explanation of the unexpected absence of German bombing reprisals against this country is that the Luftwaffe is also anticipating what is likely to happen in western Europe when the situation in North Africa eases. People think that the Germans are betting heavily on the U-boat and are cannily not expending many bombs or planes on Britons as long as they stay home. Nevertheless, the evening English radios announced the first heavy raid on Berlin most Londoners glanced a trifle apprehensively at their ceilings, as though expecting them to open and rain down an instant and furious reply. When the second record tonnage of bombs was dumped on Berliners a couple of nights later and still nothing happened here, people who had confidently dusted out the air-raid shelter and hung their siren suits on the bed post began to feel faintly creepy. At the new production of Shaw's "Heartbreak House," the air-raid scene in the third act and Captain Shotover's exultant remark, "I hope they come again tomorrow night," provoked one evening a wan titter from an audience which was only too visibly hoping that nothing of the kind would come before people had managed to catch the bus home in the blackout.

April 25

This year's Easter was a strenuous breather for lots of Londoners who were apparently determined to go places, even if it was only down to Kew to see the lilacs. In spite of official warnings that holiday transport wouldn't be augmented, trains were packed to the last inch with good-tempered crowds which, if reason had arisen to obey the printed instructions to lie down on the floor should enemy action develop overhead, would have had to subside in layers like a three-decker sandwich. The milling throng at most of the big stations also demonstrated the popular belief, which the railway companies have never either O.K.'d or denied, that during the war holders of third-class tickets who can't find room in their own compartments may sit in any empty first-class portion of a train. In the rush on the eve of the Easter break, indignant red-tabbed military and gold-braided naval gentlemen, commuting home after their day in Whitehall, frequently had to stand in jammed corridors while happy third-class passengers rode comfortably and righteously on first-class plush.

Even those Londoners who patriotically obeyed the injunction to stay home over the holidays found themselves in trouble. Apparently, the official notion of a stay-at-home va-

cation, which is being widely publicized this year, since at
any moment British railways may find themselves handling a
vast surplus of more vital material than vacationists and
their suitcases, implies a deck chair in your own back yard
and a nice walk around the block for a change of scenery.
Adventurers who tried to tap their city's resources and enjoy
a watercress tea at Richmond or Hampton Court, even if
they couldn't make it winkles at Southend, decided after
hours of queuing—often fruitlessly—for buses, food, and
drink that a trip to Tibet would possibly be easier on shoe
leather and tempers.

The lifting of the ban on the ringing of church bells
added, of course, to the general holiday enthusiasm. This has
been consistently agitated for by a good many people, including A. P. Herbert, whose new book of verses, *Bring Back the
Bells,* came out the day the ban was ended with a patness
which would have made any press agent happy. This morning, however, lots of Britons who cocked expectant ears toward the long-silent belfries must have been a trifle disappointed. Many bells needed a little fixing after their
prolonged rest, and most of the hearty chaps who used to
ring them are away in the services. The hastily organized
dingdonging which summoned British families, decked in
their last spring's new suitings, to church may have been fal-
tering, but it sounded good to anybody who looked back to
the perilous days when a single peal would have meant not
matins at eleven but invasion barges on southern beaches
right now.

May 9

The African victory came so suddenly that astonished Londoners had hardly enough breath left to cheer with. The
news of the all-out offensive had already put everyone in a
mood of confident expectation, but the fall of Tunis and
Bizerte was so far in advance of schedule that the first jubila-

tion was just faintly dazed. By evening, however, most citizens had got over the shock sufficiently to put on their hats and go forth to celebrate. In spite of official warnings that enemy resistance hadn't ended yet, beaming Britons insisted on talking, over their victory pints, as though the boys had rolled Africa up in a bundle and were now on the European road to Berlin.

All this excitement was the climax of a growingly cheerful week. The American success at Mateur had already been enthusiastically played up by the papers and welcomed as warmly by the public, which bought its evening penny worth of good cheer from news vendors who had chalked their boards with such amiabilities as "Go it, Uncle Sam" and "The Yanks are coming and the Jerries are running." Everyone seemed particularly pleased, too, that the French had been in on the Tunisian triumph.

Shabby as the town may be, the parks have once again put on their not especially abundant but still gay floral show to gladden weary eyes. The tulips near Wellington Barracks draw throngs of Whitehall clerks, who come at lunchtime to eat their sandwiches and to admire. Spring has also had its effect on the sheep in Hyde Park, who have been taking advantage of the absence of railings, removed to augment the nation's scrap-metal pile, and strolling out into the roadways, where they have been known to lie down in front of nonplused jeeps. As one more indication that spring is here, and also as a gesture of confidence in London's new barrage, a couple of ducks have trustingly nested in one of the big reserve water tanks near Bond Street. They seem to like it fine.

Although the expected renewal of the blitz is still lacking, the theatres cautiously continue to start their evening performances at six-thirty. So far, the most important event of what has been a healthy theatrical season was the offering of two new Noel Coward plays, which opened at the Haymarket last week. Mr. Coward, looking well indeed after an illness that apparently came close to casting him as a blithe spirit elsewhere, was rapturously received by his public and very nearly as handsomely by the critics, who invited him to step right up into the distinguished playwrights' gallery between Mr. Congreve and Mr. Wilde.

The first of the plays, "This Happy Breed," is a sort of junior "Cavalcade," showing the familiar middle-class family, with hearts of pure Empire teak, taking events like the Abdication and Munich in their stride. The second play, "Present Laughter," is the one which evoked the comparisons to Wilde. It is Coward at his entertaining best, both as author and actor.

May 16

Bromidic as it may sound, British hearts have been too full for words over the final Allied victory in North Africa. The press and radio did plenty of noisy exulting the day the great news arrived, but in the homes that sent the boys out the thankfulness was so quiet that a caller from Mars might have had difficulty deciding whether the inhabitants were on the winning or the losing side. West End parties were fairly gay that evening and the pubs ran out of beer a little earlier than usual, but Piccadilly Circus has often been a good deal rowdier on a prewar boat-race night. Perhaps the public reaction would have been more obviously jubilant if the Prime Minister had been here to announce the glad tidings with one of those galvanizing speeches of his. As it was, Mr. Clement Attlee, who, as deputy, had the job of making the conventional announcement to Parliament, would certainly have further misled the listener from Mars. This visitor might easily have concluded, but for the cheers from the floor of Parliament, that Mr. Attlee's measured piece of oratory was no more than a judiciously composed statement on municipal drainage. Maybe the real ovation is being saved for Mr. Churchill on his return. Meanwhile, during these last few days, Londoners' smiling faces have told the story as well as any words could.

It seems appropriate that today, when the bells are ring-

ing all over England, should have been set aside for celebrating the third birthday of the Home Guard, that army of
dogged citizens who may not be as seasoned or as photogenic
as the Eighth and First Armies but to whom Britons have
equally sound reasons for being grateful. Last week's May
weather and breath-taking events in Africa turned the
thoughts of many people back to another May, when the
evacuation of the moment wasn't from Cape Bon and when
the question everybody was asking wasn't the current
"Where do we go from there?" but "When are they arriving
here?" Mr. Churchill's broadcast, warning that it's still possible they will arrive here, may even have sounded like good
news to the home guards, fresh from reading their birthday
good wishes in the press, which told them what a fine show
they would have put up in an invasion if an invasion had
ever taken place. In answer to Mr. Churchill's remarks, lots
of the old-timers, who back in 1940 were sitting on hilltops
nursing Grandfather's sporting rifle and looking for Germans, probably began to finger their new Sten guns with
fresh hopefulness.

May 28

Some erudite Briton has just dug up the fact that 1946 will
be the bimillenary of the invasion of Britain by Rome in the
summer of 55 B.C. Lots of less erudite Britons are merely
hoping that this summer will neatly wipe out the score for
their woad-stained ancestors, even if it is three years too
early. On the whole, however, there's not much speculation
about where and how the revenge will take place, and it is
only in conversation with the Continent's exiles in London
that one begins to think of the second front not as a military
maneuver but in terms of flesh and blood. On tablecloths in
Soho and Bloomsbury it has been demonstrated with passionate conviction that here, right by this fork or that spoon,
is the only place for an Allied landing, which Kurt—or

Hendrik or Jean or Demetrios—will naturally be there to help along if he's still alive.

Londoners, more calmly waiting to see what the conference in Washington has cooked up for their own Berts and Georges, talk mostly about the increasing power of the air offensive. There have been occasional protests from the Church and elsewhere over the frankly jubilant way in which the press whoops about the tonnage of bombs that has been dumped on German cities. Certainly the average man's sober conviction that it's a bad job which has got to be done doesn't stop him from wincing over the gruesome thought that the Dortmund bombing must have made his own worst blitz night seem almost like a party. All the same, German propaganda wails about terror raiding can't be expected to make much impression on Londoners, not to mention the inhabitants of Coventry, Hull, Plymouth, and other English cities which got hell in the days when the Nazis seemed to be the only boys who could dish it out.

London's recent crop of nocturnal sirens revived local suspicions that something unpleasant in the way of retaliations was going to start at last, but all that the majority of Londoners received was a headache from lack of sleep. The first couple of nights of intermittent sirens and gunfire had everybody wide awake and wondering whether to reach for his dressing gown. By the fourth night, most people were back in the old routine of hunting up the earplugs, drawing the eiderdown over their heads, and trustingly leaving the whole thing to the boys in the ack-ack batteries. Britons on the south coast, however, haven't had such minor visitations. Recent hit-and-run raids on seaside towns, against which it's difficult to provide protection, have been nasty enough to justify their citizens' feeling better, whatever the bishops say, when they hear the Fortresses roaring out over the Channel some of these bright mornings.

Usually there is less public grousing over the Ministry of Food than over any other government body, but its scheme for the distribution of the new ration books caused a nation-wide protest. It's encouraging to note that the row arose not because Lord Woolton had taken a new crack at the national diet but because, according to millions of country dwellers, he was going to waste their precious working time by compelling them to make a trip to the district town to get their ration books. Fuming rustic householders swamped both the Ministry and their M.P.'s with plaints that the journey, probably a dozen miles of slow country bus ride, with hours of waiting in a queue at the end of it, could be dispensed with if the competent Women's Voluntary Services ladies were allowed to handle the distribution in each village. Since the allocation was to be made in alphabetical order, a busy housewife responsible for a bunch of evacuees all with different surnames would have to make the trip several days running. The Ministry has bowed before the storm and ruled that one or two delegates from each village may collect the whole community's cards and stagger home with them. This is the same system that is being employed in factories.

Something which should cheer the populace, when it finally gets its books, is that food, clothing, and chocolate coupons have all been assembled under one cover. This sensible new arrangement will do away with the old complicated one of several sets bouncing around in handbags and the fairly frequent spectacle of addled shoppers muzzily proffering their food points in a dressmaker's shop.

June 13

Englishmen who get to the radio too late to catch the synopsis of the day's events given at the beginning of the news broadcasts now merely ask earlier arrivals, "Has anything happened?" A simple shake of the head is all the answer they need to understand that the news everybody is waiting for—the invasion of the European mainland—hasn't yet begun. Until it does, not even several more Pantellerias are likely to get them very excited. The daily papers, reduced to guessing in the dark, have the somewhat aimless air they had in peacetime August days when they were merely waiting for the first autumn crop of political crises. As one newspaper expressed it, "The sense of standing on the verge of what, with the Russian campaign, will constitute the greatest military operations in the history of the world is both impressive and oppressive."

There was a rather widespread and certainly quite unjustifiable feeling of disappointment over the fact that Mr. Churchill hadn't seen fit, in his report last Tuesday to the Commons, to furnish an obliging hint about the direction from which the invasion is likely to come. Nonetheless, most people felt cheered by the little he was able to tell them and profoundly relieved that he was there to tell it. The loss of a Lisbon transport plane had done nothing to make people feel any easier about his absence. Right now, it's not only the conventional clucking old ladies who are hoping to goodness that the Prime Minister won't find it necessary to make any more long and dangerous hops for quite a while.

July 11

With his customary instinct for the proper gesture, Mr. Churchill quietly took his family to the theatre to see "Watch on the Rhine" the night that the first landings on Sicily were being made. Less well informed Britons, who merely took themselves to bed that night and learned the first sparse details the following morning, were relieved to hear that something had finally happened to take their minds off last week's uneasy watch on the upper Donetz. Ever since the new German attack on Russia began, Londoners have been fretful at finding themselves back on the sidelines while a pal did all the fighting. Reading between the lines, most people felt that the Russian battle wasn't going nearly so well as they would have liked. That uneasiness is not past. The popular impatience for the Allies to catch up with the timetable may have been increased by recent news-

paper stories, which gave the impression that air bombardment had softened Sicily weeks ago into a pat of butter
meekly waiting for the Allied knife. The first communiqué,
with its bleak warning that the operation wasn't likely to
prove such a pushover, was therefore a sobering check to any
premature optimism.

Earlier in the week, General Sikorski's death * had been la-
mented as a disaster not only to the Allies in their conduct
of the war but to the whole world after the war. A great
many people wish that his particular brand of disinterested
statesmanship was right now unravelling the unhappy
French political tangle, which seems to be causing as much
impassioned discussion as the Soviet-Polish affair a while
back. Those who tried to understand the situation in Algiers
and the scrappings among the factions of the all too aptly
named Fighting French that preceded General Giraud's visit
to the United States didn't succeed very well. They are not
at all comforted by the new turn of events. It is difficult, as
they point out, to see exactly what will be accomplished by
putting an ocean between the two principal protagonists.

Last week, in the House of Commons, the Parliamentary
Secretary for the Ministry of Information was given a rough
ride because of the government's suppression of a Gaullist
newspaper, *La Marseillaise,* which was published in London.
Members pointed out that the extinguishing of this publication, accomplished by the simple method of withholding its
supply of paper, looked unpleasantly like political maneu-
vering, especially since the anti-Russian Polish news sheets
printed here have been allowed to get off with only a warning. General de Gaulle often seems to be his own and his
cause's worst friend, but lots of non-political British haven't
forgotten that he chose to join forces with this country at a
moment when bets were being freely taken against its survival. After the death of Darlan, people were far too ready to
believe that from then on everybody was going to live happily ever after. Now they sometimes think that it might be

* Wladyslaw Sikorski, chief of Polish fighting forces on the Allied side, was
killed in a plane crash.

better if the French were allowed to manage their affairs themselves.

July 26

[*July 25, Mussolini deposed by the Fascist Grand Council and placed under arrest.*]

Needless to say, this is a one-topic city today. Some Londoners heard late last night, and the rest of them early this morning, the news that Hitler's "utensil," as the British Broadcasting Company's announcer disdainfully phrased it, had fallen off the Axis shelf. Although it is far too early for anyone to say what the news will mean to the Allied timetable, it's safe to guess that most families will be bringing out the monthly ration of Scotch tonight to celebrate what to even the most cautious looks like the beginning of the end. The invasion of Sicily, which had at first seemed a highly promising dress rehearsal on Europe's doormat for the more elaborate performance to be given inside the house, now appears to have been far more important than anyone had anticipated in its effect on Italian morale and, consequently, on the Fascist government.

The Canadian part of the Sicilian show was particularly gratifying to the English, who for more than three years had found themselves in the apologetic position of a host who had asked the boys over for a hunting trip and then couldn't show them any real sport. Not even the stiff check before Catania really damped the general optimism. Londoners have great faith in the Eighth Army, and they're apt to say, "Monty's there," as though that took care of everything. A while back, of course, they were saying, "Monty's here," even though the General's visit was supposed to have been an official secret, to the annoyance of Fleet Street and the mystification of the crowds who gathered to cheer the familiar beret in its peregrinations through the city. Maybe the General didn't share the War Office view that he should understudy the invisible man during his stay. Instead of skulking about town in mufti, he took himself shopping and to theatres looking as though he had just stepped from a tank at El Alamein. The most unobservant Londoner couldn't, and didn't, miss him.

Until yesterday, however, the bombing of Rome, even more than the progress in Sicily, was for most people the big news of the week. From now on, naturally, there won't be much discussion of whether or not it was advisable. At the outset, it appeared that most Britons regarded it as a regrettable necessity. Inevitably, the correspondence columns of the *Times* were filled with a heated debate on whether irreplaceable antiquities or human lives were more precious and whether the damaged Basilica of San Lorenzo rated higher aesthetically than the bombed cathedrals of Canterbury and Coventry. In general, people doubted that the material results of the raid were worth its political and psychological dangers. At any rate, those who know their Italy and had been worried about the threat to the little walled cities and the villas with Tiepolo ceilings are considerably heartened today. Mussolini's resignation, they feel, will mean a speedier end of the bombing of the places they loved so well.

A good many London office workers plan to spend their holidays this summer helping the Home Guards and schoolboys get in the harvest, which is, according to early reports, a knockout. That is excellent news. But harvest time means that the early and chilly English autumn can't be far behind, and Britons' thoughts are not unnaturally turning to the fuel problem and speculation about the season's prospects. The prospect right now would appear to be a gloomy one. Last year's exceptionally mild winter saved the Ministry of Fuel's skin and the public from chilblains, but there's no guarantee that it will be repeated and no point in dodging the fact that the coal situation is bad. Mr. Ernest Bevin raised a storm last week when he told the Mine Workers Federation at Blackpool that, at a time when a full-scale invasion of the Continent is in the offing, production is so far behind demand that he would be forced to order lads of sixteen into the pits. Public reaction was so shocked that it seems likely the Bevin plan will have to be considerably modified. Possibly the country's disapproval was colored by the practical objection that the young miners would have to spend the coming crucial six months learning the trade and consequently not making much of an improvement in the coal supply.

The problem, of course, will be not only to keep the home fires burning but also to stoke the liberating ones which everyone hopes will soon be spreading across Europe. A campaign has already been started to educate Britons in the important new idea that they must not only keep their own families warm, fed, and clothed but must help warm, feed, and clothe strangers they'll never meet in towns and villages that they will probably never see. Coincident with Bevin's desperate proposal came the announcement that fifty thousand tons of British coal a week would have to be shipped to Sicily and that the public would have to do with less chocolate, since most of the supply was being earmarked for occupied Europe against the day the great handout begins.

Possibly the thought of what the coming winter will be like in country districts, where fuel supplies are apt to be skimpy, has been responsible for the rush of evacuated children back to London, although the recent absence of German bombers over the capital and their unpleasant habit of attacking reception areas instead may have had a good deal to do with it. On an average, some eight hundred children are returning to London every week. This is creating quite a situation for the County Council schools, which are having as tough a time trying to squeeze homing scholars into inadequate substitutes for blitzed premises as the village schools had in 1939. Now that signposts, which had been tucked away in the days when an invasion of this country seemed imminent, are appearing again and nothing but the local accents are heard in many village playgrounds, returning week-

enders say that rural England has, superficially at least, an almost prewar air.

August 8

When the good news about Orel and Catania reached the
headlines, a London bus conductor, nearly falling off his
top deck as he leaned over the side to read them, shouted
the tidings to his fares and added a hoarsely appreciative
"Our lads've got their tails up this time, all right!"

Not only the Allied armies but the stay-at-homes have had
their tails up this last cheerful week. Britons who in 1940
felt resentfully that Italy had played them a trick as low as a
bookie's welshing at the races are now calmly certain that it
won't be long before the culprit is haled to justice between a
couple of bobbies. When that happens, however, the problem
of deciding what's to be done with the Italians is likely to
make people hotter and angrier than the chase, judging by
the worrying in the press and the discussions of ordinary citizens.

Before the M.P.'s took themselves off for the summer re-
cess, there was a short debate in Parliament on our policy toward Italy which was remarkable chiefly for the skill, tact,
and good humor with which Mr. Eden (whose stature appears to be increasing enormously, by the way) parried the
Opposition's attacks and reiterated the Government's stand
that nothing but unconditional surrender would satisfy it.

August 15

[*August, first Quebec Conference.*]

The sightseeing Londoners who can always be found peering
hopefully into Downing Street for a glimpse of a cigar proba-

bly weren't very surprised to learn that they had been peering for nothing last week and that their bird had flown
again. Mr. Churchill's jaunts have become so routine that
only the destination of this one excited much local comment. One or two journals, which last time had implored
him not to make any more risky hops for a while, soothed
their readers by saying that, just as any traveller should, the
Prime Minister had undoubtedly asked himself the question
"Is my journey really necessary?"

There are plenty of people here who wish that such a
question had been tacked up over Marshal Stalin's desk and
that he had answered yes. The satisfaction over the choosing
of Canada as the scene of the latest conference has been
matched by the disappointment that once more there are no
Russian feet under the conference table. Until something is
done about this, most intelligent Britons will very likely
continue to feel that the table is not well balanced at all and,
what's worse, that it won't be a very good one on which to
rough out the first blueprint of the grave new world that is
to follow the war.

The air offensive directed against Fortress Europe from
this country was on such a scale last week that people in the
south found themselves lying awake hour after hour, staring
through the window into a sky which seemed to have become one vast, roaring airplane engine. They said, cheerfully
and sleepily, that it was just like old times except that the
planes are headed out this time instead of in. In London,
however, it's become so unusual to hear a plane that when
one does go over by day, pedestrians stand gaping up as
though they expected to see Blériot in one of those novel
flying contraptions.

Possibly because there is official alarm over the notions,
which are gaining ground, that the blitz won't visit us again
and that the European phase of the war may be over by
Christmas, Mr. Herbert Morrison issued new fire-watching
orders last week. These told the public that plenty of unpleasantness may still be ahead, and they should make it harder for slackers to dodge serving on the fire-watching shifts if

they work in a danger zone. In the future, everybody will be responsible for keeping the office fires from burning instead of sitting cozily by the home ones. Mr. Morrison has, however, been chivalrous toward women fireguards; he has promised them that they won't have to serve in buildings infested with rats and mice, animals which apparently can still cause an Englishwoman to blanch even while taking little things like exploding incendiaries in her stride.

Though there's been no criticism of this tart government reminder that it can still happen here, and though there's perhaps even a sneaking feeling of relief among bored civil-defense workers, lots of city people hope that the long, suffocating, depressing blackout may be relaxed somewhat this winter. Double summer time ended today, and millions of citizens were mournfully reminded, as they set back their clocks, that before long they will find themselves wrestling with folds of black bombazine round about tea time and skinning their shins on curbings in the gloom when they take the dog for a late-afternoon stroll. It's being hopefully pointed out that workers waste time getting back and forth in the completely darkened streets and that the poor ventilation which is the result of all the blackout devices used in factories does as much harm to manpower as any other factor.

September 3

Today's brief, early-morning announcement of the landing in Italy was a fine fourth-anniversary present to everybody here. Millions of Britons later observed the day by taking themselves to church, but so far the general mood has seemed as much pugnacious as prayerful. Certainly the national desire to hit the Germans hard and get the thing finished as soon as possible has never been stronger, and until this morning there had been disappointment over the failure to follow up Sicily with another sock even closer to the

bull's-eye. Mr. Churchill's Quebec speech—all the more eagerly awaited after its postponement, which led people to
think it was being delayed so that it would coincide with
some big news—didn't seem to calm the public's impatience
at the prevailing quiet on the Western front. When he finally did go on the air, the first few minutes of his speech
were lost because of bad weather, which added nothing to
the happiness of his listeners. There was, however, universal
relief at the implication that next time the Russians were
going to sit in on the talking as well as the fighting.

One rumor that had a run straight through August was
that something was going to happen shortly across the Channel. This was mainly the result of a ban on visitors in the
southern coastal districts. The ban didn't, as was hoped, cut
down railway travel, since vacationists simply clogged the
lines to East Coast resorts instead of South Coast ones, but it
started the usual whispers about leaves being cancelled,
ports chockablock with invasion barges, and the entire population of such-and-such a town knowing for a fact that those
in command were only waiting for the full moon before
dropping the handkerchief. Naturally, the public was
gloomy over the fact that August had departed without our
opening a second front in France or elsewhere.

Londoners who weren't scared off by notions of getting
scrambled up in an invasion effort and who ignored the government's suggestion that they take their holidays in the
backyard vegetable patch are returning to their jobs with
tans they certainly worked hard to acquire. The hit-and-run
raiders who dropped in to machine-gun bathers on the
beaches last year haven't been so active this summer, but the
difficulties of travelling to a place and finding something to
eat and drink when you finally get there have been almost as
arduous. Most excursionists started off by queuing for their
railway tickets and went right on queuing for everything
until it was time to go back to London, there to receive the
slightly smug condolences of neighbors who had stayed put
and enjoyed the dancing in the parks, the open-air theatres,
and other attractions provided by their boroughs. At some

places, such as Blackpool, to which industrial Lancashire flocked, there were few reminders of the war except high prices, but at other resorts bathers still had to dodge the 1940-vintage barbed wire and reckon on stray mines being part of the local flora. At the seaside towns, it seems, the local housewives couldn't buy a kitchen spoon or a cake tin. The entire supply had been bought up by resourceful visiting children to make sand castles with, since buckets and spades were almost unprocurable.

September 19

The midweek's deepening anxiety here over the outcome of the Salerno battle would have been an anticlimax to the wild excitement over Italy's surrender, if there had been any wild excitement. On the night the news of the capitulation broke, there seemed to be little to-do beyond a few private parties and a spurt of business in the pubs, which opened for the evening, conveniently enough, soon after the exultant newspapers appeared on the streets. Some Londoners remarked that it would have harmed nobody and cheered everybody to hang out the flags, ring the bells, and fire off the Hyde Park guns, in the Moscow manner. As it was, almost the only official attempt to cash in on the emotional opportunities of the occasion was the concert which B.B.C. promptly broadcast, apparently aimed at putting its listeners in the right frame of mind with such triumphant music as Elgar's "Land of Hope and Glory." People were kept bounding to their feet for one national air after another, including "The Red Flag," which the orchestra played in a manner as piously soulful as though it were a hymn written by an Anglican bishop.

Next day, according to the press, all the remaining Soho Italian restaurant keepers (maybe conscious of olive oil and Parmesan cheese once more as much as of political regimes) dutifully remarked that they were "very please' indeed" by the news. A Strand bookseller filled his window with hastily dusted-off copies of guidebooks for Rome, Naples, and Milan, along with an earnest injunction to read up on the beautiful old Italian cities. Plenty of people must have been happy at the notion that they could think of them as beautiful old cities and not as enemy objectives which our bombers visited last night. That, however, was as far as anyone's enthusiasm went. The subsequent discovery that the Germans hadn't been backward either in dusting off *their* guidebooks to the peninsula was therefore not such a shock as it might have been. As the news grew worse, there were queues of worried people on every corner waiting to buy papers. On the whole, the nation's reaction was admirably steady, but the relief over the brighter turn of events this weekend was nonetheless tremendous.

[*September, Mussolini taken from jail by German rescue party.*]

There is still considerable disappointment and perplexity over the Il Duce affair. How such a valuable cat was allowed to get out of the bag (if he was ever in one) is certainly an item that everyone hopes Mr. Churchill will touch upon in his forthcoming report to Parliament.

Coal and housing have been big topics both in the week's news and in Londoners' conversation. The Nottinghamshire miners' strike, in support of an eighteen-year-old lad's refusal to be drafted for work underground, cost the country sixty thousand tons of coal while it lasted, but it was less serious than the news that the output of coal fields all over Britain is steadily dwindling. This situation has been attributed variously to long working hours, to the low meat content in miners' rations, and to the dangerous notion that the war is now going so well that everyone can afford to take things a trifle easier. Maybe the touch-and-go aspect of the affair at Salerno, coupled with the increasing belief that the Italian campaign will be a tough one, will knock this complacency in the head.

Though the problem of the home fires looks as if it will be acute enough this winter, there are even worse headaches right now for the numberless citizens who can't find a home to have a fire in. The housing shortage is universal, even in rural areas, where agricultural workers have been agitating for more cottages for almost a year. Of the three thousand modestly promised by the government, exactly two have been completed. They were formally opened the other day by Mr. Ernest Brown, Minister of Health, with considerable fanfare and presumably a lot of disappointment among the two hundred eager families who showed up to make application for them. District authorities have now been empowered to take over the cottages of weekending Londoners for local families who need to be in the neighborhood seven nights a week instead of one or two. This scheme hasn't progressed very far, from all accounts, but unhoused Londoners think it would be a fine idea if it were extended to the shuttered town houses of the well-to-do parties who skipped to hotels in unbombed areas way back in 1940.

October 24

This week's sudden burst of air-raid sirens has been more of a nuisance than a menace, which may be just what the Nazis intended. Either the bothersome things start screeching early and keep you from getting to sleep, or they wake you out of a sound slumber in the small hours. Nobody seems to have been seriously upset by them, however, and there are even people who claim that the alarms give a certain fillip to the stale monotony of the civilian's daily lot. Mr. Churchill must have felt that way when he remarked, after visiting an ack-ack gun site Friday night, that he had "much enjoyed the shooting." The other evening, when the alert sounded as the streets were filling with crowds that had just come out of cinemas and eating places, people merely stood listening to the crackling guns, shouting excited instructions to the night fighters they fancied were somewhere around, and generally carrying on as though they were at a cup final. In what may be an officially inspired attempt to make the public take a less nonchalant view of whatever is brewing in the way of unpleasantness this winter, the press has been dropping dark hints lately about a new German secret weapon which the enemy may try out quite soon. Most Londoners probably believe that it's nothing more than a newspaper yarn, remembering that the gas scare didn't come to anything. At any rate, they seem unmoved by rumors of rocket shells about to be lobbed into their midst from the French coast, apparently on the theory that nothing could be much nastier than having bombs dropped from straight overhead.

Last week, Lord Woolton, Minister of Food, kept his promise to share the first fruits of the African victory with the public. Piles of oranges appeared in the shops, with orders that they were to be doled out only to children, at the rate of two pounds for those up to five years old and one pound for those between five and sixteen. Their elders shared vicariously in the bounty, for they received a boost to their own spirits from watching the kids blissfully getting sticky round the ears.

November 7

The Moscow conference was naturally this week's liveliest topic of conversation. The general satisfaction with its results seemed to give away the fact that nearly everyone had had secret qualms about its success but now felt something like a hostess who had mixed a lot of different people at a party and unexpectedly scored a triumph. Anthony Eden's personal popularity has received a big boost from his share in it. Perhaps the only shadow of disappointment was the absence of a more definite statement about the future of Germany after the armistice. Lots of ordinary Germans, it is agreed, are anxious to hear just what is in store for them—

whether they are going to live in a partitioned Germany, or be led wholesale to the executioner, or be policed for the rest of their lives, or allowed to work out their own destiny. Probably only the most violent Vansittartites here feel that the first three answers are the best ones. The more general hope is that the new European Advisory Commission will before long issue a statement which will give the German people a tangible, compelling reason to lay down their arms.

Meanwhile, even more cheer is being spread by the good news from the Russian battlefront. Dangerous and officially discouraged though such optimism may be, many Londoners are talking as though the end of the war might come any time, shopkeepers now appear to think that their dwindling stocks of this and that may last until peace, and people in general are consoling themselves with the belief that this is positively the final winter of fumbling about in the foggy blackout.

The event which probably raised British spirits more than anything, however, was the recent repatriation of prisoners, which seemed to lift a corner of the dark curtain of war for a few brief minutes. The homecomers arrived almost unheralded, and Londoners didn't get much of a chance to welcome them unless they happened to be at one of the big railway stations, where Red Cross workers had a busy time sorting out the men who were to be driven across town to their homes. One repatriated cockney, who hung his head out of the automobile in which he was riding and beamingly shouted "Wot cheer!" to every passerby, including a brigadier general in Whitehall, got only a series of outraged glares in return. He finally remarked to his driver that everybody seemed to have got bloody unfriendly since he'd been away. He was assured that if "Repatriated Prisoner" had been written on his forehead, even the general would have been shouting "Wot cheer!" back at him. Most of the returning Londoners seemed surprised that the bomb damage was not greater.

Both East and West Enders have now got a chance to say what they think of the plans for repairing London's battered face after the war, because the London County Council's Housing Plan is on view at the Royal Academy. Mr. Churchill and the bombed-out House of Commons, too, have been discussing, as earnestly as any suburban housewife, how they want their new home built. They have decided that what they prefer is a duplicate of the cozy old original, with not enough seats to go round and a minimum of floor space, though with an improved ventilating system. There were no takers, it seems, for the suggestion that the House move to the country, away from the Thames fogs. Parliamentarians and ordinary citizens have been staunchly united in disliking the thought of being anything but Londoners; judging by the comments on the County Council's plans, most people have no wish to be included among the half million souls who, according to the plan, will move away. A poll taken of urban housewives showed an overwhelming preference for houses instead of flats. In the middle of a global war, the British dream is still of a little box behind a hedge, though the planners point out that lots of big boxes will probably have to be the answer if the London of tomorrow isn't to become one vast, sprawling suburb.

November 19

Although the press declared that the fall of Leros wasn't a major military disaster, it couldn't take the sting out of what was a profound disappointment. If the campaign in Italy had not slowed down to what looks like a crawl, there might have been less gloom over the capitulation of Leros. As it was, the general impression seemed to be that the high expectations at the opening of the Italian campaign have failed to materialize, and it seems certain that Parliament will shortly be asking those critical questions which are already being asked in lots of less formal London gatherings.

It may be, though, that the Government won't be entirely displeased if the unfamiliar taste of bad news jolts the public out of feeling that the end of the war is just around the corner. Several speakers, including Mr. Churchill and Mr. Morrison, have lately issued warnings that for some time to come civilians are likely to be getting more opportunities for practicing with the stirrup pump than for tacking up victory bunting. In all the chat about whether the Germans will shortly try out something new and nasty, the only point on which everyone seems agreed is that the capital will be the natural and inevitable target. Some of the guesses about what might be cooking have a wild, Wellsian flavor. (The old Wells movie, "The Shape of Things to Come," was revived here recently, and its prophecy of a bomb-devastated London just made the audience giggle.) The public reaction continues to be sensibly calm, but A.R.P. workers report that after the last few night alerts the streets were noticeably emptier than usual, presumably because people don't fancy sticking their heads out and achieving the honor of being the first to get cracked by any secret German weapon which may happen to be on hand.

The refusal to ease up on the blackout by so much as a glimmer has been taken by many citizens to mean that there may indeed be new and perhaps unpleasant visitations. The announcement of the decision about the blackout was somewhat softened by the Home Secretary's statement that municipal lighting systems were being checked over for the big moment when the lights go on again on armistice night.

On the home front, millions of Britons thought that the best news of the week was the appointment of Lord Woolton as the Minister of Reconstruction. The only regretful voices to offset the chorus of satisfaction were those of the housewives who apparently considered that they had lost their best friend, for the accession of Woolton to the Ministry of Reconstruction meant that he had to resign the portfolio of Minister of Food. There is hope even for these mourners, though, since the Prime Minister's definition of Britain's reconstruction job as "food, work, and homes for all" seems to show that Woolton's eye will still be on the national larder for some time to come. Seldom, if ever, has a Minister bowed his way offstage (even if only to take up another starring part) in the applauding atmosphere of a successful first night; such departures generally resemble a post-mortem.

On the whole, the food situation here would appear, from the consumer's viewpoint, to be in fairly tidy shape for the new Minister to take over. The blackest spot right now is the reduction of the milk ration to two pints a week for an adult, which, with a virulent gastric-influenza bug laying out Londoners as neatly as any secret weapon could hope to do, is bad news indeed.

"This is the Army," with its New York cast, is playing for three weeks at the Palladium to standing room only. On the Tuesday matinée attended by the King and Queen and their daughters, the audience spent all the time that they weren't laughing, which wasn't much, in cocking an eye at the Royal Box to see how the young princesses were enjoying the Gypsy Rose Lee strip-tease act and similar adult frolics. Even Princess Margaret Rose seemed to think that they were fine. The show, which is going to the provinces shortly, has done more for Anglo-American understanding than the carloads of print turned out by the propagandists. The Palladium audiences are demonstrating the simple fact that laughing with an ally is one of the best ways of getting to feel that he's a nice fellow to have around.

December 5

The three-power conference had been expected for so long by most people here, especially those who have learned to look knowing whenever Mr. Attlee gets up in Parliament to answer questions which would ordinarily be handled by Mr. Churchill, that there was no great excitement when the news of the Cairo meeting was announced. There was, on the contrary, a sense of disappointment, for while everyone was pleased that Generalissimo Chiang Kai-shek was present, Marshal Stalin's absence was much regretted and generally considered "not pally." The regret didn't last long, though, since before the week was over the Marshal, as pally as you please, showed up in Teheran to meet President Roosevelt and Mr. Churchill. *This* was the conference everybody had been waiting for and, even though the decisions arrived at were not announced for several days, the mere fact that it was held was enough to cause a great and instant lifting of local spirits.

It's harder to assess the effect of the Berlin raids on Londoners. A city which has been through the hell of persistent blitzing is likely to react in two ways to the information that an enemy city is now receiving an even larger dose of the same treatment. There is naturally the school of thought which says that Berlin got just what it deserved—a perfectly logical attitude. Thinner-skinned citizens, however, while regarding the raids as a magnificent feat, don't care to dwell on the bloody results. At any rate, despite all the jubilant press and radio accounts, the raids don't appear to have anything like the tonic effect on Londoners that the capture of just one little Italian hill by Monty's Eighth Army boys does. Next to the news of the Teheran conference, the high spot of the week was the break-through in Italy.

The Moscow press may continue to refer to the coming European second front, but the English press scarcely lets out a peep about it nowadays. Only occasionally does some occurrence suggest future military activity in a new sector, such as this week's new call-up of brand-new young doctors who, it is rumored, will serve at field dressing stations somewhere in Europe. This latest harassment of the London hospitals, which have somehow kept going despite the blitz, evacuations from bombed-out establishments, and earlier military raids on their personnel, means that half of the junior house doctors now on their staffs will be called into the services after only three months' experience in the wards instead of the usual six. This may be hard on military patients, but it will be even harder on civilians, who are already finding London no place to be seriously sick in. Evacuees returning from the country have increased the already acute crowding in the hospitals, and the civilian patient who can afford a nursing home is likely to have a tough struggle before he can find a place to get rid of his appendix.

December 19

The news of Mr. Churchill's illness has naturally overshadowed everything else in Londoners' minds this past week. Though all the papers pointed out that there was no apparent cause for alarm, the public didn't seem at all reassured, and at least one journal, the religious little *Daily Sketch,* seemed to share this view to the extent of devoting its whole front page to a photograph of the Prime Minister with a solemn verse from the Psalms under it. What with this sort of thing and the lugubrious triumph of the faint-hearted, who have always insisted that his global sorties were much, much too risky, the last few days have been distinctly uncheerful, though Mr. Churchill's apparent improvement has caused a slight lifting of spirits.

In the middle of their anxiety over Mr. Churchill's temperature, millions of Englishmen have been feverishly taking their own, for the flu epidemic has now reached worrying proportions and isn't yet at its peak, according to the *Lancet.* There have been worse epidemics, certainly, but the amount of dislocation which this one is causing is just another indication of how little slack is left in the home-front line. The current versions of influenza are the "lightning" variety, which is over in three days, and a lengthier and more unpleasant brand, which usually keeps the victim's temperature wobbling around 103 for a week or so. Both sorts leave people with a vicious cough, so at the moment every movie theatre, restaurant, and public vehicle is in a continuous and explosive uproar.

The new Minister of Health, Mr. Henry U. Willink, has as big a job to do in this new emergency as he had when, as special commissioner of the Ministry, he was called upon to

find housing accommodations for people made homeless by
the blitzes, and he is tackling it just as vigorously. His
scheme, already functioning in London boroughs and country districts, makes it possible for a distraught householder
whose entire family is prostrate and whose sink is stacked
with unwashed dishes to apply to the local Women's Voluntary Services, or similar good angels, who will come round
and do the chores, mind the children, and fetch the medicine. The British Restaurants are also organizing a mobile
canteen service of hot dinners just as they did when blitzes,
rather than bacilli, were interfering with the public's cooking arrangements.

One good effect of the epidemic is that it has stopped the
mild amount of worrying over that new secret weapon German propagandists keep talking about. Now that the influenza bug is openly laying people out right and left, there is
no inclination to speculate on what similar device the Germans may be privately concocting. The irritating greeting of
the moment is "Have you had it?" and those who can still
say no seem resigned to the possibility that they won't be
able to much longer.

The holiday shoppers are finding, naturally enough, that
there is less and poorer stuff to buy than there was last
Christmas and that what there is costs more. In a word, everything from toys to cosmetics is expensive and nasty. Gift
hunters declare angrily that what the shops offer is trash but
buy it, just as angrily, because there's nothing else. The
rocking horses of earlier days are in keen demand, and antique dealers are rubbing their hands cheerfully, for plenty
of shoppers are deciding that something old but honestly
made is better than something new and shoddy. Though the
average citizen never so much as sniffs the black market,
most of the Christmas poultry is admittedly going to it, and
the Ministry of Food so far seems unable to remedy the situation. For the benefit of Britons buying legally and mournfully on the white market, the papers give cheerful recipes
telling how to stuff your ration of frozen beef so that by closing your eyes and not thinking you might imagine it's tur-

key. The theatres, however, are gallantly keeping up the Christmas spirit with such offerings for children as "Peter Pan," "Alice in Wonderland," and that hardy holiday perennial "Where the Rainbow Ends." The theatrical treat for parents is the Lunts in Robert Sherwood's new (and non-Finnish) version of "There Shall Be No Night," which opened last week among a shower of bouquets from the critics.

1944

January 2

WITH THE SCHARNHORST SUNK, the magnificent Russian victories piling up, and the reassuring photograph of Mr. Churchill zippered up in his fire-fighting suit again, Londoners felt that the new year was getting off to a good start. Their enthusiasm over the naval triumph was heightened by the feeling that at last an old score had been paid off, for Britons have never forgotten the day in February, 1942, when the *Scharnhorst,* along with the *Gneisenau* and the *Prince Eugen,* steamed down the Channel right under their affronted noses. "If we'd got the *Scharnhorst,*" people were saying then, "it would have been something." Well, they've got it, and it certainly is something.

The immense din of outgoing bombers which the capital recently heard on more than one fine morning provided a very inspiring sort of overture to 1944, too. All the same, Londoners who saw the year in by storming one of the packed places around town or by bringing out the precious bottle of Scotch or Algerian wine at home couldn't wish each other a happy new year with a completely light heart. Now that the invasion seems so imminent, the conventional salutation sounded faintly ironic. There have been many other occasions when everyone you met confidently told you that the invasion of Europe would start next Wednesday at the latest, but the announcement of the new team of commanders appears to have really convinced the public that things will begin to move before their new calendars shed many more leaves.

Londoners seem to feel that things will get hot again at home just as soon as they warm up elsewhere, but their attitude remains nonchalant enough to annoy Doctor Goebbels. When a taxi had a particularly noisy blowout the other day, one of the apocryphal London hawkers, now peddling rare bobby pins and rarer elastic to Oxford Street matrons, is supposed to have said to a customer, "Hit must be the secret weapon, lidy."

Another slight clue to just how happy this new year may turn out to be was provided by the government's announcement that repairs to gas masks will be made free of charge for the next two months. Though this precaution possibly belongs in the knock-on-wood category, Britons thoughtfully hunting up their almost forgotten masks felt that it might also be an official hint that the Nazis have a few more tricks to try before they are forced to give in.

The latest attempt to remedy the coal situation, which still remains serious, is meeting with some criticism. Mr. Bevin's scheme for drawing numbers out of a hat, and putting all the youngsters with the corresponding numbers on their national registration cards to work digging coal for King and country, went into operation last week. As a result, many youths who may have wanted to pilot a Spitfire or drive a tank will soon be going down into the pits in the coalfields. This is a fairly stiff dose of democracy for England to swallow, and one which may have as healthy an effect on its class psychology as on its coal production, for boys from all ranks will wield picks and shovels together without any distinguishing marks other than a fine, democratic film of grime.

There have been complaints, however, from pre-service training units, which point out that their cadets, instead of being allowed to enter the services for which they have been pointing, are now likely to be snatched away willy-nilly and sent to the mines. This situation can be avoided only if the young men plump for one or another of the services before they reach registration age, and apparently nothing can help any of the present batch of disappointed intending Montgomerys or Tedders who will shortly be turning up in the mining villages. Whatever the effect of all this upon the social future of England may be, the rate of production is not likely to be increased immediately, for miners can't be made overnight. Luckily, though, this winter so far has not added to the Ministry of Fuel's worries by turning in any temperatures low enough to make householders, shivering as they are, particularly lavish with the coal scuttle.

The return of children to London has been very noticeable lately. Pantomimes ring with juvenile whoops again, harassed parents herd their young through the shops, and altogether it's a lively contrast to the days when rusticating mothers smuggled their young into town to visit the dentist and gave a sigh of relief when the risky outing was over. Nobody claims that it isn't still risky, but at least the mass homecoming is a cheerful sign of greater confidence.

January 16

The big show which everyone expects quite soon now is naturally still the major topic of conversation. Everyday the papers carry enough prophecies, hints, and rumors to make Allied plans perfectly plain to Berlin—that is, should any of the prophecies, hints, and rumors happen to be true. The prize for second-front headlines, by the way, should certainly go to the *Express* for its solemn statement that "Racing Men Fear Invasion May Cut Programme." This referred to the worries of the Jockey Club, which had announced larger entries than last year's for the Derby, Oaks, St. Leger, and the two Guineas but was afraid that the railways might be too busy carrying materials of war to have any time or room for racegoers. This crisis hasn't exactly rocked the country, since most people don't expect to be in the mood for caring whether the Derby is run at Ascot or Newmarket or even on some other planet.

The clothing ration quota, it has been announced, is to stand unchanged for the next twelve months. This put a satisfactory end to some nasty rumors that there was to be a cut. Every now and then, one of these minor domestic rumors gets around and manages to stir up quite a storm. Just recently, for instance, it was said that lipsticks and nail varnish were to be taken off the market after January 1st—a threat which caused acute feminine consternation everywhere, including, naturally, such places as machine shops and messrooms. Nail varnish isn't to be manufactured any more, sure enough, but the Board of Trade has helped the morale of the female half of the population somewhat by announcing that there would be a small increase in the amount of cosmetics released for consumption.

January 30

Londoners, normally as good-tempered a crowd of people as you could hope to find anywhere, are beginning to show the strain of these first keyed-up days of a year which by now every statesman must have hailed as one of fateful decision. Tired bus conductresses, who have one of the most gruelling jobs on the women's home front, are apt to bawl out passengers on the least provocation. Shop assistants snap at customers who timidly ask for half a pound of something which isn't there, and the customers go home and snap at their families. Naturally, a lot of the native good humor and manners is still around, but the surface impression is that everybody's nerves are frayed. Possibly it's the inevitable hangover of the winter's flu epidemic, plus four years of wartime diet, but it seems more likely to be an inevitable result of simply waiting for something to happen.

The recent night in which London underwent two air raids was certainly the noisiest in months. Plenty of citizens, as their beds quaked, must have wondered if this was the answer to everyone's question whether heavy raiding is to be expected again. The damage turned out to be nothing much, but the racket from the ground defenses was quite up to standard.

Raids or no raids, people keep on moving back into town. More and more Londoners who left during the blitz are opening up their homes again or trying to find new ones—a firm enough reply to those dark German threats of retribution any day now. The government recently took some notice of the migration back to London by increasing the amount that anyone could spend for essential repairs from one hundred to two hundred pounds, but since it didn't also increase the number of men with ladders and pots of paint, the process of putting an apartment messed up by the blitz into livable shape is apt to be difficult. How newly married couples succeed in fixing up a nest for themselves, even if they find one, is something of a mystery. Most things made of linen require precious clothing coupons, and furniture, either new or in auction rooms, is selling at prices which even the dealers admit are fantastic. The problem of getting homes and furniture has been called one of the reasons for a sudden and surprisingly sharp drop in the number of marriages—a phenomenon more gloomily attributed by the church to the chilling effect of the usual wartime increase in the number of divorces.

February 13

Anxiety over the Anzio beachhead battle was, of course, the overshadowing emotion of this weekend. For once, the Russian news didn't act as a bracer. Human nature being what it is, the continued Russian successes seemed to intensify the local gloom, because, even after making allowances for the difficulties of the terrain in Italy, people couldn't help but contrast their ally's roller-skate advance with the depressing tidings from the Italian front. It was also inevitable that people should begin to wonder, assuming that the Anzio landing can be regarded as a sort of provincial tryout, how much tougher the real big performance is going to be. It won't displease those at the top, though, if the idea that there may be worse ordeals than Anzio ahead does filter into the public mind. The opening of the second front has been a newspaper gag for so long that stay-at-home civilians have got into the habit of talking about it as blithely as though it were still just that. The Anzio setback has provided a reminder that all news isn't likely to be good news.

A verbal battle is going on between the school of thought which holds that Rome should be tenderly treated by Allied gunners and those who think that a military advantage in the hand is worth two Michelangelo frescoes on the wall. Perhaps worried families weren't precisely in the mood last week for figuring out whether they would rather know that St. Peter's or their Bert was all right, but Archbishop Lang, the former Archbishop of Canterbury, found time to lead the chorus of anxious concern over the fate of Rome— concern which, judging by the extreme solicitude the Allies were showing for the Monte Cassino Monastery, seemed hardly necessary.

The subject also came up last week in the House of Lords' debate on the ethics of wholesale bombing, and the official answer was that the systematic obliteration of German cities must and will go on. Lots of not particularly sensitive English, though they realize that this is true enough, have an uncomfortable feeling that the press and radio are overdoing the gloating. A B.B.C. announcer, carolling the tonnage of bombs dropped on Berlin, sometimes makes people think that they might be listening to a broadcast of rugby scores back in the good old days.

February 27

Once more London finds itself a blitz city. A city officially enters that class when people ring up their friends the day after a noisy night to find out if they're still there. The recent raids are nothing like the old affairs, which began late in the afternoon and went on, with occasional lulls, until morning, but they are nastier, in a way, because they are concentrated. Everything happens in a hurry and without a break; there are none of those nice ten-minute breathers during which your insides can get back into place. As one fire-watching matron feelingly remarked, "It's a little like having a baby in an hour—gratifying afterwards but highly uncomfortable while it's going on." The fact, incidentally, that compulsory fire-fighting has been stepped up since the 1941 blitz means that far more citizens are finding themselves, willy-nilly, in ringside seats for the return engagement.

It seems strange and a bit dreamlike to hear broken glass being shovelled out of the gutters again and to see a display of fluttering rayon stockings in a shattered shop window being guarded by enough policemen to make a Hope Diamond feel reasonably safe. The crowds who are taking shelter in the tubes these nights, however, have plainly decided that what is happening is no dream. They begin standing in line for shelter tickets quite early at some stations, and travellers often have a hard job struggling past the bundles of bedding, the new babies howling their indignation, and older kids who well remember the time when they *always* went to bed under the Bovril advertisements.

Restaurant proprietors and theatre managers have been stoutly telling the press that business is fine, despite the sound effects. Diners-out, however, seem to be more on the lookout for a good, modern, steel-and-concrete building with a deep shelter handy than for excellent cuisine in a place where there isn't much protection overhead. Many of the theatres have announced that in the future their evening performances will begin around five o'clock instead of six, so that their audiences will have a chance to duck home before anything starts.

The most noticeable effect of the past, unrestful week is that people look tired—especially the women. It is too early to gauge the psychological effect of the raids, but the Germans may have picked a good time to reopen the attack, because waiting to be the jumping-off place for a critical operation hasn't been particularly restful, either. Also, after the inexplicably rosy mood of a while back, in which bets were being made on how soon the war was going to end, there has been the inevitable, chilling reaction, which came when Britons realized that matters in Italy weren't going with the speed expected. Now, to all of this, there have been added not only the dangers but all the small, exasperating irritations of a blitz. Citizens who had once again grown accustomed to windows which kept the draughts out and to gas which came on when they turned the tap have been gamely relearning the half-forgotten lessons of the past.

In the general preoccupation with the blitz, Mr. Churchill's warning, contained in his statement on the war, that pilotless planes and rocket shells might soon be heading toward England from the French coast, passed without much comment. Most of us seemed to feel that we had enough to worry about right now with planes which did have pilots. Nobody appears disposed to treat this new blitz with anything but marked respect. About the only people who take a cheerful view of it are the youngsters, who are having a fine time collecting "flutterers," the strips of silver paper which are dropped by the raiders to interfere with the detecting instruments that are part of London's defense. Suburban backyard trees, tricked out with the silvery ribbons, often look like Maypoles, and the kids think it's fun.

March 19

London can't quite decide whether it's in for a blitz again or not. When the fire-bombers came back on Tuesday night, people figured that this marked the end of the peaceful moonlight nights and the beginning of a week or two of noisy ones. Moreover, the Germans' new dislike of what, in the old blitz days, used to be glumly called "a nice bombers' moon" has resulted in a sharp swing back to popular favor for bright nights. After the baby blitz that hit the city toward the end of last month was abruptly cut short—just when everybody had decided that it would probably keep right on squalling—Londoners began regarding the full moon with the same affection that householders have for a trusty watchdog. Sure enough, as soon as it waned, the bombers came back to deliver what was officially called "a sharp attack." The knowing, however, who expected them to go on delivering more of the same until the next moon came round, were confounded by the fact that the nightly alerts have been short and that there has not really been much bombing. The citizens most let down were those who had checked up on their sand buckets and hastily memorized the instructions for dealing with the small anti-personnel bombs which are often thrown in with the incendiaries for good measure.

In Tuesday's raid, by the way, the new plan for speeded-up fire-fighting came into operation. Under this system, pumps are sent to the scene of trouble as soon as fires are spotted by the National Fire Service observation posts. Previously, no fire was considered bona-fide until it had been reported through wardens and fire guards to officials with authority to decide which blaze had priority, by which time, indignant Londoners complained, their homes were in danger of being a bona-fide heap of ashes. On Tuesday, the new system was said to work fine for subduing that unpleasant red glare which couples, homeward bound after dinner or a movie in town, used to watch light up the sky from wherever the sirens had happened to catch them. Another change in the local bombing situation, now that the raids are generally over by midnight, is that people, instead of going home to bed after a raid, now wander about looking for a good blaze to gape at. At one big incident the other night, the fire-fighters had to fight the crowd before they could tackle the blaze —which perhaps made some of the veterans think back longingly to the old 1941 days when the bombers came late and the citizenry was by then tucked out of the way in shelters.

There's been no new government evacuation scheme, but children leave for the country in batches after every fairly hot night. The human memory being what it is, a couple of quiet nights cause parents to think that maybe things aren't going to be so bad—a conviction that persists until the next noisy barrage joggles them again.

According to wardens, there's considerable feeling, especially in working-class districts, over adult evacuees who had the money to take themselves out of bomb range in the big blitz but who moved back into London when things quieted down. The returning rusticators answer, quite legitimately, that they were officially requested not to hang around without good reason and possibly bother the civil-defense services by becoming casualties. This apparently doesn't stop their neighbors around the corner from regarding them with a good deal of coldness. Small shopkeepers and the like, who stayed behind and kept the neighborhood's flags flying when the bombs were dropping, don't precisely hope the returned wanderers will get a warm time now that the bombs are dropping again. Wardens say, though, with a chuckle, that a slight but unmistakable quiver of pleasure runs through the corner pub when the nice, freshly washed windows of householders who ducked back during the quiet period get broken.

On the whole, people seem to be meeting the raids with the same discipline and good humor they showed during the big blitz. Ellen Wilkinson, M.P., recently squashed a whispering campaign which said that East Enders weren't taking it so well as they used to. It's quite possible that the only important difference is that both East and West Enders are now three, tired years older and disinclined, by just that much, to be deadpan over the current visitations. Anyway, it's a big consolation to highly strung civilians, who previously went through agonies trying to look as calm and collected as everybody else, to discover that when the racket starts now nobody minds saying candidly that he doesn't enjoy it.

April 2

In the bad quarter of an hour that comes before the call to battle stations, tempers, it seems, are inclined to get short in high places as well as in low. To judge by the turn of most recent conversations, Britons have somewhat anxiously been wishing that they would wake up and find that "it" had started, that they knew what Russia was thinking, that they knew what the Allied foreign policy was up to, and that it would rain like the dickens and relieve the serious drought. Though the weather is one thing Mr. Churchill has never attempted to control and is not expected to, it had been hoped that he would tackle a couple of the other problems in his Sunday-night broadcast—that he would explain, for instance, just how the Atlantic Charter, which sounded so fine from the middle of an ocean, is going to be made to work on dry land. Next day, many still confused Britons seemed to feel that they had asked for bread and had been given, if not a stone, simply a promise of thousands upon thousands of prefabricated houses, at moderate rent, after the war. Steel shares rose immediately on the strength of this prefabricated future, but people's spirits noticeably didn't.

Those who had looked forward to one of the old Churchillian trumpet blasts had to console themselves with the Cromwellian speech of the enormously popular General Sir Bernard Montgomery at the opening of London's Salute the Soldier Week, when the General doughtily invited God to scatter the Allies' enemies and the public to scatter its cash in war bonds. This seemed more in the genuine just-before-the-battle vein than the Prime Minister's contribution, about which none of the press, with the exception of the truculently loyal Beaverbrook faction, could summon up much more than polite enthusiasm.

London has been "saluting the soldier" with the usual accompaniment of crowds gaping at the rocket guns that demurely sit on view in Trafalgar Square, hawkers selling paper flags at black-market prices, endless shows of superb marching men and material, and an endless tinkle of cash flowing into the National Savings till. Since Londoners are always ready for a good procession, maybe it was a sound idea to glamorize the fighting men just when so much attention was fixed upon them, but possibly they themselves feel that the most sincere salute to the soldier will be the increase in service allowances for wives and children which the Government is expected to announce shortly.

Meanwhile, the blitz having temporarily died down, business once more seems to be flourishing in theatres, restaurants, and the like, and new shows keep popping out like spring flowers, despite the fact that the opening of the invasion may cut them down overnight. Londoners who come back from short breathers in the country say that impending events seem far more real in the rural sections than they do in the capital, which has to have a National Savings Week in order to see a tank. In remote villages, people are losing sleep because of the rumble of military traffic on the roads, and "the invasion" is now made an excuse, just as "the blitz" used to be, for the minor dislocations of everyday life, from no whiskey in the pub to the plumber turning up late because he and his bicycle got involved in a convoy.

Londoners have not yet felt the effect of the drought, which, in many parts of rural England, has been grave enough to make standing in queues for water a daily chore. England is now in the position of the hostess of a modest-sized house with an influx of guests who have run the cistern dry. An exceptionally arid season, a lack of prevision on the part of those in charge, and more and more American troops crowding in on this already overcrowded little island have resulted in a situation which is making farmers, not to mention lots of bathless householders, look worried. Reservoirs will probably be as high on the priority building list as Mr. Churchill's prefabricated homes on that wonderful day which Britons, without specifying the month or even the year, now doggedly refer to as "after it's over."

April 16

The customary official injunction to stay home over the Easter weekend, on which trains are usually packed with people who seem to imagine the government is talking to a couple of other fellows, really worked this year. The ban placed on coastal areas, forbidding them to civilians, certainly helped, but it's just as likely that prudence really turned the trick. Naturally, few people fancied getting stranded as the result of some sudden clamp-down on all civilian travel, so the travellers on the railways were mainly military. The only big civilian exodus recently was to the Bank Holiday Windsor race meeting, at which thousands of racegoers, making the short trip by every sort of conveyance, from river steamers to one-horse shays, saw the Derby favorite, Orestes, unexpectedly lose by a neck to The Solicitor and then descended on the local food supplies like hungry locusts. Even that day, however, the majority of Londoners, virtuously staying in town, strolled in the parks, took the kids to the zoo, queued up for things to eat and drink, and endlessly discussed the invasion. This still remains the preoccupation of the press and the public. Even for those who haven't a personal stake in the coming operations—and such people are extremely few—this sense of being on the brink is hard on the nerves. People are inclined to fret over the continuing quietness on the Western front and the Russian non-stop advance is gloomily contrasted with the deadlock at Cassino. Londoners have been telling each other a crop of wry jokes, such as the one in which Stalin rings up from Dieppe and says, "Come on over, the bathing's fine." Nevertheless, most people, particularly since the big softening-up assault on French railheads, believe that the word to go will soon be given. The fact that Moscow hasn't been critical of any delay has also been taken as reassuring by people here.

Meanwhile, there have been angry words over the Yorkshire miners' strike, which, coming at this juncture, has caused them an almost irreparable loss of public sympathy. Other important domestic news, however, such as the passage of the education and health bills, which will alter millions of British lives if they go through, might be about happenings on Mars, for all the interest Britons are apparently taking in it. Right now, almost every Londoner's fidgety and completely uninformed chat is of moons and tides.

May 7

A visitor to this city who had managed to get in before the last pre-invasion drawbridge was hauled up would probably be able to deduce nothing much from its appearance. Londoners, whatever they feel is coming in the near future, are getting on with their day-to-day existence in an almost ostentatiously normal way. After the tense chattiness of the past few weeks, most people have settled down to a calm, quiet wait, and even speculations on likely invasion dates and places have mercifully petered out. Now there appears to be a conspiracy to pretend that this is just another spring, instead of the spring everybody has been waiting for since Dunkirk. Although no one knows if he'll be able to keep them, private and public engagements are imperturbably being made for the next few weeks. The Royal Academy's private preview, which in peacetime opens the London social season, went off much as usual last week. Women are cheering themselves up with uncouponed new spring hats at dizzy prices which the Board of Trade, whose members are possibly husbands as well as officials, have promised to bring under control. The grass around the display of tulips in Hyde Park has been worn bald by the feet of garden lovers, who are taking advantage of their lunch hour to forget the war for five minutes and revive their memories of the Chelsea flower show. Traffic on the streets seems thicker than usual, most of its liveliness being contributed by American jeeps and glossy staff cars. Cinema managers report ruefully that there has been a sharp drop in business—something that is not entirely attributable to the longer spring days. While waiting in a deceptively placid way for events to occur, the public apparently does not want its mind taken off them. The mood of the moment here resembles the trusting calm which descends on a man in the hospital for an operation who, after months of anxiety, realizes all at once that there is nothing for him to do but lie back and leave everything to the professionals.

Londoners were last week introduced to an architectural blueprint of what large areas of Britain are going to look like after the war. The first of Mr. Churchill's promised prefabricated steel houses for newlyweds has, like a squat mushroom, suddenly sprung up in the shadow of the Tate Gallery. While its aesthetic appeal is limited, lots of housewives who go to see it will think its labor-saving devices are much better-looking than anything in the Tate. It is being emphasized that such houses represent only a temporary solution of the postwar housing problem, which, on this bombed island, will certainly be acute—a reassuring guarantee to those apprehensive lovers of rural England who were beginning to visualize bungaloid growths sprawling all over the green countryside.

The Royal Academy show, like the budget, was comfortably free of shocks, and, in this most critical of problem years, free of problem pictures, too. At the preview, the greatest crowds seemed to collect around Augustus John's portrait of General Montgomery, a work which didn't flatter either John or Montgomery, and around Dame Laura Knight's detailed interiors of bombers and aircraft factories. A popular subject picture, in the good old Academy tradition, entitled "The Week's Ration," showed a good-humored butcher quizzically regarding two mutton chops and somebody's weekly one-and-tuppence meat allowance. This struck an almost painfully topical note in a week in which news of the letup on meat rationing in the United States had caught Britons trying not to look too envious, and at the same time becomingly grateful for their one-and-tuppence worth of frozen lend-lease pork.

May 21

Living on this little island just now uncomfortably resembles living on a vast combination of an aircraft carrier, a floating dock jammed with men, and a warehouse stacked to the ceiling with material labelled "Europe." It's not at all difficult for one to imagine that England's coastline can actually be seen bulging and trembling like the walls of a Silly Symphony house in which a terrific fight is going on. The fight everybody is waiting for hasn't started yet, but all over England, from the big cities to the tiniest hamlet, the people, at least in spirit, seem already to have begun it. There is a curious new something in their expressions which recalls the way people looked when the blitz was on. It's an air of responsibility, as though they had shouldered the job of being back in the civilian front line once again. It's evident in the faces of women looking up thoughtfully from their gardens at the gliders passing overhead, in the unguarded faces of businessmen wearily catnapping on trains on their way home to all-night Home Guard duty, in the faces of everybody except the young fighting men themselves. The troops look unfailingly cheerful and lighthearted, as though they didn't know that anything unusual was afoot, and it is obvious that they are in wonderful physical shape.

Life is reminiscent of the blitz in other ways, too, for now, as then, people are keyed up to withstand something which they have often imagined but never experienced, and there is the same element of uncertainty about what is coming. The ordinary civilian seems far less worried, however, about possible bombs, long-distance shelling, or gas attacks than about such problems as how the dickens he is going to get to and from work if transport is seriously curtailed. It has already been announced that trains may be suddenly cancelled without warning, but there is a vague promise that motor-buses for essential workers will take their place wherever possible. Stay-at-home Britons seem resigned to the probability that their second front will consist mainly of humdrum hardships, including more inconvenience, fatigue, and doing without. The idea that London, during the invasion, will come in for heavy air attacks seems to have faded away, oddly, and there is even less worrying over any secret weapon that may be up the German sleeve for D Day. It is plausible to lots of English that the Germans may stage a token invasion or series of parachute raids. This would mean that, since the Army's attention would be engaged elsewhere, the Home Guard would be expected to take charge of the situation.

Already, in the country, the milk and the mail arrive late, delivered by a somewhat bleary-eyed milkman or postman who explains that he has just finished standing his watch with the all-night guard, which once more has been established. The shadow of the second front falls across day-to-day happenings in even the smallest community. One country-dwelling lady who recently decided that she must have some urgent plumbing repairs done in her home was warned by the contractor that he and his plumber's mates were all Home Guards. He pointed out that if anything happened (there isn't a village in England which doesn't proudly imagine that it's all-important to the Nazis), the boys would just drop her new water tank smack on the lawn and she would be left bathless until the fighting was over. It is often in just such a ridiculous way that English families begin to realize what it may be like to have the battle of Europe right on their doorsteps, involving not only big and historic issues but also small and homely ones like baths, trains, the morning paper, and the day's milk.

There has been, so far as can be judged, no panic buying of food. The authorities have announced reassuringly that the situation is in good enough order to make anything but temporary local shortages unlikely. Moreover, in case any village gets cut off from its source of food supply, it has its own iron rations stored away in barns and other places, with plans for their distribution already organized by the squire, the vicar, and the schoolmaster. Villagers may not be hungry this summer, but they are likely to be thirsty for their traditional pint at the end of the day's work. In many rural districts, beer is so scarce already that pubs only open certain days of the week. This is due in part to the labor shortage and second-front traffic priorities and in part to the presence everywhere of troops who cheerfully drink the place dry before the locals can put on their clean corduroys and toddle round to the Dog and Pheasant.

Whether or not the High Command hopes to confuse the enemy with constant troop movements, they are certainly succeeding in confusing the village know-it-alls. The pretty girls hardly have time to get excited over the news that the Yanks have moved in before the Yanks are succeeded by the Canadians. When word gets around that the Canadians are leaving, too, there is much head-wagging over the rumor that something is really starting this time, but by next afternoon the English troops have arrived.

The peaceful charm of the English countryside is now mostly something that the English, too, read about in books. Like the phrase "weather permitting," the unspoken phrase "second front permitting" is, more and more, tacked on to all minor plans for the future, from a lunch date for next week to a village flower-show announcement that a regimental band will play—if the regiment is still there, that is.

In this dreamlike pause, the big London railway stations, crowded with men in uniform who have rushed up for a few hours' leave, are the only places where the invasion seems real and pressing and dramatic. The women who have come to see their men off nearly always walk to the very end of the platform to wave their elaborately smiling goodbyes as the train pulls out. Sometimes they look to one as though they're standing on the extreme tip of England itself, fluttering their gay, undeceiving handkerchiefs, and possibly they look that way to the boys hanging out of the windows to wave back at them.

June 4

Although the British have had the news from Rome to cheer them and the recent Churchill speech to puzzle them, the really big news for them is the fact that it's still C Day and not yet D Day. In the curious hush of the moment—a hush that is not merely figurative, since Londoners haven't been awakened by sirens for a month—it seems as though everyone is existing merely from one ordinary day to the next, waiting for the great, extraordinary one. Until the invasion begins, even the most momentous domestic happenings are bound to fall flat. For example, Lord Woolton's first important offering as Minister of Reconstruction, his White Paper dealing with the problem of maintaining full employment after the war, created as little stir as if it had described plans for preventing unemployment among the Hottentots rather than among the men who will be coming back from the invasion. In contrast to the enormous interest the public showed in the Beveridge plan, the lack of excitement over Lord Woolton's plan was remarkable.

Civilians have already had a foretaste of the interruptions in the routine of existence which the invasion will bring, for the railways, as was threatened, have been quietly withdrawing services here and there under the very noses of commuters, who frequently arrive at the station in their city clothes only to find that there are no trains to take them to the city. Furthermore, over the recent Whitsun weekend, many of the determined holiday makers who went to look for trains to take them out of London were disappointed. Among the successful ones were those who headed up the Thames, which suddenly had a prewar boom in punts, or went to see the horses run at Ascot. Few of Ascot's traditional frills remain, and the Bank Holiday crowd in the formerly exclusive Royal Enclosure munched sandwiches like any cheerful tripper party on Hampstead Heath.

Other Londoners spent what they felt to be their last breather for some time to come watching the Australians play cricket at Lord's, where a record crowd enjoyed what the weather bulletin described as a heat wave. Newspapers aren't allowed to comment on the weather—at least until the information is too dated to help the enemy—but as a conversational topic in the countryside its behavior has recently run a close second to the invasion. Dismayed rural folk have been bewailing a series of disastrous May frosts, which wiped out the famous Vale of Evesham berry and plum crops and blackened the blossoms of what promised to be a record yield in Kentish orchards. The fruit growers regret that the official secrecy on weather conditions was not relaxed for once to give them a warning which might have helped save some of the fruit. The loss in this particular year, when all England is crowded out of both house and larder, is a serious one. Then, to add to the joys of a rollicking farmer's life, the drought has damaged the hay crop, and this, in turn, will affect the milk yield. Although these headaches naturally figure in a good many of the discussions after opening time in the village pub, the one unfailing topic, as much there as in London clubs and bars, is the invasion.

In coastal hamlets, where one can see the Channel simply by toiling up a chalk track to the downs, the coming invasion is felt to be very much a local affair. So, in a way, is the fighting in Italy. Gaffers who have taken Sunday strolls to the local Roman villa or earthworks all their lives have seemed to accept, with a cozy sense of familiarity, the fact that their grandsons were now slogging up the Appian Way. All the little churches will be open for prayers and improvised services when the invasion signal is given. The local folk, especially in southern parts, think that they will get a hint of what is afoot long before those slow London chaps read it in their newspapers. It's true that the peace of the countryside is rent day and night with every variety of loud noise, but they nevertheless expect to recognize the real thing when it comes. Any particularly heavy coastal barrage put up against the German reconnaissance raids these nights has wives excitedly jabbing sleeping husbands in the ribs and saying, "Wake up, Dad! It's started!" Tiny coastal communities, where cars never even bothered to stop in peacetime, proudly expect that when it does start they will find themselves in the front line, just as they have always been in the hundreds of years that Englishmen, in one pattern of warfare or another, have been slipping away across the Channel on other D Days.

June 11

[*June 6, Allies land in Normandy.*]

For the English, D Day might well have stood for Dunkirk Day. The tremendous news that British soldiers were back on French soil seemed suddenly to reveal exactly how much it had rankled when they were beaten off it four years ago. As the great fleets of planes roared toward the coast all day long, people glancing up at them said, "Now they'll know how our boys felt on the beaches at Dunkirk." And as the people went soberly back to their jobs, they had a satisfied look, as though this return trip to France had in itself been worth waiting four impatient, interminable years for. There was also a slightly bemused expression on most D Day faces, because the event wasn't working out quite the way anybody had expected. Londoners seemed to imagine that there would be some immediate, miraculous change, that the heavens would open, that something like the last trumpet would sound. What they definitely hadn't expected was that the greatest day of our times would be just the same old London day, with men and women going to the office, queuing up for fish, getting haircuts, and scrambling for lunch.

D Day sneaked up on people so quietly that half the crowds flocking to business on Tuesday morning didn't know it was anything but Tuesday, and then it fooled them by going right on being Tuesday. The principal impression one got on the streets was that nobody was smiling. The un-English urge to talk to strangers which came over Londoners during the blitzes, and in other recent times of crisis, was noticeably absent. Everybody seemed to be existing wholly in a preoccupied silence of his own, a silence which had something almost frantic about it, as if the effort of punching bus tickets, or shopping for kitchen pans, or whatever the day's chore might be, was, in its quiet way, harder to bear than a bombardment. Later in the day, the people who patiently waited in the queues at each newsstand for the vans to turn up with the latest editions were still enclosed in their individual silences. In the queer hush, one could sense the strain of a city trying to project itself across the intervening English orchards and cornfields, across the strip of water, to the men already beginning to die in the French orchards and cornfields which once more had become "over there." Flag sellers for a Red Cross drive were on the streets, and many people looked thoughtfully at the little red paper symbol before pinning it to their lapels, for it was yet another reminder of the personal loss which D Day was bringing closer for thousands of them.

In Westminster Abbey, typists in summer dresses and the usual elderly visitors in country-looking clothes came in to pray beside the tomb of the last war's Unknown Soldier, or to gaze rather vacantly at the tattered colors and the marble heroes of battles which no longer seemed remote. The top-hatted old warrior who is gatekeeper at Marlborough House, where King George V was born, pinned on all his medals in honor of the day, and hawkers selling cornflowers and red and white peonies had hastily concocted little patriotic floral arrangements, but there was no rush to put out flags, no cheers, no outward emotion. In the shops, since people aren't specially interested in spending money when they are anxious, business was extremely bad. Streets which normally are crowded had the deserted look of a small provincial town on a wet Sunday afternoon. Taxi drivers, incredulously cruising about for customers, said that it was their worst day in months. Even after the King's broadcast was over, Londoners stayed home. Everybody seemed to feel that this was one night you wanted your own thoughts in your own chair. Theatre and cinema receipts slumped, despite the movie houses' attempt to attract audiences by broadcasting the King's speech and the invasion bulletins. Even the pubs didn't draw the usual cronies. At midnight, London was utterly quiet, the Civil Defence people were standing by for a half-expected alert which didn't come, and D Day had passed into history.

It is in the country districts just back of the sealed south coast that one gets a real and urgent sense of what is happening only a few minutes' flying time away. Pheasants whirr their alarm at the distant rumble of guns, just as they did when Dunkirk's guns were booming. On Tuesday evening, villagers hoeing weeds in the wheat fields watched the gliders passing in an almost unending string toward Normandy. And always there are the planes. When the big American bombers sail overhead, moving with a sinister drowsiness in their perfect formations, people who have not bothered to glance up at the familiar drone for months rush out of their houses to stare. Everything is different, now that the second front has opened, and every truck on the road, every piece of gear on the railways, every jeep and half-track which is heading toward the front has become a thing of passionate concern. The dry weather, which country folk a week ago were hoping would end, has now become a matter for worry the other way round. Farmers who wanted gray skies for their hay's sake now want blue ones for the sake of their sons, fighting in the skies and on the earth across the Channel. Finally, there are the trainloads of wounded, which are already beginning to pass through summer England, festooned with its dog roses and honeysuckle. The red symbol which Londoners were pinning to their lapels on Tuesday now shines on the side of trains going past crossings where the waiting women, shopping baskets on their arms, don't know whether to wave or cheer or cry. Sometimes they do all three.

June 18

[*June, first pilotless planes—"buzz bombs"—over England.*]

Once again the civilians of this island find themselves, as they expected, back under fire in the front line—all civilians, that is, living south of an imaginary line drawn from Bristol to The Wash, an area all parts of which, for security reasons, are now lumped together in air-raid reports as southern England. Up to Thursday the people of this section, like those of the rest of England, were thinking about the Battle of Normandy and not much else. On Friday, however, when it became evident that Hitler's secret weapon had stopped being a joke and had entered the active nuisance class, the new attacks on southern England by pilotless planes naturally took up a good deal of local conversation. Wardens and fireguards, arriving at their jobs rather bleary after a night of unfamiliar sights and noises, had guessed that something queer was up and there was general approval when Mr. Herbert Morrison, later in the day, made no bones about it in his official statement. Nobody seemed inclined to make any bones, either, about the new element of danger introduced by the weapon, even though the universal conviction is, as one man put it, that "the Jerries have got a nuisance there but not a winner." People know that the pilotless plane can't affect the outcome of the invasion one jot, but also they are resigned to the fact that it may easily make life here uncomfortable and hazardous in a new sort of way. What principally bothers the southern English at this moment is a certain illogical, Wellsian creepiness about the idea of a robot skulking about overhead, in place of merely a young Nazi with his finger on the bomb button. Mothers are dispatching delighted youngsters to school these days with instructions for them to duck into the nearest doorway should they see an odd-shaped, winged missile which, repu-

tedly, hums like a motorbike and is lit up at the tail and otherwise carries on suspiciously. Tin hats which have been
hanging dustily in closets with the family gas masks are also
being hauled out, since wherever there is an anti-aircraft
barrage, daylight alerts will again be unhealthy. Annoyance,
altogether, would seem to be the dominant public emotion,
though lots of English might sneakingly admit that they
don't feel displeased to be in it with the boys in Normandy,
even in such a relatively minor way.

Until Thursday's sudden burst of sirens, what had surprised the average individual most, and perhaps slightly disappointed him, was that the everyday routine of life had
been so little changed by the invasion. Transportation, for
instance, which everybody thought would be badly snarled
up, turned out to be affected far less than worried travellers
had feared. The Southern Railway has been bringing its
mob of hurrying business people into London every morning as blandly as if it didn't also have an invasion on its
hands. London itself, since D Day, has seemed more normal
than it had for months before. There's a lot more room on
its pavements, for one thing, now that the uniforms, both
British and American, have thinned out, and the effect of
their departure upon the average citizen's ability to get
about town is staggering. Civilians lifting a timid finger for
a taxi are overwhelmed when two or three attentive cabbies
race up, and they are unsettled by the novelty of being able
to buy a meal or a seat in a cinema with ease. Any newsreel
theatre showing pictures of the landings in France, however,
draws enormous, if quite unexcitable, audiences.

People seem remarkably calm about the invasion as a
whole, though they feel that the Allies are doing fine and
there was real enthusiasm over the great American recovery
at the beachhead near Carentan. Possibly the general sober-
ness is due to the feeling that the worst fighting is still to
come, or possibly it is due to the fact that the nearness of the
operations seems to have dawned on the public at last and
with a shock. Except for a short time at the beginning of the
war, most English families have done their worrying about

soldiers who were a long way off, but now postcards from France are beginning to drop into their mailboxes as casually as though the troops had gone to Brighton for the weekend. Possibly the first impact upon civilians of the wounded—not neatly tidied-up cases returning after months of hospitalization but weary, bloodstained men straight out of battle—has also helped to bring home the fact that war has moved in just across the street. Incidentally, an official warning has just been issued, aimed at curbing the impatience of the families of wounded men, who are advised to find out if the train service is reliable before they rush to his bedside, if there is any accommodation to be had at their destination, and if their man is in serious enough shape to justify the expedition at all.

July 9

Londoners, who hadn't been called Southern English since about the time of King Canute, felt better-tempered after the Prime Minister's statement on the flying bomb had made it all right to call them Londoners again. The censorship rulings, which, ever since the robots started, had made it necessary for press accounts to imply that they had fallen into a complete vacuum, infuriated the already angered people who knew that they had fallen in their streets and who wanted the credit for it. Now Londoners feel that they can put in their places not only those pushing people in the real Southern England who have been inclined to think that London wasn't getting half such a warm time as they were but also those Northerners who kept on writing down anxiously to ask if they were in ashes. The real answer, which should disappoint Dr. Goebbels, is that London is having no picnic but that it isn't in ashes, either. The city is uncomfortable and harassed but doggedly getting its first wind. It is also as garrulous as a village suddenly plagued with some peculiar flying pest. In the un-British flow of matey chat that is always set off by danger, total strangers gossip like neighbors on a country green about how many of "those things" have buzzed over their rooftops, what the bombs have damaged, how to deal with them, and so on. At the moment, everybody's inevitable flying-bomb story is by no means the least trying feature of the new development. People are adapting themselves with courage and humor to being under fire again, but the courage and humor are three years older and wearier than they were.

Already life is settling down to a recognizable routine, punctuated day as well as night by sirens. Nobody bothers much about the daytime ones, unless the sound of a robot can also be heard. In many big offices, stores, and other public places there are independent warning systems, which do not go off until a bomb is almost overhead—a time-saver that enables one to keep on quietly working or shopping until the roof-spotters think it's advisable for one to duck under cover. Under cover is usually away from glass, which has been causing a great many eye injuries. Restaurants with skylights and charming mirror-glass decorations aren't so popular as they were a while back.

The behavior of crowds is nonchalant to the point of idiocy, official warnings notwithstanding. Housewives standing in queues with their baskets glance up, when they hear a robot coming, with no more than the uneasy expression of a woman who has just discovered a wasp in the room. (A flying bomb, as it passes overhead, makes a loud, harsh roar which convinces you that the beastly thing has roosted on your chimneypot.) When it finally goes off, farther away then anybody expected, there is, of course, a general sigh of relief. The women in the queues once more give their attention to kippers or cherries, errand boys whistle, and the traffic seems to move forward more buoyantly.

People fancy that there is a definite rhythm to the bombardments—which appear to warm up at certain hours and slacken off at others—and that there are definite paths along which the robots cross the coast. Be that as it may, the daily round of life here tends to be jerky and subject to unpredictable interruptions. Theatres and cinemas, which have gamely decided to keep open, are naturally hard hit. Several well-established shows have folded in the past few days. The little Windmill Theatre girl show, however, is still proudly advertising its 1941 slogan, "We never closed." Hardy souls who take in a cinema are apt to feel like moving over and talking to the gentleman fifty-seven seats away for company. Restaurants don't seem so badly affected. After all, people with work to do must eat, but at night most sensible Londoners—at least, those who don't go to shelters—stay home. Incidentally, citizens still cling to the early blitz habits and leap automatically, when the sirens sound, to adjust a bad blackout, in case "those chaps up there" notice it.

The cockles of Cockney hearts have been thoroughly warmed by the help that Americans are giving in the new ordeal. This time, they feel that it isn't only supplies and encouragement coming across an ocean, it's American arms and shovels getting to work right here to dig them and their friends up out of the wreckage of their homes. A family feeling is promoted, as only the queer, uncomfortable bond of being bombed together can promote it.

Everybody is glad that mothers and children are being encouraged to leave town, for there's no easy, optimistic feeling that things are likely to get better quickly. Mr. Churchill's advice to the civilian army to get on with its job and keep its head well down is nevertheless being cheerfully followed. At the same time, people are trying to digest the Prime Minister's warning that the shape of things to come may easily be heavier, faster, and a lot more unpleasant. But whatever else happens, bad haters though Britons are, the flying bomb seems certain to harden British hearts on the question of the postwar treatment of Germany. Londoners make jokes about what they call the doodlebugs; after an assault, they get up from the pavement, dust their knees, straighten their hats, and move off with the slightly embarrassed smile of someone who has been caught leaping for dear life from a mad bull, but there is a look in their eyes which would make any bull or any German thoughtful. It's a safe bet that they won't forget the flying bomb when it comes to the payoff.

July 23

[*July, bomb plot against Hitler fails.*]

When the first reports of the crisis in Germany started to filter through, people here seemed determined not to allow themselves to think how good the news might actually be. The feeling appeared to be that if Germany was starting to crack up behind the lines, it was fine, but that if she wasn't, there was no point in doing any premature cheering. Even the most skeptical Londoners, though, soon began to feel that howsoever things might turn out, they looked pretty good at the moment, and their spirits reacted smartly. There's still no extreme optimism and, as the doodlebugs rasp overhead, lots of citizens remark grimly that the Nazis in the Pas-de-Calais don't seem to know about the rumored disaffection. Germany's internal troubles, at any rate, are everybody's absorbing topic of conversation right now, even eclipsing Montgomery's eagerly awaited breakthrough in Normandy—an event which stirred up an enthusiasm that was temporarily checked by the gloomy discovery that bad weather isn't always on the English side of the Channel.

Londoners can't help paying a certain amount of respectful attention to the robot bombs, but the city appears to have settled down to its inconvenient new routine very calmly. As a matter of fact, it's something of a problem for the authorities to get people to abandon that calmness and to duck, when the occasion arises. The Ministry of Homes Security recently issued some hints to the citizens, telling them, among other things, not to feel sheepish, during a raid, about being the first to take precautions, since Londoners are apparently more frightened of appearing frightened than they are of the bombs. The fear of rising from your knees and finding that the man behind you is still nonchalantly upright and that the doodlebug has exploded two miles away is something only a few narrow escapes will cure. A newspaper cartoon recently showed one Londoner saying to another, "It's ridiculous to say that these flying bombs have affected people in the slightest," as they walk along a street on which every pedestrian in sight, including themselves, has sprouted an alert oversized ear.

During the past fortnight, lots of things have joggled back to at least an approximation of normal. In the first, unsettling week of the robot bombing, many plays closed, including the Lunts' production of "There Shall Be No Night," but most of the ten theatres still open report that receipts are looking up. All the big stores, factories, and offices now have their own roof spotters, to announce approaching danger, but they announce it in a variety of ways, and there will probably soon have to be some sort of standardization. Many spotters ring bells, but on one West End street the shops are warned by a thin, tooting noise that sounds like the horn of a French railway guard. At one railway station, the usual tinkling bells are supplemented by a lady announcer who coos over the microphone, "Enemy raiders are overhead. You are advised to take cover," in the same emotionless accent she uses to impart the information that the ten-fifteen will leave from Platform 8. Everybody hopes that Mr. Morrison will soon come forward with the official method of warning he has promised, because now it's quite possible to stroll placidly along under the impression that three bells means "danger past" when, in the part of town you happen to be in, three bells means that danger is uncomfortably present and that it's no time for placid strolling.

An evacuation of children and mothers has been successfully in progress for the past two weeks. The already overtaxed railways have coped nobly with the job of removing two hundred thousand persons from the danger zone. Judging by their spirits at the railway stations, many of the children felt that fate was awarding them the summer holiday which the grownups had said they couldn't have this year. There was, apparently, rather less hilarity in some of the towns which received them, notably in the coastal districts, where landladies, since the tourist ban had just been removed, were hoping to wind up a disastrous season by filling their best front double bedrooms with something more profitable than London schoolchildren. On the other hand, there have been indignant protests from the many willing reception areas, whose inhabitants resent the press publicity which has unfairly linked them up with the reluctant few. Meanwhile, any kids left in town spend their nights in Anderson or Morrison shelters at home, in the tubes, or in one of the newly opened deep shelters which finally have been made available to the public. Priority for these last is given to families who have been blasted out or have no adequate shelter. A large number of Londoners prefer to hunt up the ear plugs and stay right in their own beds, acting on the philosophical theory that appointments in Samarra are kept, as often as not, by trying to dodge them. But the main thing which sustains everybody these tricky days is the belief that Montgomery's and Bradley's boys will soon have the Nazis moving so fast they won't be able to give much thought to setting up bomb-launching platforms.

August 13

The news from across the Channel looks so good right now that it has crowded the flying bombs not only off the front pages of the London newspapers but, to everybody's relief, out of most conversations. Actually, the good feeling began about a fortnight ago, with the optimistic Churchill speech. Everything seems encouraging enough, in fact, to justify the people who not long ago were talking soberly of "next year" but now are beginning to say that the collapse of German resistance will come this autumn. No one even seems to mind much that the British sectors in France haven't as yet provided the most spectacular headlines. The only real damper on the beaming Londoners' spirits is the difficulty of speeding the boys on to Paris with a pint, since there's a beer drought in the capital and in most of southern England. The contagious confidence is helped along, naturally, by the fact that fewer flying bombs are coming over at the moment. Faces which a week back were showing signs of strain are again ironed out, but most Londoners seem stolidly resigned to the possibility that, though the welcome lull probably means that London's defenses are getting on to their job, the Nazis may simply be cooking up something bigger and nastier. Nine out of ten people think that the threatened V-2, or double-size, bomb will materialize unless the Allies, like the hero in an old-time movie, get to the launching sites just as the villain's hand is about to press the button.

Meanwhile, the evacuation of mothers and children is continuing, and, what with their exodus and the departure of people who have no good reason for staying in London and those who always go somewhere in August anyway, the city is beginning to have an almost empty look. The West End streets seem particularly quiet, since the doodlebugs (a name, by the way, that has stuck) have frightened off the up-for-the-day class of woman customer who used to come into town for a perm and a bit of shopping. All the same, the city doesn't seem especially empty to people who are trying to rent a small flat. Everybody expected rents to come down after the robots began to arrive, but they are still high, and only occasional top floors, which don't seem very attractive nowadays, are on the agents' books. Until the casualty and damage figures were given out by Churchill, no one really had much idea what mischief the bombs were doing outside his own neighborhood. The censorship is still strict and usually it is only from chance conversations, or from glimpses through a train or bus window of that familiar rash of green tarpaulins spread over the roofs of blasted houses, that you learn that a place has been having a bad time.

Taking advantage of the lull in the bombing, a new revue, cheerfully christened "Keep Going," opened this week. It served, at least, to bolster the dwindling list of plays. Recently, a short season of ballet was crowded to the doors with rapt fans, who were happy to be intent, for a change, on a *pas seul* instead of on the Pas-de-Calais. The sporting life of the country, after a brief period of uncertainty when the doodles first came over, has also got back into its stride. On Bank Holiday, Lord's drew vast crowds to watch the cricket. There have been occasions, on other grounds, when the gentlemanly tempo of the afternoon has been upset by the players' having to hit the turf and the spectators' having to dive under their seats. The Eton and Harrow match was cancelled because the headmasters didn't want to risk sending their boys to London, but most other traditional sporting events have been held as usual. There was a drop in attendance at the greyhound courses around town during the first week of the robot raids, but now they're as crowded as ever, and the patrons don't even bother to look up when the doodles go over. Judging by the attendance at the few surviving race meetings, British enthusiasts have apparently decided that since death can find them anywhere in southern England these days, they'd just as soon be found laying a bet on a promising horse.

Londoners who are back with their holiday tans report that the old bomb snobbery which used to flourish in the blitz days is once more evident in rural districts. Residents of tiny southern villages where, perhaps, a bomb has blasted a field and killed a few hens are inclined to be proudly certain that they are the ones who are getting the really tough part of the battle and deflecting it from "those cockneys." What is really tough for country dwellers, though, is the job of getting house repairs made, because so many local workpeople have been drafted up to London to assist in the rehabilitation of the severely hit districts. The most serious damage in some little English towns has been caused not by bombs but by modern armies negotiating streets more suitable for knights in armor riding on palfreys. The battered Saxon bridges and sagging Tudor doorways which record the progress of skidding British tanks and American trucks

through the countryside will keep the local bricklayers busy
for a long time after they get back from London. This unexpected devastation is accepted cheerfully by the townsfolk.
Like Londoners, they now believe that this is the last summer, and the pretty girls wave more fervently than ever to
the tanks and trucks that go rumbling by on their way to
make that belief a certainty.

August 27

Londoners, as might have been expected, neither danced in
the streets nor chanted the "Marseillaise" when the first reports of the liberation of Paris reached here at lunchtime on
Wednesday. Stolid as ever, they merely picked up a paper
and hurried on to the usual scramble for something to eat.
There was some excitement worked up later in the afternoon, but the first reaction, perhaps because the occasion
was so deeply emotional, was as quiet as the first reaction on
D Day. To lots of English, apparently, the word from France
marked a kind of spiritual end of the war, since it cancelled
out that black June 14th four years ago when the Germans
marched into Paris and this country united to pretend that
it wasn't beaten. Wednesday's news made Londoners feel as
though they were waking up from a long and horrible dream
and returning to a sanity so overwhelmingly good that it had
to be taken slowly. It wouldn't surprise anyone now if the
final victory itself is greeted with that same queer, recuperative hush before the city goes mad and starts tearing itself
apart.

More immediately festive on the surface than its citizens,
London's buildings quickly broke into a flutter of tricolors.
Nobody appeared to mind when one confused building su-
perintendent ran up the Dutch flag instead. The Abbey and
St. Paul's, which, like most of the people, apparently required a little time before they got going, didn't ring their
jubilant peals until Thursday—the first time the cathedral

has uttered a sound since June, when it was decided that the bells might drown out an approaching robot. By Wednesday evening, however, everyone's determination to celebrate couldn't have been cramped by a whole covey of flying bombs. Soho, where the Fighting French meet at such convivial centres as the completely Gallic pub with the unsuitable, Anthony Trollope name of the York Minster, naturally was the most high-spirited part of town. The Rumanian news took care of any headaches the next morning, and even the subsequent discovery that there were, after all, some Germans left in Paris didn't seem to affect the general happiness. No matter what history may decide, Paris was liberated on August 23rd, as far as London is concerned.

At the moment, children are again a major problem to the London authorities, for, however stirring the news may be from other battlefronts, the battle of London is still grim. For some reason, many parents who weeks ago sent their youngsters away to safe billets have decided that the war news is good enough to warrant bringing them back. In spite of Mr. Churchill's plain speaking and the plain evidence of the robots themselves, some cockneys seem convinced that a dead Londoner is better any day than a live yokel. The newspapers are waging a campaign to get the children who are still here to leave and the ones who have already gone to stay put. In a story about a hundred and forty-nine children who hadn't been evacuated from one school, the *Daily Herald* referred to them as a hundred and forty-nine candidates for crippledom. Possibly the unpopular business called compulsion is the only thing that will do the trick. There's every evidence that informed circles take the V-2 threat more seriously than the great uninformed do. The other day, Mr. Willink, the Minister of Health, urged expectant mothers to leave; certain other special groups, such as hospital patients, are being quietly but steadily removed every day. These steps can, of course, be interpreted simply as precautions against the current attacks, but it is noticeable that the papers are not being officially discouraged from printing a good deal of fairly creepy talk about V-2. There are even some rumors that, instead of being a bomb, V-2 may be an incendiary fog sprayed from planes or something involving splitting the atom.

September 16

Londoners end most of their casual conversations these days with the cheerful cliché of the moment, "Well, it won't be long now." They seem to enjoy just saying it. Even though a lot of people here believe that the Germans will try to hang on into the winter and that guerrilla opposition probably will go on for a time after organized resistance collapses, everybody is intoxicated by the realization that the end is now months, rather than years, off. There was little disappointment the other day when a rumor of German capitulation turned out to be false; Londoners philosophically felt that since they had waited so long they could easily wait a bit longer.

The partial lifting of the blackout was in itself enough to raise everyone's spirits. On the morning that the news of this was announced, nobody here or anywhere else in England, it is safe to say, got around to discussing the real war news. In town, the general improvement in manners was beautiful to see. Shop people, instead of snapping that there was none of this or that, said it with a big, happy smile. There won't be any great blaze of brilliance in London even after the lights go on, because street lighting isn't to be augmented much. For most people, though, it will be a satisfying novelty to be able to pick out the cozy, curtained windows of their own home instead of stumbling up the next-door steps by mistake, and the happiness people have displayed over the prospect of even a small glimmer showing ahead down the long dark tunnel of their street as they come home has been rather pathetic.

The supposed end of the flying bombs contributed much, of course, to everybody's cheerfulness. During the first few

incredible days that passed without the familiar roar overhead and the sudden, sickening silences as the things coasted
down, people were glancing up uneasily at the sky now and
then as though they had come out with their umbrellas and
couldn't understand why it didn't rain. For the first time in
ten nightmarish weeks, lots of Londoners climbed into their
own beds and slept the sleep of the just and dog-tired. Vanished friends reappeared, and once more it became difficult
to get a movie seat, book a hairdressing appointment, or buy
the little food extras which had been easy for determined
people to hunt down while the town was so empty. Just the
same, there was much surprise and a good deal of criticism
over the finality of the government statement that the battle
of London had been won for good and all. Though hardly
anyone expects V-1 to reappear as a major menace, some people think that V-2 is still a serious threat. Nevertheless, so
short is human memory that many householders are now re-
fusing to take delivery of the indoor Morrison shelters for
which they were clamoring at the height of the flying-bomb
attack, only a few weeks ago. What is more, the tone of the
statement was so encouraging that, in spite of an official footnote warning evacuees to stay put, several thousand London
mothers concluded that the war was over and decided not to
languish in the wilderness another moment. The Ministry of
Home Security has been issuing stern announcements that
there will be no more government financial assistance if the
day ever comes when they want to move out again, but the
naïve official astonishment over the wholesale return of people who had been told that London was now perfectly safe is
itself fairly astonishing. This reading of public psychology
may have tragic consequences should any further unpleasant
surprises arrive; the immediate results are merely such in-
conveniences as trains crammed to the roof with family parties firmly going home to daddy.

The stand-down of the Home Guard from their emergency duties was another slight slackening in the civilian
cable which encouraged the feeling that the end couldn't be
far off now. After receiving the stand-down order, the mem-

bers of one country platoon rather wistfully set about destroying some menacing orchard wasp nests with their little hoard of Molotoff cocktails, the homemade bombs concocted in 1940 to throw at German tanks.

Whatever trials are still in store for London, the present quiet seems blissful. It's nice, as one citizen put it, that windows are once more things to look through instead of flying glass to duck from. People are going out nights again to eat and to take in a show, and the much-depleted list of plays is picking up. The Old Vic repertory company gallantly opened before the official all-clear was given, launching a season of Shakespeare, Shaw, and Ibsen at a time when most managements were temporarily putting up the shutters. Laurence Olivier, Ralph Richardson, and Dame Sybil Thorndike are the stars, if there can be said to be any, since, in true repertory fashion, the players alternate in the fat and slender parts. They opened in a new theatre (the Old Vic itself was blitzed in the early days) amid doodlebugs and all the production difficulties which the raids entailed. The only thing that saved "Richard III" from being played in lounge suits was the determined efforts of a few young students from the Bristol Art School who, when the flying bombs played havoc with the costumers' workroom staff, came up to town and, while the air-raid sirens blew, stitched away enthusiastically at velvet robes. The project not only is giving London the first solid intellectual theatrical treat it has had for months but looks as if it might even provide a permanent nucleus of that national theatre about which there has been so much chat for so many years.

October 1

[*September, British airborne troops defeated at Arnhem.*]

It was bad luck that the Government happened to issue its long-awaited White Papers on social security and demobilization at a time when everybody's attention was painfully fixed on Arnhem. This past week was not one in which many Englishmen could turn their attention to a design for Britain at peace. Words of any kind were difficult to utter and countless English families paid the story of the courageous stand at Arnhem the tribute of saying absolutely nothing as they sat at their radios listening to the tired broadcasters who had come back to tell what happened. The story of Arnhem, which already has become a proud part of English history, was being read to school children before the week was out. Even though people had gone around for weeks saying that the battle would get tough when it got near Germany, it was a jolt when they realized how right they had been. One immediate reaction seems to be that nobody is as eager now to trot out his hunch about when the war will end as he was a while back. Those who do make predictions tend to be as cautious as Mr. Churchill was the other day. The Prime Minister's speech, even though he refused to be over-rosy, made everybody feel better, because it did the job of bringing Arnhem and the rest of the war picture into the proper perspective. Many people here were especially glad that he dealt with the Burma campaign and with figures on British casualties and the percentage of British troops in the Allied armies—sore subjects that have long provided the Nazis with fine material for propaganda in their little tries to split the Allies. Now that the Prime Minister has given the facts on these matters, the folks at home, not to mention the boys over there and particularly the forces in Burma (who sometimes bitterly speak of themselves as "the forgotten men"), should feel relieved.

London's biggest local disappointment in a long time was the change-over from the blackout to the dimout, which has turned out to be merely a washout. Since the Germans have from time to time repeated their first-night joke of sending over a stray robot or two, catching Londoners with their blackout down, most people now think it is easier to leave their windows blacked out as usual. The street lighting also looks much as it always did—that is, nonexistent—but the entrances to the corner pub and the local movie now throw a cautious welcoming glow into the gloom. Suburbanites who rashly leave their flashlights at home when they come into town to see the illumination are lucky if they only graze a knee in the blackness. With a winter ahead which may or may not bring with it permission for a real lighting up (or the return of the basic petrol ration for which the Beaverbrook press is yelling), the reaction of Londoners to tales of twinkling lamps in Manchester and other such fortunate cities is decidedly sour.

October 29

The multitude of British, glumly suspecting that this Christmas might not bring peace on earth after all, brightened up slightly when Colonel Llewellin, the Food Minister, announced that at least there would be a little more food for the holidays. To the accompaniment of a good deal of public hurrahing—which Lord Woolton, his predecessor, probably listened to rather wistfully from his thorny new perch in the Ministry of Reconstruction—Colonel Llewellin promised a Christmas bonus of fats and meat for everyone, extra sweets for the children, and an extra allotment of tea for people over seventy.

Lots of Londoners felt that the prospect of better Christmas dinners was hardly enough to make up for Lord Woolton's coincident announcement that many of the eight hundred thousand houses that were damaged by flying bombs will not be completely repaired until spring. Shortage of materials, labor difficulties, and good old departmental muddle are blamed for the disappointing showing of the housing program in its first real test. Building reconstruction is the biggest domestic issue for this government, and possibly for many a government to come. Angry questions were asked in Parliament last week. Meanwhile, autumn winds are beginning to moan through countless windows and roofs still only temporarily patched up after two or three months. The authorities are trying to cope with this situation, which in many districts of the city is desperate. The armies of workmen who were recruited from the provinces to do these rush jobs have created a housing problem themselves. They are being lodged in rest centres and air-raid shelters and fed from canteens that were hastily set up in such queer places as the Chinese section of the Victoria and Albert Museum.

November 16

[*September, Germans begin bombing with V-2 rockets.*]

Prime Minister Churchill's statement, which made it all right to talk out loud about V-2 instead of cautiously referring to it as if it were something supernatural which had dropped in somehow and made a big hole in the back yard, came as a relief to the inhabitants of southern England. The Government's secrecy and the ordinary public's silence since the first of "those new things" arrived have both been amazing. The new bombs had been expected for so long that by the time they did turn up a lot of people here had reached a state of skepticism and for a while they thought the distant, unheralded explosions were anything from a stray robot to a thunderstorm. Even when it became apparent that the V-2 was a reality, nobody mentioned the thing by name in public. Perhaps because of deliberately planted rumors, the first big, mysterious explosion was ascribed to a bursting gas main, and that fiction was solemnly maintained for days by people who must have known better but who wagged their heads and said that it was extraordinary how many gas mains had been reported going up lately. This conspiracy to gloss over a topic which everybody was naturally longing to discuss gave most people's faces a taut look which suggested that they themselves were on the verge of exploding. To the strain of this self-imposed censorship was added a flood of anxious letters from relatives in other parts of England who had heard the usual elaborate stories of disaster.

Now that the secret is out, the great question is whether the rocket is worse than the robot bomb. Jumpy folk are inclined to believe that they prefer the robot because it could at least be detected by the defenses in time to sound a warning. The V-2, with nasty abruptness, just arrives. "If I'm going to be killed," one lady remarked, "I would like to have the excitement of knowing it's going to happen." However, the majority of Britons philosophically declare that nights without sirens are worth the hazard of unpredictable bolts from the stratosphere. So far, morale has stood up well under the V-2s, and there has been nothing approaching the dismay that the flying bombs created. There has been little or no precautionary evacuation of people from London. The city continues to be jammed with cheerful crowds who you might think had never heard of any rockets more deadly than the ones shot off on Guy Fawkes Day. Practically all the grumbling during the period of censorship was directed at the Government's policy of silence, since the British always feel aggrieved if bad news is withheld. It is possible that this particular bad news will turn out to be worse than anybody imagines before the newest blitz is over, but at the moment people say that the V-2 raids will be like the V-1 raids— nasty while they last and another bad mark on the German side of the book when it comes to the payoff.

Londoners were delighted to hear that Mr. Churchill was in Paris, but, as always, they were relieved when he was safely home again. The great success of the visit was regarded as a plain indication that the widely known differences of opinion between the Prime Minister and General de Gaulle would be straightened out. The announcement that France would take part in the postwar discussions was received joyfully here. Those in a position to know think that the decision to give France a place at the conference table is something for which Anthony Eden was responsible, since his patient efforts to bring two stubborn personalities into line were the foundation for the spectacular edifice

which was publicly dedicated in Paris on Armistice Day.
The *entente cordiale,* which has had its ups and downs in
the past five years, is definitely an *entente cordiale* once
more. The British, who didn't like the French after Dunkirk, changed their minds after D Day, but the warm emotion generated by the liberation of Paris cooled off a bit
when inept propagandists rushed over photographs of
blooming Parisian mannequins instead of thin French children. English women, trying to figure out how they would
fill the gaps in the family wardrobe with the few clothing
coupons at their disposal, were naturally not overjoyed to
hear that Parisian women were facing war's rigors in tower-
ing turbans and dresses with voluminous sleeves that would
use up a three-month British clothing coupon allotment.
Since more realistic reporting eventually proved that this
was by no means the whole story, there was unrestrained
pleasure over Churchill's welcome in Paris—a welcome in
which even the most insignificant Briton felt included.

Another reason for beaming faces was President Roosevelt's reëlection. In spite of the keen interest taken in the
election by a nation which is beginning to think about an
election of its own again, British speculations on its outcome
had been as studiously cautious as those on the V-2 bombings. When the returns started coming over, however, Londoners walked around looking as though they had heard
good news from the front. In the glow of relief, Dewey's gra-
cious acceptance of defeat won him more friends than anything he had said during the campaign. By evening, the glow
was, in many cases, physical as well as mental, since innumerable monthly bottles of Scotch were sacrificed to make a
Roosevelt holiday. Londoners think that if the President
ever makes the trip to England that the newspapers hint at
from time to time, he will get as big a hand here as Churchill got in Paris.

December 3

The publication of the Government's portly, statistical White Paper on the British war effort made it possible for the average person here to figure out with depressing exactness just how uncomfortable certain aspects of his life had been during the past five years. Because of the length of the document, the newspapers considerately boiled it down and gave it to their readers in easily assimilable summaries. The complete White Paper is a staggering collection of facts which ranges from the number (small) of ounces of fresh fruit and the number (large) of pounds of potatoes that are being consumed each week by British civilians to the number of fighter planes coming off the assembly lines and the number of heifers in calf. Statistics usually aren't particularly engrossing to anybody except statisticians, but this lot had for most people the fascination of a medical handbook about some disease from which one is still suffering. Mr. Churchill's refusal to prophesy last week that Europe would be on the out-of-danger list before next summer naturally didn't raise anybody's spirits. Still, now that the cost of the war in cash and flesh and blood (representing the war's large hopes for the future and its small, irritating deprivations for the present) is on the record, the British have the feeling that there is no reason any longer to fear that they will be misinterpreted when they say, as they frequently do in private, that they're tired to the bone and would like to think that the end is actually in sight. The nation's deep fatigue is particularly evident on train journeys, when civilians, as well as service men and women, fall asleep almost as soon as they sit down in the train. Doctors say that they are kept busy dishing out tonics to workers who really need the unprocurable prescription of a long rest from blackout, bombs, and worry.

All elements in the community affectionately joined to-

gether last Thursday to wish Mr. Churchill well on his seventieth birthday. Most of the papers were inspired to birthday tributes in verse. The *Times'* vigorous and somewhat
Popeish effort included this stern couplet: "Let Churchill
take the milestone in his stride/And treat a birthday as a foe
defied." The Prime Minister's stock has never stood higher,
and it is likely to soar still higher if he has success with the
housing question, which he announced last week he intended to take a hand in. This is perhaps the hottest question the Government has to face on the home front at the
moment. Critics of the prefabricated bungalows which have
been promised as temporary relief say that the things are too
small to encourage the raising of families and that the rentals will have to be far too high because of weaknesses in the
Government's scheme for acquiring the land they are to be
built on. Mr. Churchill's recent appointment of his son-in-
law, Duncan Sandys, as Minister of Works to tackle this
problem has met with a mixed reception from the public,
which hopes that Mr. Sandys will be quicker than his predecessor in putting roofs over people's heads again. Many people tend to feel uneasy because Mr. Sandys has had no experience in housing matters. Others, who think that he made a
good showing in his job as head of the committee set up to
devise defense measures against the flying bomb, are optimistic. In any event, his new work isn't likely to be made simpler by the fresh V-bomb threat to British homes.

As southern Englanders adjust themselves to the V-2,
their memories of last summer's V-1 have become conveniently blurred. One of the West End cinemas is showing a
short documentary, with horridly realistic sound effects, on
the flying bomb and the defense put up against it. The other
evening, the audience laughed and cheered at the beginning
of the film, but when a robot was shown groaning and popping into the foreground and there was suddenly that familiar cut-off of the engines and that dreadful silence before the
explosion, you could have heard a pin drop in the theatre.
People shut their eyes and grabbed the arms of their seats,

trying to overcome an absurd, almost uncontrollable urge to crawl under them.

December 17

Last week, the inescapable fact that the season of peace and good will is at hand sank, belatedly, into the public consciousness. There were enormous crowds in every shopping center. The gift hunter's wild expression and vacant eye are more noticeable than ever this year, for anything worth buying needs either coupons or a fat pocketbook, or both. Even books, the customary happy solution, aren't very easy to find. Classic standbys, which everybody wants, seem to have melted away, and anything new and good is limited by the paper shortage to small editions, which are quickly exhausted. The toys look as though they had been knocked together out of an old sugar box by a ten-year-old with his first fret saw, and the prices are painful. "I'm giving my children clothes, and they'll have to like it," one mother grimly told a friend the other day. With luck, children may be consoled by once more finding the traditional orange and nuts in the toe of their stocking, since the Food Minister has promised a supply of both these delicacies. Already greengrocers are slipping bulging paper bags to regular customers, many of whom would have been surprised in prewar days if they could have foreseen what a thrill the sight of a pound of peanuts (the amount allotted to each family) would someday give them.

The children also have been remembered by the theatres, which are tempting nervous out-of-town parents to take the risk of bringing the youngsters in to see "Peter Pan," Robert Donat's musical play "The Glass Slipper," or one of a number of pantomimes. The current sellout in entertainment for all ages is Laurence Olivier's handsome Technicolor film "Henry V," a sumptuously mounted affair with a score by William Walton. Londoners have been finding it a heartening escapist dip into a comfortable past, when wars were simple affairs fought only by armies.

December 28

A holiday bonus of fats and sugar gave most people here a little glow of physical satisfaction, but it was not on the whole a very comfortable Christmas. As friends and acquaintances kept telling each other, it didn't even seem like Christmas. In spite of the barrows of holly, which streetcorner venders hawked at stiff prices, and the appearance of some skimpy turkeys, few people were inclined to get into the right mood. This feeling of depression, which affected everybody except the children, was, at least in part, a reaction from last summer's hope that this might be a peacetime Christmas. Now there is not only no way of knowing when the men in uniform will return but the new conscription regulations indicate that thousands of additional men may soon be in the service. Down in the tubes, the shelter-dwellers, who had probably hoped to spend this Christmas night above ground, were making their customary pathetic attempts to decorate the unfestive platforms and bunks into some semblance of Christmasy cheer. In fact, the inevitable toast, "Well, here's to the last wartime Christmas," was seldom offered with conviction. The belief that the way will be hard and long now appears to be as universal as the Government, fearful of any complacent slackening off on the home front, could wish. There is no doubt that the news of the big German offensive * and the even grimmer news of its early successes were enormous shocks to the public. People stood on the street reading the papers with expressions of incredulity. The first comment was that the offensive was probably good news in the long run, since it was forcing into action reserves of German men and material, but later on

---

* The Battle of the Bulge (December 1944–January 1945), the last major German counteroffensive.

people agreed gloomily that it will almost certainly make the long run longer. Although it is officially denied that the new conscription order has anything to do with events on the Western Front, most people are sure that it has and that it means at least another year of fighting.

1945

January 14

THE NEWS OF THE CHANGE in Field Marshal Montgomery's command and the more cheerful outlook on the Western Front gave a big boost to British spirits, which had been beaten down by the German breakthrough, the Greek and Polish troubles, freezing weather, and the latest visitations of the V-bomb family. Montgomery's name seems to affect people here much the way a four-leaf clover does the superstitious. They have complete confidence in his talents as a military commander.

The ordinary citizen is, at the moment, chiefly concerned with local and immediate anxieties. Not the least of these is the latest lethal sample of what the official communiqués now call V-bombs—a deliberately vague term which can mean either robots or rockets. Censorship is still very strict about mentioning the affected districts. The blanket designation "Southern England" is being used once more and is once more worrying friends of people who live in Kent, Sussex, and other southern counties as much as it worries county people who wonder if the revival of the term means that London is having another bad time. Since the Government's admission that the rockets had landed in this country made it unnecessary to go on talking about them in whispers, the question whether they are harder on the nerves than the robots has been much discussed and usually answered in the affirmative. People dislike the newcomers' nasty and unpredictable habit of plunking out of the blue with a truly appalling explosion which leaves the air thrum-

ming and twanging like a plucked guitar string. Still, as
someone remarked the other day, they arrive so abruptly you
don't have time to get scared—you're either dead or simply
startled.

Outwardly at least, the London crowds seem to be not especially troubled by the danger, although the tubes are
again filled up every evening with shelterers who feel happier if they are sleeping deep. The theatres and cinemas are
losing the business of customers who feel that it's better to
take precautions than be sorry, but the V-bombs have not affected such established sellouts as the Lunts, who have
opened at the Lyric with their usual much-admired performance in a not much-admired play called "Love in Idle-
ness." The big funny-man shows starring the English comedians Tommy Trinder and Sid Fields are also booked for
weeks ahead. Even the audiences at the musicals appear to
have come out dressed to meet any emergency, from bombs
to a long tramp home. It is rumored that in the Midlands
and the North the prosperous manufacturers' wives are regularly putting on long evening dresses, but the women in the
London theatre audience usually look as if they had come
straight from their jobs. The young things who go out and
dance at night get themselves up rather more festively and
every dance place in London is jammed with boys and girls
on leave. If they have money to burn, they dance at the Mi-
rabelle, Manetta's, the Four Hundred, or one of the big hotels. Those who can't afford such places dance at the Stage
Door Canteen or at one of the big dance halls, where you
can have hours of swing for about half a crown. Dancing is
having a healthy boom right now despite the menace in the
stratosphere.

January 28

Ministries concerned with such civilian preoccupations as
food and clothing have noted in the past that grumbles from

the public always coincide with good news. When there's a
bad spell of bombing or the Allies have a setback, the complaining letters dwindle to nothing. As soon as things begin
to look better again, however, the English go back to their
normal, everyday worrying about the baby's shoes, the eter-
nal frozen cod at the fishmonger's, the shortage of sheets, and
other familiar domestic problems. Judging by the atmosphere here this past week, the letters must be rolling in
nicely once more. The Russian advance has raised the spirits
of the English to a level which would not have seemed possible only a month ago. In spite of V-bombs, icy weather, and
the accompanying coal shortage, London is full of beaming
faces. Even those diehard Tory elements which still view the
Soviet Union with either covert or fairly open alarm are
keeping quiet at the moment, since it's difficult to sound
grateful and suspicious at the same time. The papers, which
are as afraid of unchecked optimism as they are of despair,
warn their readers that the Russians must stop somewhere,
but it is obvious that most Londoners have decided that any
halt in the drive from the east will be brief. A short time
ago, the end of the war seemed hopelessly far away, but right
now it seems beautifully, unbelievably close to every tired
man and woman in this island of tired people.

February 18

[*February 4–11, Churchill, Roosevelt and Stalin meet at
the Yalta Conference.*]

The Crimea, which most of the British had associated with
Florence Nightingale and a military disaster, last week became a name which every Briton associated with a hope.
The success of the conference seemed the most encouraging
omen for the postwar world that people here, wearied by the
present and frightened of the future, have yet laid eyes on.
They appeared to be especially pleased by the announce-

ment that the headquarters for the reparations commission would be in Moscow. There is no tendency at the moment, with V-bombs thudding down, to think kindly of the Germans, but the British, like amiable topers who can foresee just which drink will hit them, know their own weakness. It had been feared that somehow, somewhere, the fatal national tendency to be too easygoing might result in a toning down of the retribution which many of us seem now convinced Germany must make. The English of this generation will never forget the years of bombing, but they are afraid of forgiving too easily or too soon. The Russians, they are sure, are not likely to do either, so they are relieved to know that Moscow will preside over the till into which the debt is to be paid.

The Polish proposals also appear to have satisfied nearly everybody except the London Poles, whose dissatisfaction surprised no one in diplomatic circles and lost them sympathy elsewhere. The apparent readiness of the Soviet Union to coöperate on this as well as other matters was really the main reason for the beaming Yalta face which one saw everywhere about town last Tuesday. Few Englishmen, of course, believe that all ideological differences between the three big nations were adjusted at Yalta or that an era of beautiful good will toward all men will automatically begin with the peace. Still, the meeting has brought the first solid assurance that the partnership will work as well in peace as in war. The English press and the English public are inclined to give President Roosevelt most of the credit for bringing off this triumph.

Unfortunately, the satisfaction over the conference's declaration on liberated Europe is not matched by satisfaction over the way Allied policy is working out right now, as far as liberated European stomachs are concerned. Millions of shocked English families are suddenly aware of the desperate food situation in France, Holland, and Belgium. They are now realizing, a little shamefacedly, that their own wartime table, spread with unrationed bread and adequate if not plentiful rations of fats and meat, must look like a feast to many people on the other side of the Channel. The Allies' announcement that food would roll into Europe over the first bridgehead was believed here, and the early photographs and stories of the citizens of Paris and Brussels in their best clothes and in a gay, celebrating mood were misleading; people here forgot that the amount of expensive luxury goods in a city's shop windows is not an accurate gauge of a country's well-being. Now that it is realized that although the captive maiden is certainly rescued, she is fainting on our hands, there is considerable uneasiness and criticism. Many English seem to feel that the stocks of essential foodstuffs which were carefully built up here in the days when an invasion of this country looked imminent and when the Luftwaffe might have done devastating things to the sugar or fats ration overnight can safely be drawn upon now to relieve the increasingly distressing situation on the Continent. The informed and influential *Economist* says that several thousand British Army trucks now serving Army needs in Great Britain might be sent across the Channel to ease the transport situation. Intelligent English recognized that the urgency of the problem is the keeping alive not only of French, Belgian, and Dutch bodies but of French, Belgian, and Dutch good will toward the Allies for years to come. If the Government instituted a temporary cut in food allowances here, the move would be understood and even welcomed by all but the most heedless.

So far, the only practical opportunity of showing sympathy for those in the liberated countries has been the welcoming of five hundred Dutch children—the first batch of an expected twenty thousand—who arrived the other day for what is described as a recuperative holiday. Thousands of families offered to take the children. Many of the volunteers had only just finished tidying up the spare room recently vacated by English youngsters who had been evacuated from the cities. Nevertheless, for the first few weeks, the children will stay in a hostel, where the feeding of starved and queasy stomachs can be supervised. The Women's Voluntary Services workers who met the children at the boat took with them plenty of warm blankets in case the visitors were literally in rags, but they found the little boys and girls dressed —and this was rather more heartbreaking—with painful, passionate neatness in the very clean, carefully patched results of an obvious scrounge around the family wardrobe. Workers who had had experience in dealing with Spanish and Jewish child refugees in the old days sadly recognized things which they had forgotten—the dreadful grayish pallor, the look in the eyes, the tears of the youngest ones, who thought that the press photographers levelling cameras were a firing squad. The ghastly results of living on four hundred and fifty calories a day (the wartime British daily calory consumption is three thousand) were plain enough to make plenty of British parents feel that, all in all, theirs had been an unbelievably lucky war.

March 11

The two little words "They're over" made Thursday night seem big and beautiful to Londoners. It was apparent to everybody who heard the news of the Rhine crossing on the radio that this was a moment of the war that had the genuine flavor of victory. However, by the next day there was singularly little excitement in evidence. Most people, remembering the many setbacks in the past, particularly the German counter-offensive in Belgium, appeared determined to accept the good news warily. That morning's papers were for once less cautious than their readers, and came right out and said that it was now only a matter of weeks until the final collapse of the Nazis. Such prophecies made painfully interesting reading to people who have relatives in German prison camps. With the Nazi castle unmistakably beginning to crumble, thousands of English families, like thousands of European families, are understandably worried about the men who are still behind barbed wire somewhere in the middle of the German catastrophe. One of their greatest fears is that the inevitable disorganization of transportation by bombing may keep the precious, almost life-saving Red Cross parcels from getting through to the prisoners. There was some reassurance the other day in an announcement that a road convoy of foodstuffs had left Switzerland in an attempt to reach the prison camps. Nevertheless, the ironic fact is that the good war news is causing a great deal of private grief and worry.

The first photographs that really show the results of Allied strategic bombing in Germany have just been released here, and they have further convinced Britons that the Reich's days are numbered. Londoners, who have had plenty of experience in calculating piles of rubble in terms of human misery, are apt to whistle incredulously at the shots of Cologne street scenes. The evidence of what the enemy is trying to withstand makes it easier for people here to accept the latest crop of V-bombs and the sudden return of piloted bombers in a series of small and apparently merely vindictive attacks. The bomber raids were the first of the kind on England since last June, and many people had got so accustomed to being bombed by robots that the idea of being bombed in the old-fashioned way seemed almost as strange as a Jules Verne fantasy. However, the new attacks appeared to be less disconcerting than the coincident guarded official statement that as yet a return to a full blackout was not being considered. General opinion has held for months that the Nazis, as their defeat gets closer, would do their best to make it as hot as possible for the civilian population of England.

During the war years, more and more Londoners have taken to reading poetry, listening to music, and going to art exhibitions, although there is less and less of all three to be had in this shabby, weary capital. Most of the poets are too personally involved in the war to have attained that state of impersonal tranquillity which generates good poetry. Louis MacNeice, whose most recent collection, *Springboard,* was quickly sold out, is working at the B.B.C., C. Day Lewis has a job at the Ministry of Information, Stephen Spender is a

full-time fireman, and most of the younger poets are in uniform. Several have been killed, among them Alun Lewis,
who was considered one of the most promising. The output
of good poetry is small, but the public hunger for it is pa-
thetically great. The demand for music is probably not
much greater now than it was in peacetime, but it looks
greater because the supply of concert halls and orchestras is
sadly limited. Since the Queen's Hall was bombed, the Albert Hall has become London's leading musical center. Mi-
chael Tippett's important new oratorio, "A Child of Our
Time," the child being that young Polish Jew who killed a
Nazi in Paris several years ago, was given there recently. People line up at the National Gallery every day for the lunchtime concerts organized by Myra Hess. There isn't much to
see in the way of paintings at the Gallery right now except a
collection of things by war artists. The old masterpieces are
still laid away in their secret mountain hideout. They will
probably be among the last evacuees to return home.

March 24

Peace in Europe, a prospect that was looming perceptibly
larger last week, is now being talked about and thought
about by intelligent English in somewhat the way a man
might contemplate approaching matrimony. The grave new
responsibilities of the state occasionally seem more overwhelming than its blissful aspects. The most blissful aspect
of the peace, of course, will be the end of the waste of life—
not only the large-scale waste of young men's lives all over
the world but also the sad, steady dribbling away of civilian
lives in England as the bombs continue to fall. It is now officially disclosed that rockets have been hitting London, but
Londoners would feel happier if someone in authority could
disclose the date on which this bombing may be expected to
stop. There is a gloomy school of thought which considers it
possible that rockets, launched from isolated pockets of re-

sistance, may keep on coming over long after the order to cease fire is given. Most English, when they talk of peace, think first of quiet nights, bright lights, and the return of the menfolk, although, remembering the war in the East, this last is a hope of which families speak with caution.

Some of the responsibilities of the future are already in sight. The government warned months ago that the feeding and clothing of the people in the liberated countries would be a strain so severe that it would have to be shared by all Allied stomachs and backs. That strain, it seems, has now begun. When the disturbing truth about the food situation in Europe was realized here, it was widely and sincerely suggested that the British ration be reduced so that food could be sent over to the Continent. The government seems to have dryly taken people at their word. Colonel Llewellin, the Minister of Food, announced the other day that the meat ration would probably have to be cut, and perhaps fats and sugar as well, and that the entire security margin of food stocks, which was never as comfortably large as most people had imagined, had already been shipped to the liberated countries.

Colonel Llewellin's revelation, in the course of his announcement, that meat stocks were so low that only immediate requirements could be met and that henceforth the country would be living from sheep to mouth came as a shock. Housewives have an uneasy memory of the lean days of 1941, when the meat ration sank, as it may again, to the shillings-worth-a-week level, on which families subsisted but felt remarkably empty. If the proposed cut does come, and, in spite of vague and soothing government stalling, most people feel convinced that it will, miners and workers in other heavy industries will be particularly hard hit. Such workers have never been given an extra meat ration, but they are supposed to get additional meat in canteen meals. A cut in meat would be especially serious because allotments of cheese, the usual protein substitute, have already been ordered reduced after April 1st. Two other items have just been taken off the market—rice, one of the standbys for stretching out the family's meat allotment, and dried milk, an equally useful commodity. Many people who are not at all scaremongers think that this may be just the beginning, for this densely populated island, of a postwar period which could make the war years seem, in retrospect, almost comfortable. Audiences at the Laurence Olivier film, "Henry V," tend to snicker mournfully when one of the French nobles before the battle of Agincourt observes, "But these English are shrewdly out of beef."

April 1

This year, the joyful Easter promise of a resurrection of life seems startlingly applicable to temporal affairs. Every dazzling headline is a promise that the hard, dark years are nearly over and that at any moment now the incredible word of Victory may come. The oddly touching impression one is apt to get here—of a city struggling toward a gaiety in which it still hardly dares believe—has perhaps been heightened during these last days of perfect weather and perfect news by the fact that everybody who isn't carrying a paper seems to be carrying a bunch of flowers. Last September, when many people believed that the end of the war was within touching distance, the street hawkers did a roaring trade in Allied flags to hang out. This spring, with more justifiable confidence, Londoners are, instead, buying Cornish daffodils, violets, or forsythia from the heaped corner barrows. Even the shabby, peeling window boxes in the woefully down-at-heel residential streets are sprouting little green plants again for the first time in years, as though the owners had felt suddenly that some gesture was required.

If it were not for these impulses to carry something bright and to spruce up one's home with something fresh, no one would know that people here expect to wake up any morning and find that the war in Europe is all over. There was more visible exhilaration during the extraordinary, keyed-up days right after Dunkirk. Now that the end is practically at hand, the supernormality of the English is surprising. While there was considerable excitement and a good deal of relief when the British Second Army swept into Germany at last, London is far from being in a mood for wild celebrating. For one thing, it is still possible that the Germans may send all they have in known and unknown forms of air attack against this country as a final gesture of despairing malice. Increasingly few people hold this gloomy view, however. It is simply difficult for Londoners to forget that they will be under some sort of fire right up to the last minute.

Londoners whose war jobs took them out of the city or who could afford to move their children out of bombing range are now beginning to return to town, and, as a result, the prices of London property are starting to show the same alarming upward curve they developed after the First World War. Depressed couples in search of a small family house in which to settle down as Londoners once more are finding that the good things are prohibitive in price and that the moderately priced houses appear to have received a little too much attention from the bombers. The new government limit on house repairs is ten pounds, so the problem of getting a dirty, leaking house into habitable shape is a difficult one. However, some amateur house-decorating help is available. For example, the charwoman's husband, on leave from the Navy, may oblige with a little distempering, or a friendly air warden may come around in off-duty hours and do a bit of carpentering.

The returning middle-class people, who normally could afford a neat little house in Kensington or Chelsea, are discovering that today's abnormal prices are beyond them and wondering whether it will turn out that they are a forgotten group for whose needs the government housing program will not provide. It is still not satisfactorily clear how fully or how soon the government will be able to provide for even its most important customers, the fighting men, many of whom may be freed before long to come home and ask tiresome questions about such matters. As in every European country,

shelter and food will be the big primitive questions of the
immediate future, and it will be against a background of the
government's success or failure in answering them that the
people will go to the polls to decide the color of the next
chapter in England's political history.

There is really, of course, only one big question among
Londoners right now, and it does not concern shelter or
food. People feel that everything can wait until after that almost unbelievable hour when the lights go on again, when
the sirens scream for something which will not be an air
raid, and when everyone can express in his own way, with
tears or embraces or Scotch or silence, his own version of the
Te Deum.

April 15

Because the British have been prepared for the last few
weeks to receive the good news which obviously nothing
could spoil, the bad news knocked them sideways. President
Roosevelt's death came as a stupefying shock, even to those
Britons whose ideas of the peace do not run much beyond
the purely personal ones of getting their children home
again, a roof back over their heads, a little car back on the
road, and plenty of consumer goods in the shops. To the
more internationally minded, the news seemed a crushing
disaster. People stood in the streets staring blankly at the
first incredible newspaper headlines which appeared to have
suddenly remodelled the architecture of the world. They
queued up patiently for succeeding editions as if they hoped
that something would be added to the first bald facts to
make them more bearable. The flags hung limply at half-
mast along Whitehall, where knots of lugubrious people
gathered at the entrance to Downing Street, hoping for a
glimpse of Mr. Churchill as he came back from adjourning
the House of Commons' business of the day. The Prime
Minister will pay his formal tribute on Tuesday, two days

before his expected war statement, which, according to some excited speculation, may contain the announcement that German organized resistance is over.

On the first shocked day after the President's death, one frequently heard the observation that at this juncture even Mr. Churchill could almost have been better spared than Mr. Roosevelt. It was a strange remark to hear in England, but it was a perfectly sincere one. The fact is that many people feel that the Prime Minister's supreme job was to steer this country safely through the Second World War, as it was the job of the only recently mourned Lloyd George to steer it through the First World War. Loyal and grateful Britons know that no other leader could have done it as well as Mr. Churchill, but they believe that if, by sad chance, it had been he who had caused Friday's tragic headlines, England's postwar policy would have continued roughly on the same tracks. The postwar policy of a United States without Mr. Roosevelt is hard to predict on this side of the Atlantic. People here might find more comfort in the situation if they were at all familiar with the new President, but they are not. The average Englishman, who knows little about American domestic politics, feels as lost as the average American would if Mr. Churchill were to be suddenly succeeded by some relatively unknown Conservative. The evening papers came out with photographs and hastily dug up biographies of President Truman, which Londoners read noncommittally. They glanced at the adjoining headlines, which said that Allied troops were reported only fifteen miles from Berlin, with ironically little apparent emotion and as though Berlin were a village on another planet. Mr. Roosevelt's death will sober still more what would in any event have been a sober V Day. The universal expression of profound personal sorrow, however, has far outweighed the sense of political uncertainty or the worries about the San Francisco Conference. No Briton has forgotten those dark times when the only cheerful thing seemed to be Mr. Roosevelt's voice coming over the radio late at night, and no Briton will ever forget. Elderly people with long memories say that they remember no such dazed outburst of general grief over the death of any other foreign statesman, or, for that matter, over many English ones. At the end of that sad Friday, innumerable people cancelled whatever plans they had made for the evening and stayed quietly at home because they had no heart for going out.

It is all very different from what every one of us had expected the last few days of the European war to be like. Earlier, there had been much cheerfulness over the fact that the V-bomb attacks had apparently already ended. Hardly anybody seems inclined to believe that the Nazis are still contemplating some last, horrific attempt on Britain. This feeling of security has raised a formidable new problem for the government, which has to convince thousands of evacuee Londoners that though the bombing danger may be past, home is not yet the best place. The reason, of course, is that there are a number of homes which are still anything but snug, but it is going to be hard, now that V Day is in sight, to make restive Londoners stay put and wait for the orderly process of being moved back under the government scheme instead of simply hopping on the first homeward train. Still another sign, this time political and not quite so bright, of the nearness of what people hopefully call the peace has been supplied in the last week by the unpeaceful spectacle of Cabinet Ministers' forgetting their Coalition neutrality and indulging in a wordy party set-to. Labour's Bevin has accused the Conservative Party of having been unready for 1939, and the Conservatives' Brendan Bracken has tartly reminded the Socialists that because of their hampering refusal in earlier days to support rearmament or conscription, they have no particular cause to pat themselves on the back either. This breaking down of impartiality at a high level looked to many people as though the elections were near at hand and the Coalition was having its last gasp.

Since Friday's heavy blow, many, too, seem to be coming around to the idea that the political parties in this country should stick together, at least until after the San Francisco Conference and maybe on into the confused shadows of the future. National unity in wartime is essential and people increasingly appear to feel that it may be equally essential in the perils of peace. But at the moment, everything here for anybody who bothers to think is subordinate to this crushing loss, which came at a time when people's minds were keyed only to victory. Trying to realize that this disaster has happened, and trying not to think what it may mean to the world, has temporarily clouded the feeling that the sun is very nearly shining.

April 29

If the San Francisco Conference is the big worry of the moment, the big sensation, which also has to do with the future, because it brings up the subject of our treatment of the conquered, is the revelation of the horrors of the German concentration camps. It has taken the camera to bring home to the slow, good-natured, skeptical British what, as various liberal journals have tartly pointed out, the pens of their correspondents have been unsuccessfully trying to bring home to them since as far back as 1933. Millions of comfortable families, too kind and too lazy in those days to make the effort to believe what they conveniently looked upon as a newspaper propaganda stunt, now believe the horrifying, irrefutable evidence that even blurred printing on poor wartime paper has made all too clear. There are long queues of people waiting silently wherever the photographs are on exhibition. The shock to the public has been enormous, and lots of hitherto moderate people are wondering uncomfortably whether they will agree, after all, with Lord Vansittart's ruthless views on a hard peace. While the violent revulsion has not produced any particularly helpful answers to the question of what is to be done with the Germans, it has suggested one or two things that might not be done with them. Plenty of angry Englishmen would like to know that German prisoners of war here would no longer draw double the

rations a civilian gets. After photographs of Buchenwald's
walking skeletons, Britons were understandably incensed by
the thought of Nazis growing plump in English prison
camps. If, as some people think, the sudden piling on of the
horrors is an attempt to prepare the British and American
publics for the stiff terms Moscow seems determined to im-
pose on Germany, it has certainly succeeded here. Whatever
the Russians ask, it will not be enough to wipe Buchenwald
and the rest from shocked British minds.

Aside from the communiqués, there are other cheerful
signs that V Day is not far ahead. The other day, workmen
started pulling down the surface shelters in the streets—an
operation which Londoners watched contentedly. People are
still inclined to tap cautiously on wood whenever they say
that it seems funny without the V-2s, which it is now permis-
sible to report fell repeatedly on London and were probably
the worst ordeal the population has had to stand. The guarantee that it was really all over came on Monday with the
long-awaited and almost symbolic order to turn up the lights
again. The order did not apply to street lighting, which apparently needs some fixing before it can function once more,
but it was expected that at least homes, hotels, and night
spots would be twinkling and festive. The order, however,
was the biggest flop of the war. The West End streets were
full of people strolling along to see the lights; they must
have thought it funny that about all they could see were the
usual slivers of light glinting from the houses of citizens who
had been drawing the curtains every evening for five and a
half years and could not get out of the habit even now. One
or two restaurants took the blackout stuff off their swinging
doors and the big hotels were lighted up, but on the whole
London looked about as dutifully murky as usual. The St.
James's Street clubs were among the few buildings which
daringly left their big windows uncurtained. Passersby
stopped and stood on tiptoe to peep at the old gentlemen sedately reading their *Times* and sipping their coffee in what
was to Londoners a wildly fascinating setting—a lighted

room which was throwing its brightness far into the street without attracting the attention of a warden.

Possibly the old gentlemen were brooding over the Budget report, which was to be published the following day and turned out to be the mixture as expected, inasmuch as there were no new reliefs of any importance but no new burdens, either. The figures on net incomes, prewar and war, which were given in the Budget provided much food for brooding in these clubs. Seven thousand people had net annual incomes of six thousand pounds and over in 1939, the report said, but there were only eighty in that category in 1943. The figures showed an increase of three million persons in the group which earns between two hundred and fifty and five hundred pounds a year. Some of the things that Socialist orators in Hyde Park have long been clamoring for on Sunday mornings seem to have come about not through a bloody revolution but through a very bloody war.

May 12

[*May 7, V-E Day; the war ends in Europe.*]

The big day started off here with a coincidence. In the last hours of peace, in September, 1939, a violent thunderstorm broke over the city, making a lot of people think for a moment that the first air raid had begun. Early Tuesday morning, V-E Day, nature tidily brought the war to an end with an imitation of a blitz so realistic that many Londoners started awake and reached blurrily for the bedside torch. Then they remembered, and, sighing with relief, fell asleep again as the thunder rolled over the capital, already waiting with its flags. The decorations had blossomed on the streets Monday afternoon. By six that night, Piccadilly Circus and all the city's other focal points were jammed with a cheerful, expectant crowd waiting for an official statement from

Downing Street. Movie cameramen crouched patiently on the rooftops. When a brewer's van rattled by and the driver leaned out and yelled "It's all over," the crowd cheered, then went on waiting. Presently, word spread that the announcement would be delayed, and the day, which had started off like a rocket, began to fizzle slowly and damply out.

When the day finally came, it was like no other day that anyone can remember. It had a flavor of its own, an extemporaneousness which gave it something of the quality of a vast, happy village fête as people wandered about, sat, sang, and slept against a summer background of trees, grass, flowers, and water. It was not, people said, like the 1918 Armistice Day, for at no time was the reaction hysterical. It was not like the Coronation, for the crowds were larger and their gaiety, which held up all through the night, was obviously not picked up in a pub. The day also surprised the prophets who had said that only the young would be resilient enough to celebrate in a big way. Apparently, the desire to assist in London's celebration combusted spontaneously in the bosom of every member of every family, from the smallest babies, with their hair done up in red-white-and-blue ribbons, to beaming elderly couples who, utterly without self-consciousness, strolled up and down the streets arm in arm in red-white-and-blue paper hats. Even the dogs wore immense tricolored bows. Rosettes sprouted from the slabs of pork in the butcher shops, which, like other food stores, were open for a couple of hours in the morning. With their customary practicality, housewives put bread before circuses. They waited in the long bakery queues, the string bags of the common round in one hand and the Union Jack of the glad occasion in the other. Even queues seemed tolerable that morning. The bells had begun to peal and, after the storm, London was having that perfect, hot, English summer's day which, one sometimes feels, is to be found only in the imaginations of the lyric poets.

The girls in their thin, bright dresses heightened the impression that the city had been taken over by an enormous family picnic. The number of extraordinarily pretty young girls, who presumably are hidden on working days inside the factories and government offices, was astonishing. They streamed out into the parks and streets like flocks of twittering, gaily plumaged cockney birds. In their freshly curled hair were cornflowers and poppies, and they wore red-white-and-blue ribbons around their narrow waists. Some of them even tied ribbons around their bare ankles. Strolling with their uniformed boys, arms candidly about each other, they provided a constant, gay, simple marginal decoration to the big, solemn moments of the day. The crowds milled back and forth between the Palace, Westminster, Trafalgar Square, and Piccadilly Circus, and when they got tired they simply sat down wherever they happened to be—on the grass, on doorsteps, or on the curb—and watched the other people or spread handkerchiefs over their faces and took a nap. Everybody appeared determined to see the King and Queen and Mr. Churchill at least once, and few could have been disappointed. One small boy, holding onto his father's hand, wanted to see the trench shelters in Green Park too. "You don't want to see shelters today," his father said. "You'll never have to use them again, son." "Never?" the child asked doubtfully. "Never!" the man cried, almost angrily. *"Never!* Understand?" In the open space before the Palace, one of the places where the Prime Minister's speech was to be relayed by loudspeaker at three o'clock, the crowds seemed a little intimidated by the nearness of that symbolic block of gray stone. The people who chose to open their lunch baskets and munch sandwiches there among the flowerbeds of tulips were rather subdued. Piccadilly Circus attracted the more demonstrative spirits.

By lunchtime, in the Circus, the buses had to slow to a crawl in order to get through the tightly packed, laughing people. A lad in the black beret of the Tank Corps was the first to climb the little pyramidal Angkor Vat of scaffolding and sandbags which was erected early in the war to protect the pedestal of the Eros statue after the figure had been removed to safekeeping. The boy shinnied up to the top and took a tiptoe Eros pose, aiming an imaginary bow, while the crowd roared. He was followed by a paratrooper in a maroon beret, who, after getting up to the top, reached down and hauled up a blond young woman in a very tight pair of green slacks. When she got to the top, the Tank Corps soldier promptly grabbed her in his arms and, encouraged by ecstatic cheers from the whole Circus, seemed about to enact the classic rôle of Eros right on the top of the monument. Nothing came of it, because a moment later a couple of G.I.s joined them and before long the pyramid was covered with boys and girls. They sat jammed together in an affectionate mass, swinging their legs over the sides, wearing each other's uniform caps, and calling down wisecracks to the crowd. "My God," someone said, "think of a flying bomb coming down on this!" When a firecracker went off, a hawker with a tray of tin brooches of Monty's head happily yelled that comforting, sometimes fallacious phrase of the blitz nights, "All right, mates, it's one of ours!"

All day long, the deadly past was for most people only just under the surface of the beautiful, safe present—so much so that the government decided against sounding the sirens in a triumphant "all clear" for fear that the noise would revive too many painful memories. For the same reason, there were no salutes of guns—only the pealing of the bells and the whistles of tugs on the Thames sounding the doot, doot, doot, dooooot of the V, and the roar of the planes, which swooped back and forth over the city, dropping red and green signals toward the blur of smiling, upturned faces.

It was without any doubt Churchill's day. Thousands of King George's subjects wedged themselves in front of the Palace throughout the day, chanting ceaselessly "We want the King" and cheering themselves hoarse when he and the Queen and their daughters appeared, but when the crowd saw Churchill, there was a deep, full-throated, almost reverent roar. He was at the head of a procession of Members of Parliament, walking back to the House of Commons from the traditional St. Margaret's Thanksgiving Service. Instantly, he was surrounded by people—people running, standing on tiptoe, holding up babies so that they could be told later they had seen him, and shouting affectionately the absurd little nurserymaid name, "Winnie, Winnie!" One of two happily sozzled, very old, and incredibly dirty cockneys who had been engaged in a slow, shuffling dance, like a couple of Shakespearean clowns, bellowed, "That's 'im, that's 'is little old lovely bald 'ead!" The crowds saw Churchill again later, when he emerged from Commons and was driven off in the back of a small open car, rosy, smiling, and looking immensely happy. Ernest Bevin, following in another car, got a cheer, too. Herbert Morrison, sitting unobtrusively in a corner of a third car, was hardly recognized, and the other Cabinet Ministers did no better. The crowd had ears, eyes, and throats for no one but Churchill, and for him everyone in it seemed to have the hearing, sight, and lungs of fifty men. His slightly formal official broadcast, which was followed by buglers sounding the "cease firing" call, did not strike the emotional note that had been expected, but he hit it perfectly in his subsequent informal speech ("My dear friends, this is your victory . . .") from a Whitehall balcony.

All day long, little extra celebrations started up. In the Mall, a model of a Gallic cock waltzed on a pole over the heads of the singing people. "It's the Free French," said someone. The Belgians in the crowd tagged along after a Belgian flag that marched by, its bearer invisible. A procession of students raced through Green Park, among exploding squibs, clashing dustbin lids like cymbals and waving an immense Jeyes Disinfectant poster as a banner. American sailors and laughing girls formed a conga line down the middle of Piccadily, and cockneys linked arms in the Lambeth Walk. It was a day and night of no fixed plan and no organized merriment. Each group danced its own dance, sang its own song, and went its own way as the spirit moved it. The most tolerant, self-effacing people in London on V-E Day were the police, who simply stood by, smiling benignly, while soldiers swung by one arm from lamp standards and laughing groups tore down hoardings to build the evening's bonfires. Actually, the police were not unduly strained. The extraordinary thing about the crowds was that they were almost all sober. The number of drunks one saw in that whole day and night could have been counted on two hands— possibly because the pubs were sold out so early. The young service men and women who swung arm in arm down the middle of every street, singing and swarming over the few cars rash enough to come out, were simply happy with an immense holiday happiness. Just before the King's speech, at nine Tuesday night, the big lamps outside the Palace came on and there were cheers and ohs from children who had never seen anything of that kind in their short, blacked-out lives. As the evening wore on, most of the public buildings were floodlighted. The night was as warm as midsummer, and London, its shabbiness now hidden and its domes and remaining Wren spires warmed by lights and bonfires, was suddenly magnificent. The handsomest building of all was the National Gallery, standing out honey-colored near a ghostly, blue-shadowed St. Martin's and the Charles I bit of Whitehall. The floodlighted face of Big Ben loomed like a kind moon.